THE LONDON FURNITURE MAKERS
from 1660–1840

The London Makers of
CABINET & UPHOLSTERY WORK
in the Newest Fashion & Most Genteel Taste

Buroes, Bookcases, Cloathes Presses and Chests
Dining, Writing and Toilet Tables, Card Tables
Tea Tables, Sophas and Chairs of all sorts
Fashionable Four Post and Standing Bedsteads
with hangings of Silk, Stuff or Cheney washing
materials. Sconces, Pier and Looking-glasses
all in the neatest manner
at Reasonable Rates

AS ANY IN TOWN

THE LONDON FURNITURE MAKERS

FROM THE RESTORATION TO
THE VICTORIAN ERA
1660–1840

By

SIR AMBROSE HEAL

A record of 2500 cabinet-makers, upholsterers, carvers and gilders with their addresses and working dates illustrated by 165 reproductions of makers' trade-cards

with a chapter

By R. W. SYMONDS, F.S.A.

on the problem of identification of the furniture they produced illustrated by some hitherto unpublished examples of authenticated pieces

DOVER PUBLICATIONS, INC.
NEW YORK

/

Published in Canada by General Publishing Company, Ltd., 30 Lesmill Road, Don Mills, Toronto,
Ontario.

Published in the United Kingdom by Constable
and Company, Ltd., 10 Orange Street, London
WC 2.

This Dover edition, first published in 1972, is an
unabridged republication of the work originally
published by B. T. Batsford Ltd. in 1953.

International Standard Book Number: 0-486-22903-3
Library of Congress Catalog Card Number: 72-87434

Manufactured in the United States of America
Dover Publications, Inc.
180 Varick Street
New York, N.Y. 10014

In the 100th anniversary year
of the author's birth,
and in his memory,

this new reprint edition of
The London Furniture Makers, 1660-1840
is dedicated by his sons to
The Worshipful Company of Furniture Makers.

August, 1972   A.S.H.

                                    J.C.H.

INTRODUCTION

THE APPROACH TO THE STUDY OF ANTIQUE furniture during recent years has shown a marked tendency towards the consideration of individual pieces, their provenances and the identification of their makers. Wider generalisations on style and period have now been narrowed down to more exact appreciation of detail and dates which in turn have focussed attention on characteristics of certain of the lesser-known cabinet-makers and the influence which these have had upon fashion in furniture. The development of this tendency towards more critical examination has shown itself more particularly in recent publications by some of the leading authorities on the subject who have broken fresh ground and given us the results of much original research in these directions.

Previous to the opening of the present century the moderately informed member of the general public would have been at a loss to instance the names of more than five or six furniture makers or designers and those would probably have been confined to the men whose work had become familiar through the publication of their pattern books. Formerly the vague term "Chippendale" was usually good enough to cover most of the mahogany furniture of the mid-eighteenth century and the pieces inlaid with satinwood banding would be generically dubbed "Sheraton." For the rest a "Hepplewhite" chair or an "Adam" sideboard would commonly suffice.

In more recent times the carefully documented work by such expert authorities as Ralph Edwards, Margaret Jourdain, Constance Simon, H. Clifford Smith, R. W. Symonds and others has brought to light the names of eminent cabinet-makers, previously overshadowed, whose work places them on a par with those craftsmen whose publications had caused them to be widely known. Thus we are now made familiar with the names of Goodison, Jensen, Moore, Vile & Cobb, Seddon and others whom we rank with any of the great master cabinet-makers. Much useful spade-work has been done on the Accounts of the Royal Household and in the archives, still providentially preserved, in some of the famous houses. But exploration at these high levels produces only a relatively small number of new names from among all those makers who were engaged in the large cabinet-making industry which was flourishing in London during the eighteenth century and of which we have much factual evidence in what remains to us of their output at the present day.

CABINET-MAKERS' WORKSHOPS Very little is known as to the size and conditions of cabinet-makers' workshops at this period but some of them, at all events, must have been on a quite considerable scale. Chippendale, we know, had been established in a little court off Long Acre only four years before he launched out into larger premises in St. Martin's Lane, and to these he soon added three adjoining houses. This gives us some idea of his rate of expansion but the mere fact that he was in a position to publish so elaborate a catalogue as his *Director* with 160 large engraved plates shows that he was conducting a flourishing concern. The list of subscribers appended to this book gives substance to the claim that he had "patrons and customers in all classes of society." The success of this publication must have been substantial and immediate for it justified no fewer than three editions within seven years of its first appearance. Another eminent firm was that of the Seddons in Aldersgate of which we have been given a vivid contemporary account by the diarist and novelist Sophie von la Roche when she was taken over their factory during her visit to London in 1786. The description of it in her book, translated under the title *Sophie in London*, is a full and picturesque one, though possibly rather over-coloured. She gives a detailed account of the various crafts she saw being carried on in the large "house with six wings" where "some 400 (!) workpeople" were employed—cabinet-makers, upholsterers, carvers, gilders, mirror makers and ormolu workers, with large timber-yard and saw-mills adjacent. While bearing testimony to the very high-class business that was being done there the writer lays stress on the fact that the Seddons' work ranged "from the simplest and cheapest to the most elegant and expensive. . . ." We know from an independent account that the house had been "a very large commodious brick building, the façade adorned by a row of nine columns." This was known as London House and was one of the fine houses which stood in Aldersgate Street: it was destroyed by fire in 1768, then rebuilt and again burnt down in 1783. Another contemporary reference to this business is found in the *Memoirs of William Hickey* when in 1791 he exported to his house near Calcutta "a very capital billiards table made by Seddons" which presumably he was obliged to abandon with his other effects when he left India in 1808.

It was evidently nothing unusual for the leading cabinet-makers in the eighteenth century to occupy fine premises. William Linnell and his successor John Linnell carried on their business at No. 28 Berkeley Square, a large double-fronted house in the north-east corner of the square which is shown on a contemporary plan* running right through into Bourdon Street. It occupied more ground space and had a wider frontage than any of the other houses in the square. The Linnells had a select and fashionable

* See Horwood's Map of London, 1799.

clientèle and their charges seem to have been similarly egregious, as would appear from a bill I have of William Linnell made out to Sir Richard Hoare of Barn Elms. This account is rubricated by Sir Richard with remarks against various items such as "extravagant charge," "too much," "deduct," while other charges are abruptly struck through in red ink. John Linnell carried out a great deal of work for William Drake both at Shardeloes and Grosvenor Square and we learn from George Eland's *Shardeloes Papers* that Mr. Drake was so dissatisfied with the bill that he submitted it for comment to another cabinet-maker who assessed the charges as excessive by 20 per cent, but despite this report the account was paid up in full. The relationship, if any, between these Linnells and John Linnell, the portraitist and landscape painter (1792–1882), has never been established. The *D.N.B.* says the artist was the "son of a London wood carver" who may have been the James Linnell of St. Martin's Lane (*q.v.*) or a relation of his.

DEALINGS WITH CUSTOMERS Now and again from early diaries and memoirs we get a glimpse of customers' dealings at furnishing shops. In October 1668 Samuel Pepys is going the rounds in search of hangings for his new bedroom. On the 15th he sets out with his wife and Deb "by coach to the upholsterer's in Long Lane, Alderman Reave's (*q.v.*), and then on to Alderman Crow's (*q.v.*) to see variety of hangings and were mightily pleased therewith, and spent the whole afternoon thereupon: and at last I think we shall pitch upon the best suit of Apostles where three pieces for my room come to almost £80." The next day they all go to see "Mr. Wren's* hangings and bed at St. James's and then to Sir W. Coventry's in the Pell Mell for our satisfaction in what we are going to buy; and so by Mr. Crow's home, about his hangings, and do pitch upon buying his second suit of Apostles—the whole suit comes to £83; and this we think the best for us." This decision to buy the second best set of "Apostles" was an economical move on the part of Mr. Pepys, as though there was only a few pounds difference in price the one he chose was a larger set which would "answer any other rooms or service."

I am told by Mr. Wingfield Digby, Keeper of Textiles at the Victoria and Albert Museum, that these "suits of Apostles" were undoubtedly taken from the well-known tapestry cartoons of Raphael's design "The Acts of the Apostles," and he judges that as the prices asked were so low, they would have been second-hand panels; the charges for these tapestries at the Mortlake factory at this date being very much higher.

On the 19th October, 1668, Pepys calls for Mr. Harman (*q.v.*) the upholsterer and took him "to take measure of Mr. Wren's bed at St. James's I being resolved to have just such another made me." Previous to this occasion Mr. Pepys had paid various visits to Harman's shop but unfortunately he never mentions the address. The earliest entry is on 23rd August,

---

* Matthew Wren, son of the Bishop of Ely, Secretary to Lord Clarendon and later to the Duke of York.

1664: "called at Harman's and there bespoke some chairs." In 1666 he goes there three times during August and September when he is choosing a bed and hangings "for my new closet." The fine bookcases which Mr. Pepys caused to be made for him by "Sympson the joiner" (*q.v.*) had already been installed at the house in Seething Lane (see *Diary*, 16th and 22nd August, 1666) and they are still a joy to the visitor in the Pepysian Library at Magdalene College, Cambridge (see Plates, pages 222 and 223).

William Whitley, in his delightful book *Artists and their Friends in England, 1700–1799,* tells how David Garrick, during one of his less prosperous phases, was furnishing his new house in the Adelphi and ran up a bill with Chippendale and Haig, as the firm was known then, "of nearly a thousand pounds and after paying off on account more than a third of this sum neglected to make a final settlement with the firm until threatened with an action-at-law." Whitley incidentally gives us a good deal of information about the craftsmen of the period and helps us to identify some of the London carvers and gilders. He mentions Norris in Long Acre "the picture keeper and frame maker to William and Mary" whom we knew of already when Mr. Pepys employed him to frame his prints (*Diary*, 30th April, 1699). Another eminent frame maker we meet with was Gossett in Berwick Street (*q.v.*); he worked for Gainsborough and Hogarth and was probably a brother of Isaac Gossett, the famous wax modeller. These makers of carved and gilded picture frames were the same craftsmen who produced the fine wall mirrors and girandoles which were so characteristic of the period.

Here and there we pick up stray references to customers' dealings with the master furniture makers of the eighteenth century. *Nollekens and His Times,* written by "Rainy Day" Smith in 1828, and so admirably edited and annotated by Wilfred Whitten (1920), provides us with many gossipy anecdotes of the shopkeepers of Joseph Nollekens' days. Among others he relates the oft-quoted incident of Mr. Cobb (*q.v.*), the pompous upholsterer of St. Martin's Lane, when he was neatly snubbed by George III in the library at Buckingham House. Elsewhere Smith describes the elaborately painted ceiling "believed to be by the hand of Hogarth" at the house in Litchfield Street occupied by "Banks the cellaret maker" (*q.v.*) who was occasionally employed by Cobb. A passing reference to "Gainsborough's friend Collins of Tothill Fields the most famous modeller of chimney tablets of his day" is of more present interest to us since the famous set of Dolphin furniture in Greenwich Hospital has now been attributed to him.*

In the *Letters of Edward Gibbon* we are told of long discussions with "Ireland the upholder" over the designs for his new bookcases when the historian was moving into his new house, No. 7 Bentinck Street (1773), and how finally it was decided to make them in mahogany "painted white with a

---

* Brackett and Clifford Smith's *English Furniture Illustrated,* 1950.

light frize [*sic*] neither Doric nor Denticulated Adamic." It was in this room that Gibbon worked for the next ten years on the first three volumes of his great work prior to leaving England for Lausanne, where he completed his *Decline and Fall of the Roman Empire*. In Horace Walpole's *Description of Strawberry Hill*, and in the *Accounts* edited and annotated by Paget Toynbee, we naturally meet with the names of several of the leading furnishers of the day. In the Holbein Chamber a sumptuously upholstered bed hung with purple cloth and white satin surmounted by a plume of white and purple feathers on the centre of the tester was supplied by Mr. Cobb of the firm of Vile and Cobb (*q.v.*) in St. Martin's Lane. The same eminent firm was also responsible for the carpet in this room and for various pieces of cabinet work in the Gallery and elsewhere in the house. The "handsome crimson pattern bordered carpet" in the Gallery, however, was made to order at the Moorfields factory by Thomas Moore (*q.v.*) who had just come into prominence through having been awarded a distinction by the Royal Society of Arts for his invention of a process of carpet weaving "in imitation of those in Turkey and Persia." Moore, through the patronage of Robert Adam, was entrusted with the making of carpets at Syon House and Osterley. This Thomas Moore was by trade a "hosier and manufacturer at the Sign of the Bishop Blaze in Chiswell Street" (see Plate, page 119) and on his later trade-cards he describes himself as "Marchand fabricant de Bas & Bonneterie de la Majesté Britanique" and sports the royal arms with the cypher of George III.

Another elaborate four-poster in the Great North Bedchamber at Strawberry Hill, hung with Aubusson tapestry and bedecked on all four corners with plumes of ostrich feathers, was supplied by Strickland (*q.v.*) "nephew to the late Mr. Vile." Walpole also employed Pierre Langlois of Tottenham Court Road (*q.v.*) to supply him with various pieces of French furniture, notably two *encoignures* which he prized highly. The fine trade-card engraved for Langlois by Antoine Aveline states that he "fait toutes sortes de Commodes, Encoignures inscrutées de fleurs en bois et marqueteries...." (see Plate, page 94). Thomas Bromwich (*q.v.*), too, was brought in to supply his modish "new wallpaper" in several rooms. I have found no direct evidence that Walpole employed the fashionable cabinet-maker William Hallett (*q.v.*) though from Walpole's correspondence we infer that he admits Hallett's pre-eminence in his craft and recognises him as a leading exponent of the new Chinese taste, then coming into vogue, but with which Walpole was not in sympathy. The family group of this Mr. Hallett was painted by Francis Hayman, and his grandson William it was who figures with his young wife in Gainsborough's well-known work *The Morning Walk*.

A lively picture is drawn for us by George Eland in his admirably edited *The Purefoy Letters* of how, in the mid-eighteenth century, country house needs were largely met through the intermediary of the London carrier.

Commissions ranging from a fine sturgeon to a four-post bedstead were confidently entrusted by Mrs. Purefoy of Shalstone Manor to Mr. Zachary Meads, the Buckinghamshire carrier. The cabinet-maker usually employed by her was Mr. Belchier of St. Paul's Churchyard whose trade-card is illustrated on Plate, page 6. But on one occasion, having need for a second-hand sedan-chair "that is strong and tite," she addressed herself to Mr. Greaves at the *Golden Chair* in Warwick Lane (*q.v.*).

MAKERS' MARKS   The attribution of a piece of furniture to a particular maker has usually been a matter of difficulty owing to the absence, in nearly all cases, of any mark of identification. It is rarely that a maker's label or stamp is found upon English cabinet work of the eighteenth century. In this way we are at a great disadvantage with many other trades. The work of gold and silver smiths invariably carries marks indicating by whom, when and where it was made. The pewterers' "touches" were registered, the potter stamped his name or distinguishing device, booksellers and engravers had their imprints, scientific and musical instrument-makers often marked their products or labelled the cases which contained them as did the gun-smiths and sword-smiths; clocks and watches almost invariably carry the maker's name on their dials or on the works. Unfortunately, the general practice of labelling did not obtain in our furniture trade, and we have had no system of record in this country to correspond to the register of *Maîtres Ébénistes* that obtained in France in the eighteenth century.

Within recent years it has been noticeable that when an article of furniture has been offered in the London salerooms which does bear a maker's label it usually attracts a high price, and on the occasions when the identification of a hitherto unacknowledged maker is established on a piece of high quality a rarity value is created and collectors are on the alert for specimens from the same workshop; close scrutiny of his stock by an antique dealer will sometimes bring to light another piece bearing a similar label. An instance occurred not long ago when a remarkable cabinet was put up for sale and on the underside of one of the drawers a trade card was discovered of a maker hitherto almost unknown. Since then two other cabinets with very similar characteristics, and evidently by the same hand, have come under the hammer and been knocked down at enhanced figures. Hitherto, when the names of previously unknown makers have come to light there has been difficulty in establishing their dates, except by the general style of the piece, but that method affords no more than a rough approximation. My hope is that with this list of makers' names, and with such dates as one has been able to attach to the references, it will be more possible to identify individuals as their names arise, to establish the address at which they worked and thus to arrive at a fairly close approximation as to the date of an article.

**DIRECTORIES &
ADVERTISEMENTS**

In the absence of a register of names and marks as exists in some trades, one has been thrown back upon the task of compiling a list of such makers as can be traced by means of directories and searching for their advertisements in contemporary newspapers. These are haphazard alternatives at the best, as the London directories of the eighteenth century are diminutive volumes and by no means so complete or as accurate as one could wish. The earliest was published in 1734, though there was a *Collection of the Names of Merchants living in and about the City of London* issued as early as 1677. These meagre and unofficial publications of slim small octavo size are rather scarce, particularly those prior to 1770, and no public library has a complete set of them. Their comparative rarity arises from the ephemeral character of their usefulness; obsolete editions, having been periodically superseded by later ones, were usually destroyed. Before 1790 the London directories contained no classifications of trades with one single exception, namely *Mortimer's Director* published in 1763; consequently one is compelled to scrutinise each volume line by line in order to extract the required trade individually. This process was too protracted to be conducted in public libraries, so for convenient reference I was led to acquire such issues as I could find, with the result that I now possess a six-foot shelf of these rather scarce little books issued between the years 1740 and 1830.

Much useful information is to be gathered from contemporary advertisements in *The Daily Courant, London Gazette, Daily Advertiser, The Post Boy*, but searching through the files is a wearisome and almost endless job as so many of the "runs" in any one library are incomplete.

**TRADESMEN'S
CARDS & BILLS**

Such sources as these, however, have their use in establishing many a man's address and the date of his occupation, but they give no indication of the quality of business he was engaged upon and it is here that the trade-card is of assistance. Frequently these cards will supply an engraving of various pieces of furniture from which we can judge the style and class of the work and the period when a man was working. Below the illustration the tradesman will often list the sort of things he specialises in and notify the services he is prepared to offer. The wording in the earlier examples will give his shop sign, which was usually embodied in an ornamental frame enclosing the whole design. These decorative devices of the shop signs upon billheads and trade-cards began to fall into disuse when signboards were rendered obsolete by the numbering of the streets, a practice which was introduced in 1762 and had become to be generally adopted by about 1780. Furthermore—and this is of the utmost value in tracing the history of a firm—a man will occasionally mention on his trade-card the name of his predecessor "late Mr. So and So" or "son of Mr. Such and Such of Blank Street."

These trade-cards were often used as memoranda of accounts for goods supplied to customers and in such cases they give us a definite date. Apart from the useful purpose they serve of providing a man's name, his address, the class of business and occasionally the date of the purchase, they are in themselves decorative and interesting in design, finely engraved and with well-drawn lettering. The importance of their sociological interest as well as their value as trade records is beginning to be more fully recognised, with the result that good examples are becoming scarce. The one hundred and sixty here illustrated are selected from more than twice that number in my collection emanating from the London furniture trades alone. Those which seem to be of the least importance have been eliminated.

In addition to the trade-cards proper I have drawn upon collections of billheads. The itemised accounts on these provide useful information as to charges made to customers for various types of furniture and, of course, are direct evidence of the exact dates at which the various articles were supplied. These billheads, however, are more difficult to come by for the reason that, not possessing the pictorial attraction of the trade-card, they are more likely to have been destroyed. Occasionally a bundle will come to light, having been meticulously docketed and tied up by some careful housekeeper, and are found still besprinkled with the sand with which they had been pounced when originally stored away. Billheads come into a rather different category from the more elaborate and decorative trade-card, the latter being mainly designed to fulfil the purpose of an attractive advertisement, whereas the engraved billhead was a business-like form restricted to the name of the shopkeeper, his calling and his address. If of a date prior to the introduction of street numbering his shop sign would usually be displayed framed in a neat cartouche but in a simpler form than when introduced into the design of the more pictorial trade-card.

SHOP SIGNS   The emblems mostly favoured by the cabinet-making and the upholstery trades will usually be found to fall within one of the following categories. The most distinctive group is that where the shop sign symbolises this particular trade, The Chair, The Cabinet, The Bed, The Looking Glass, The Walnut Tree, The Blue Curtain, The Three Tents of the Upholders' Company, or else The Three Compasses, the charge which appears on the arms of both the Joiners' and the Carpenters' Companies. The largest group comprises emblems of loyalty, as The King's Arms, The Queen's Head, or Crown and Sceptre, or employs familiar heraldic devices drawn from regal blazonry and from the arms of noble families such as The White Hart, The Golden Lion, The Blue Boar, The White Swan, The Spread Eagle, The Unicorn, The Fleur-de-Lys, or The Bear and Ragged Staff, all of which were widely adopted by most of the trades, as were also such emblems as The Sun, Star and Half Moon, not infrequently used in conjunction. There remains that strange group of incongruously associated emblems which has more often been speculated upon than explained: the group to which belong such signs as The Bull and Bedpost, The Blue Ball and Artichoke, The Three Nuns and Hare, The Wheatsheaf and Speaking Trumpet, The Whale and Gate and other indiscriminate combinations. Most of these amalgamations are susceptible of the simple explanation of a tradesman taking over a shop with a well-established sign which he wishes to preserve for the sake of the goodwill attached to it and yet chooses to add to it another emblem, either more closely associated with his own business or for which he has some personal preference. In other cases heraldic terms are converted into colloquialisms and result in strange composites as in the case where the Order of the Garter was rendered by a sign-painter as a naturalistic Leg and Star, and it was so designated.

The names of certain prominent cabinet-makers and upholsterers are well known and they occur again and again in works of writers on antique furniture. Examples of the work of these craftsmen exist, the provenances are known and the pieces described and illustrated, but the sum-total of such makers' names is pitiably small compared with those recorded in many other trades. From time to time fresh names come to light and records are then required to establish identities. Working dates and addresses are tediously sought for, registers and directories sedulously examined, advertisement columns of old newspapers are combed through and eventually the desired information may, or may not, be discovered. The most complete list of master craftsmen in the furnishing trade which has so far been published is contained in the carefully documented work *Georgian Cabinet Makers*, by Ralph Edwards and Margaret Jourdain, where full particulars of the makers and their works appear in a hand-picked list consisting of eighty names; from this list I have gathered many valuable pieces of information. The authors, after defining the limits of selection which they have set for themselves, go on to say: "A concise handbook of cabinet-makers, joiners, chair-makers and the like could doubtless be compiled and might be a useful work." It was precisely with that purpose in view, of covering a wider field, that I originally began, many years ago, to record the names, addresses and dates of all the early makers of furniture as I came across them in a loose-leaf index which has now grown to twenty-three volumes and contains some 4,000 entries. Of these I have selected rather more than half as being most likely to be of service for the purpose in hand. In all probability only a relatively small proportion of these names will need to be referred to, but it is unpredictable whether the nonentity of to-day may not conceivably be of interest to some researcher in the future as fields of enquiry widen out. If only on the off-chance of it being put to some future use one is reluctant not to preserve in permanent form a record which has taken thirty years or more to put together. Hence these pages.

ACKNOWLEDGE-
MENTS

A list of various sources from which I have drawn information will be found on p. xix, but in particular I owe a great deal to the help I have received at all times from Mr. R. W. Symonds, who with unfailing good nature has put up with importunate correspondence and even allowed me full use of his invaluable accumulation of notes and cuttings, which during past years he has gathered and collated from the files of early newspapers and other out of the way sources. In addition to availing myself of their published works, I have referred many a doubtful point to one or other of the acknowledged experts previously mentioned and invariably the benefit of their wide knowledge of the subject has been readily placed at my disposal. Other helpful collaboration I have had from owners whose old houses contain furniture for which the makers' bills have mercifully been preserved or where other family records of it still exist. Enquiries in these cases have often involved the owners in considerable correspondence which has been submitted to with much kindness and has proved of the greatest help in cases where the information has been unobtainable elsewhere. To the watchful and experienced eye which Mr. Hanneford-Smith, the Director of Batsford's, has kept upon me during the process of proof-reading I owe escape from many errors which otherwise I should have fallen into.

The value and interest of the work is greatly enhanced by the descriptive commentary on authenticated pieces of furniture which has been provided for it by Mr. R. W. Symonds whose intimate knowledge in this field of research is probably unsurpassed. This is a subject which hitherto has received but little attention owing, probably, to the scarcity of pieces which can be directly authenticated. By his study and records of identifiable examples Mr. Symonds traces makers' individual characteristics which have enabled him to attribute other pieces to common origins. His deductions are illustrated with photographs which he has collected exemplifying what he calls the "hand-writing" of various cabinet-makers. These, together with his critical commentaries upon them, add considerably to our knowledge of the craftsmen and undoubtedly lend a touch of verisimilitude to my own stark records.

A. H.

Tottenham Court Road,
    London.
November 1952.

CONTENTS

SOURCES OF REFERENCES

Reference
Number

1   Tradesmen's Cards and Billheads in the Author's Collection and in various
    Public and University Libraries

2   London Directories from 1740 to 1840
3   London Polling Lists
4   London Rate Books
5   Advertisements and other Notices in contemporary Newspapers
6   Records of Insurance Companies*
7   Registers of Unclaimed Dividends of Bank Stock
8   Royal Household Accounts
9   Policy Holders of the Society for the Assurance of Widows and Orphans
10 "General Remarks on Trade"
11 "Book of Trades" (1805)
12 "The Gentleman's Magazine"
13 "Richard Smyth's Obituary" (1849)
14 Children Apprenticed by the Sons of the Clergy
15 Apprenticeship Records
16 "List of Principal Inhabitants of the City of London in 1640"
17 Declaration of the Inhabitants of London (1795)
18 List of Subscribers to Chippendale's "Director" (1754)
19 List of Subscribers to Sheraton's "Cabinet Dictionary" (1803)
20 Sheraton's List of Master Cabinet-Makers in and around London (1803)
21 Beavan's "Aldermen of the City of London" (1908)

22 Diary of Samuel Pepys (1659–1669)
23 "Artists and Their Friends" (W. T. Whitley) (1700–99)
24 "Purefoy Letters, 1735–53" (G. Eland)
25 "Shardeloes Papers" (G. Eland) (c. 1750–70)
26 Horace Walpole's Strawberry Hill Accounts (c. 1750–70)
27 "Description of Strawberry Hill" (Toynbee)
28 "Sophie in London" (von la Roche) (1786)
29 "Memoirs of William Hickey" (1749–75)
30 "Nollekens and His Times" (W. Whitten) (c. 1760–1820)
31 "Private Correspondence of David Garrick" (c. 1770)
32 "Letters of Edward Gibbon"

33 "Signs of Old London" (Hilton Price) (1903–08)
34 "London Past and Present" (Wheatley and Cunningham) (1891)

* Fire Insurance policies in the middle of the eighteenth century show that despite the frequency of fires occurring in cabinet-makers' workshops they were accepted at "normal" risks rate at 2s. 6d. per cent, but by the end of the century these came under the heading of "hazardous trades" and were charged at increased rates.

Reference
Number

35 "Old Cheapside" (*K. Rogers*) (1931)
36 "Charing Cross" (*J. H. MacMichael*) (1906)
37 "Annals of Covent Garden" (*Beresford Chancellor*) (1931)
38 "Annals of Fleet Street" (*Beresford Chancellor*) (1912)
39 "Annals of The Strand" (*Beresford Chancellor*) (1912)
40 "London Topographical Records" (*Beresford Chancellor*) (1903–08)
41 "Romance of Soho" (*Beresford Chancellor*) (1931)
42 "Memorials of St. James's Street" (*Gordon Home*) (1922)
43 "The Russells in Bloomsbury" (*G. S. Thompson*) (1940)
44 "Old London Bridge" (*Gordon Home*) (1931)
45 "Signs of Old London Bridge" (*H. Syer Cumming*) (1887)

46 "Thomas Chippendale" (*E. J. Layton*)
47 "Chippendale Furniture Designs" (*R. W. Symonds*) (1948)
48 "Life of Thomas Chippendale" (*O. Brackett*)
49 "Dictionary of English Furniture" (*Macquoid and Edwards*) (1924)
50 "Regency Furniture" (*M. Jourdain*) (1934)
51 "English Furniture Designers" (*C. Simon*) (1907)
52 "English Furniture Illustrated" (*O. Brackett, revised edition, by H. Clifford Smith*) (1950)
53 "British Furniture Makers" (*J. Gloag*) (1945)
54 "The English Chair" (*R. Edwards*) (1951)
55 "Furniture of our Forefathers" (*E. Singleton*) (1906)
56 "Georgian Cabinet Makers" (*Edwards and Jourdain*) (1945)
57 "Georgian Furniture" (*R. Edwards*) (1947)
58 "History of English Wallpapers" (*Sugden and Edmondson*) (1925)
59 "Masterpieces of English Furniture and Clocks" (*R. W. Symonds*) (1940)
60 "Old Clocks and Watches" (*F. J. Britten*) (1922)
61 "Old English Furniture" (*M. Harris*) (1935)

62 "Dictionary of National Biography" (1908, *et seq.*)
63 *Notes and Queries*, 1849 to 1950
64 Various articles in *Connoisseur, Country Life*, etc.

65 Registers of St. Mary, Woolnoth
66 Churchwardens' Records of St. Mary Woolchurch Hawe
67 Ackermann's "Repository of Arts," etc., January–June, 1825
68 Ackermann's "Repository of Arts," etc., January–June, 1813
69 "Cabinet-Makers' London Book of Prices," 1788

LONDON FURNITURE MAKERS

A Selected List of

THE CABINET-MAKERS, UPHOLSTERERS CARVERS AND GILDERS WORKING IN LONDON BETWEEN 1660 AND 1840

SUPPLEMENTED WITH THEIR DATES, ADDRESSES AND SOME
DETAILS OF THEIR WORK

SIZE OF ORIGINAL 6⅝″ × 5″   *See page 8*

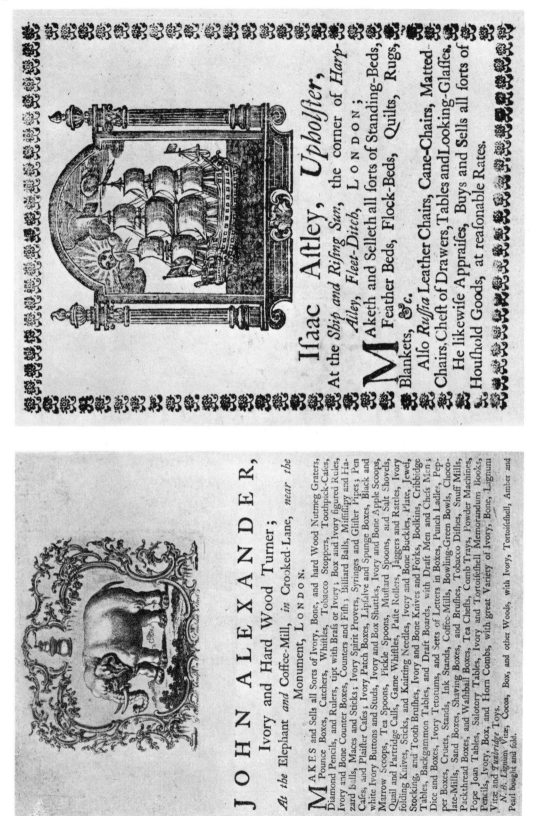

JOHN ALEXANDER,

Ivory and Hard Wood Turner;

At the Elephant *and* Coffee-Mill, *in* Crooked-Lane, *near the* Monument, LONDON.

MAKES and Sells all Sorts of Ivory, Bone, and hard Wood Nutmeg Graters, Pounce Boxes, Catchers, Whittles, Tobacco Stoppers, Toothpick-Cafes, Diamond Pencils, and Rulers, tipt with Brafs or Ivory; Box and Ivory figured Rules, Ivory and Bone Counter Boxes, Counters and Fifh; Billiard Balls, Mifinfipy and Hazard Balls, Maces and Sticks; Ivory Spirit Provers, Syringes and Glifter Pipes; Pen Cafes, and Plaifter Cafes; Ivory Patch Boxes, Liplave and Spunge Boxes, Black and white Ivory Buttons and Studs, Ivory and Box Shuttles, Ivory and Bone Apple Scoops, Marrow Scoops, Tea Spoons, Pickle Spoons, Muftard Spoons, and Salt Shovels, Quail and Partridge Calls, Game Whiftles, Pafte Rollers, Jäggers and Rattles, Ivory folding Knives, Sticks, and Knitting Needles, Ivory and Bone Buckles, Plate, Jewel, Stocking, and Tooth Brufhes, Ivory and Bone Knives and Forks, Bodkins, Cribbidge Tables, Backgammon Tables, and Draft Boards, with Draft Men and Chefs Men; Dice and Boxes, Ivory Tetotums, and Setts of Letters in Boxes, Punch Ladles, Pepper Boxes, Cruets, Stands, Ink Stands, Coffee-Mills, Bowling-Green Bowls, Chocolate-Mills, Sand Boxes, Shaving Boxes, and Brufhes, Tobacco Difhes, Snuff Mills, Packthread Boxes, and Wafhball Boxes, Tea Chefts, Comb Trays, Powder Machines, Pope Joan Tables, Salotory Tables, Ivory and Tortoifefhell Memorandum Books, Pencils, Ivory, Box, and Horn Combs, with great Variety of Ivory, Bone, Lignum Vitæ and *Tunbridge* Toys.

N. B. Lignum Vitæ, Cocoa, Box, and other Woods, with Ivory, Tortoifehell, Amber and Pearl bought and fold.

See page 4

SIZE OF ORIGINAL 8⅛″ × 5⅝″

Ifaac Aftley, Upholfter,

At the *Ship and Rifing Sun*, the corner of *Harp-Alley, Fleet-Ditch,* LONDON;

Maketh and Selleth all forts of Standing-Beds, Feather Beds, Flock-Beds, Quilts, Rugs, Blankets, &c.

Alfo *Ruffia* Leather Chairs, Cane-Chairs, Matted-Chairs, Cheft of Drawers, Tables and Looking-Glaffes. He likewife Appraifes, Buys and Sells all forts of Houfhold Goods, at reafonable Rates.

See page 7

SIZE OF ORIGINAL 6¼″ × 4¾″

LONDON FURNITURE MAKERS
from 1660-1840

(The figures, enclosed within brackets, after the dates in the following list correspond to those in the Sources of Reference given on pp. xix–xx.)

ABBOTT, ADRIAN, Cabinet-maker, of Alley, Buckingham Street, Strand.
$\qquad$ 1774 (3)

ABBOTT, STEPHEN, Cabinet-maker and Upholder, Lombard Street. 1760 (2)

ABRAHAM, JOHN, Frame carver and Gilder, Long Acre. 1709 (4)

ADAIR, —, Carver and Gilder, No. 55, King Street, Golden Square. 1790 (2)
$\qquad$ Supplied mirrors for Hartwell House. 1766 and 1778 (52)

ADAIR, JOHN, Carver and Gilder, in Wardour Street, Soho. *c.* 1763 (46)

ADAIR-WILLIAM, R., Carver and Gilder, No. 26, Wardour Street, Soho.
$\qquad$ 1784–93 (2)
$\qquad$ Executed work, sofas, etc., for the Royal palaces. 1773–1805 (52)

ADAM, ROBERT AND JAMES, Architects and Designers of furniture,
$\qquad$ Albermarle Street, 1728–1794 (62)
$\qquad$ Among the most important of the houses designed by them are Lansdowne House, Kenwood, Osterley House and Syon House.

ADAMS, GEORGE, Upholder and Cabinet-maker, No. 122, Minories.
$\qquad$ 1790–1803 (2, 18)
$\qquad$ Mentioned in Directories and Sheraton's *Cabinet Dictionary*.

ADAMS, GEORGE, Cabinet-maker, No. 37, Long Alley, Moorfields. 1817 (2)

ADAMS, —, Cabinet-maker, No. 122, Minories. 1803 (19)

ADAMSON, —, Joiner and Turner in mahogany, Fen-Church Street.
$\qquad$ *c.* 1760 (1)
$\qquad$ Makes all sorts of cabinets, looking-glasses and all sorts of mahogany goods. Funerals performed and goods appraised.

ADDISON, JOHN, Carpenter (no address).
$\qquad$ Subscribed to Chippendale's *Director*. 1755 (17)

ADDISON, ROBERT, Cabinet-maker, Hanover Street. 1774 (3)

AFFLECK, JAMES, Cabinet-maker, Parliament Street, Westminster.
$\qquad$ 1749–74 (3)

AGAR, SAMUEL, Carver, Church Street, St. Anne's, Soho. 1755 (17) 1763 (2)

AIRAY, JOHN, Upholder, Southwark. 1724 (3)
$\qquad$ Clerkenwell. 1734

AITKEN, THOMAS, Cabinet-maker, at the corner of Langley Street in Long Acre.   *c.* 1760 (1)

(Plate, page 5)

ALDERSEY, THOMAS, Glassgrinder, Cabinet-maker and Upholder.
No. 20, Tooley Street, Southwark.   1763–70 (2)
Bridge Yard, Southwark.   1772 (2)
No. 17, Brokers' Road, Moorfields.   1779 (2)

ALEXANDER, JOHN, Wood and Ivory Turner, at *The Elephant & Coffee-mill* in Crooked Lane, near the Monument.   1776–93 (1, 2)

(Plate, page 2)

ALKAN, SEFFERIN, Carver in wood and stone, Dufour's Court, Broad Street, near Golden Square.   1763 (2)
Possibly identical with the following:

ALKEN & LAWRANCE, who carried out the carvings in the Adam library at Shardeloes.   1763 (25)

ALKEN, SAMUEL, Wood carver (no address).   *fl.* 1780–1796 (49)(62)
Employed on carving mirror by Sir William Chambers and subscribed to Sir William Chambers' *Treatise.*   (49)

ALLAM, THOMAS, Upholder, Maddox Street, Hanover Square.   1748–74 (3)

ALLEN, —, Upholsterer (deceased) at *The White Swan*, West Smithfield.
His widow not designing to follow the trade.   1704 (5)

ALLEN, —, Upholstry, Cabinet and Looking-Glass Manufactory, No. 21, Little Eastcheap.   *c.* 1800 (1)

(Plate, page 5)

ALLEN, ABRAHAM, Upholsterer, designer and manufacturer of "furniture calicoes," No. 61, Pall Mall.   1809–17 (1)

ALLEN, GEORGE, Upholsterer, No. 158, Fenchurch Street, removed from No. 50, Fenchurch Street.   1802–11 (1)

ALLEN, JOHN, Upholder, Cabinet-maker and Looking-glass maker to the Bank of England, No. 50, Fenchurch Street.   1783–96 (1, 2)

ALLEN, WILLIAM, Upholder.
No. 129, New Bond Street.   1783 (2)
No. 24, Davies Street.   1790

ALLEN & DOOLAN, Cabinet and Chair maker, No. 174, Borough.
1768–74 (2)

ALPORT, RICHARD, Upholster, in the Poultry.   Died 1649 (13)

ANDERSON, —, Chair maker, Windmill Street, Tottenham Court Road.
1803 (19)

ANGEL, —, Upholster (address unrecorded).   1628 (46)

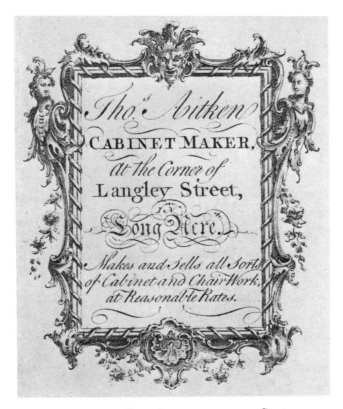

SIZE OF ORIGINAL 4⅞″ × 4″   *See page* 4

SIZE OF ORIGINAL 2⅜″ × 3¼″   *See page* 10

SIZE OF ORIGINAL 4⅝″ × 3″   *See page* 4

SIZE OF ORIGINAL 6¼″ × 3¾″   *See page* 10

SIZE OF ORIGINAL 4″ × 5⅝″ *See pages* 14, 252, 253

SIZE OF ORIGINAL 4½″ × 4½″ *See pages* 13, 236, 237

SIZE OF ORIGINAL 5⅜″ × 3¾″ *See page* 13

SIZE OF ORIGINAL 5¼″ × 4⅛″ *See page* 14

ANSELL, —, Cabinet-maker (address unrecorded).

    Supplied fine mirrors and consoles at Blenheim, designed by Sir William Chambers. 1773 (60)

ANTHONY, MARK, Cabinet-maker (address not recorded). *c.* 1690 (46)

APPLETREE, *see* DOBSON & APPLETREE.

ARBUNOT, JACOB, Cabinet-maker, on the south side of Long Acre. 1709 (4)

ARBUNOT, JACOB, Looking-glass shop, at *The Royal Cabinet* over against Church Court in the Strand. 1715 (5)
    His shop was burnt out.

ARBUNOT, JAMES, Cabinet-maker in the Strand. 1727 (5)
    "Leaving off trade."

ARBUNOT, PHILIP, Cabinet-maker, Strand. 1709 (4)

ARBUNOT, PHILIP, Looking-glass shop, corner of Villiers Street, Strand.
    "Leaving off trade." 1716 (5)

ARNE, THOMAS, Upholder, at *The George & White Lion*, in the Great Piazza, Covent Garden. *c.* 1690 (5)
    Removed to *The George* in Bedford Court, near Bedford Street, Covent Garden. 1698 (5)
    At *The Two Crowns & Cushions* in King Street, Covent Garden. 1707–12 (5)
    At *The Crown* in King Street. 1721–34 (5)
    His name is best known as the father of Dr. Arne, the composer, and of his daughter Mrs. Cibber, the actress. It was at Arne's house in King Street that the four "Indian Chiefs" were lodged when they visited London in Queen Anne's reign. 1710 (33)

ARNOLD, SAMUEL, Upholder, Gracechurch Street. 1727 (5)

ARROWSMITH, H. W. & A. (late Henderson), Upholsterers and Gilders to Her Majesty, No. 80, New Bond Street. 1840 (2)

ARROWSMITH, JOHN, Cabinet-maker, succeeded by John Hatt (*q.v.*), at above address. (*deceased*) 1759 (57)

ARROWSMITH, STEPHEN, Cabinet-maker, at *The Blue Ball & Artichoke* in Aldersgate Street. (1)

ASKEW, WILLIAM, Cabinet-maker, in Knaves Acre, Golden Square. 1749 (3)

ASTLEY, EDWARD, Cabinet-maker, at *The Clock Case* in Wych Street, near the New Church in the Strand. *c.* 1730 (1)

ASTLEY, ISAAC, Upholster, at *The Ship & Rising Sun*, the corner of Harp Alley, Fleet Ditch. 1753 (1)
                 (Plate, page 2)

ATKINS, HENRY, Cane chair makers, at *The Three Crowns*, south side of St. Paul's Churchyard. 1723 (6), 1801 (1)

ATKINSON, —, Cabinet-maker, Aldersgate Street. 1803

ATKINSON, THOMAS, Cabinet-maker, successor to Mr. Belchier (*q.v.*) at *The Sun*, ye south side of St. Paul's, opposite the clock.   1755 (1)
(Plate, page 1)

ATLEE, WILLIAM, Upholsterer, removed from York Buildings next to Mrs. Rochford's at the Upper Mews Gate to the corner of Duke Street, York Buildings.   1722 (5)

AYLIFFE & WEBB, Chair makers and Turners, No. 49, Wardour Street, Soho.
                                                                  1765 (1)

N.B. Chairs lent for Routs.

AYLIFFE & CO.   Address unrecorded.   1777 (1)
N.B. Chairs lent for Routs.

AYLIFFE & GEE.   Address unrecorded.   1785 (1), 1794 (2)
N.B. Chairs lent for Routs.
Succeeded by C. BRIDGES (*q.v.*).

AYTON, J., Carver, Gilder and Picture Frame maker, No. 73, next door to *The Coffee Mill* in Berners Street, Oxford Road.
Sells all sorts of Green and Gold Dressing Glasses, Pier Glasses, Girandoles, etc.
                                                            c. 1790 (1)

BABEL, PETER, Papier mâché frames and Ornaments maker, near James's Street in Long Acre.   1763 (2)

BAGSTER, JAMES, Upholsterer. No. 20, Piccadilly.   1790–96 (2), 1803 (18)

BAILEY, —, *see* TATHAM & BAILEY.

BAILEY, *see* TATHAM AND BAILEY, Cabinet-makers, No. 14, Mount Street.
                                                                  1809 (2)
See also BAILEY AND SAUNDERS, Cabinet-makers, No. 13, Mount Street.
                                                              1811–17 (2)

BAILEY, THOMAS, Cabinet-maker and Upholsterer in Conduit Street, near New Bond Street, Hanover Square.   1766 (1), 1774 (3)
Succeeded by VICKERS AND RUTLUDGE, *q.v.*

BAILEY & SAUNDERS, Cabinet-makers, No. 13, Mount Street.   1817 (2)
See also TATHAM, BAILEY AND SAUNDERS.

BAKER, BERNARD, Upholder, No. 23, Bedford Street, Covent Garden.
                                                    1774 (3), 1783–96 (2)

BAKER, JOHN, Upholsterer to James I (address not recorded).   (46)

BALL, THOMAS, Upholster, in Vine Street near St. James's Church. 1749 (5)

BANKS, BENJAMIN, Cabinet and case maker, No. 3, Litchfield Street.
                                                              1817–27 (2)

In *Nollekens and His Times* is a description of Mr. Banks' house with the painted ceiling thought to be by the hand of Hogarth, Vol. II, p. 167.   (30)
J. T. Smith in *Nollekens* says also that Cobb (*q.v.*) the upholsterer "occasionally employed Banks the cellaret maker."

BARBER, J., Cabinet-maker, No. 37, Red Lion Square. 1803 (19)

BARBER, JACOB, Cabinet-maker and Upholsterer, No. 18, Lamb's Conduit Street. 1817 (2)

BARBER, JAMES, Upholder, in Checker Yard, Aldgate. 1638 (46)

BARBER, JAMES, Upholsterer, in Piccadilly. 1749 (3)

BARBER, JOHN, Cabinet-maker (no address).
Subscribed to Chippendale's *Director*. 1755 (17)

BARBERRY, —, Cabinet-maker, George Street, Oxford Street. 1803 (19)

BARFORD, HENRY, Cabinet-maker and Upholder, No. 226, Piccadilly. 1779 (2)

BARFORD, RICHARD, Upholder, in Pall Mall. 1747 (5)

BARFORD, MR., Upholsterer, next door to the Earl Inchiquin's in Pall Mall. 1748 (5)

BARFORD & PICK, Cabinet-makers in Piccadilly. 1777 (2)

BARKER, JOHN, Upholsterer, No. 72, Great Titchfield Street. 1824–25 (2)

BARNES, ISAAC, Ivory and hardwood turner at *The Blue Coat Boy* opposite Buckingham Street (No. 41) in the Strand. 1777 (1, 2)
Succeeded by THOMAS BLAIR (*q.v.*).

BARRETT & WICKSTEED, succeeded by J. Ovenston (*q.v.*), Cabinet-makers, No. 53 and 54, Wardour Street. 1803 (19)

BARRON, BENJAMIN, Upholder, over against Bond's Court in Walbrook. 1732 (5)

BARRON, JAMES, Upholder and Cabinet-maker, No. 28, Little Queen Street, Lincoln's Inn Fields. 1790–93 (2)

BARRON, JOHN, Upholder, in Wood Street. 1747 (5)

BARRON, RANDOLPH, Upholsterer, Martlet Court, Bow Street. 1709 (3)

BARRON, RANDOLPH, Upholder, Martlet Court, Bow Street. 1712 (5)

BARRON, RANDOLPH, St. Martin's Lane. 1727 (5)

BARRY, A., Upholsterer, No. 7, Vere Street, Oxford Street. 1803 (19)

BARRY, E., & SON, Upholsterers and Cabinet-makers, No. 64; Newington Causeway, near the Turnpike. 1826 (1)

BARTLETT, EDWARD, Cane chair maker, Russell Street, Drury Lane. 1709 (3)

BATESON, DAVID, Cabinet-maker and Upholder, No. 128, High Holborn. 1794–1817 (2)

BATESON, WILLIAM, Upholder and Cabinet-maker, Queen Street, Bloomsbury. 1774 (3)
No. 114, Russell Street, Bloomsbury. 1790–94 (2)

BATLERSON, —, Cabinet and Chair maker, in Berkeley Row, Berkeley Square.
1744 (57)

BAXTER, ANTHONY, Cabinet-maker (?), at *The Naked Boy* in Henrietta Street, Covent Garden.   1735 (23)

Mrs. Purefoy, of Shalstone, commissioned him on various occasions regarding a four-post bedstead and quilted hangings.

BAYLEY, DANIEL, Cabinet-maker (deceased), Aldermanbury.   1729 (5)

BEACHCROFT, SAMUEL, Upholder, at *The White Hart*, Mark Lane, Fenchurch Street.

Bankrupt.   1727 (5)
Deceased.   1731 (5)

BEALE, J., Cabinet-maker, No. 5, Old Bailey.   1803 (19)

BEARD, ARABELLA, Cabinet-maker and upholsterer, No. 157, Fenchurch Street.   1794 (19), 1803 (2)

BEATY, FRANCIS, Cabinet-maker, Bull Inn Court, Strand.   1774 (3)

BEAUCHAMP, GEORGE, Cabinet-maker, No. 18, St. Paul's Church Yard.
1783–1803 (19) (2)

BEAUMONT, JOHN, Cabinet-maker, No. 45, Beech Street, Barbican. 1803 (19)

BEAUMONT, WILLIAM, Carver and Gilder, at *The King's Arms*, Leicester Square.

"Nephew and successor to the late Mr. Vialls" [*sic*].   1788 (1)
See *Strawberry Hill Accounts*, p. 105.   1790–93 (2)
William Vile (*q.v.*) was in partnership with John Cobb at No. 72, St. Martin's Lane.   He died in 1767.

(Plate, page 5)

BECKWITH & FRANCE, St. Martin's Lane.   1796 (2)

BECKWITH, SAMUEL, Upholsterer and Cabinet-maker, No. 5, Rathbone Place, Oxford Street, from St. Martin's Lane.   1801 (1)

See also FRANCE & BECKWITH.

BEDFORD, BENJAMIN, Upholsterer, late of Pall Mall, bankrupt.   1710 (5)

BEDWIN, —, Upholsterer, in Oxford Road.   1747 (5)

BEESLY, EDWARD, Turner, at *The King's Arms*, opposite the Wax-work in Fleet Street.   1787 (1)

"The Wax-work" was Mrs. Salmon's famous gallery at *The Golden Salmon*, No. 189, Fleet Street.

(Plate, page 5)

BELCHER & GRAY, Cabinet-makers, Brownlow Street, Holborn.   1770–83 (2)
Pulteney Street, Golden Square.   1784 (2)

SIZE OF ORIGINAL $3\frac{7}{8}'' \times 5\frac{1}{8}''$ *See page* 14

Charles Blyde

Late Foreman to. Mess.rs Gally & Baker

AT THE

Chair and Tea-Chest

in Knaves Acre.

Cabinet Maker and Upholdterer.

Appraiser and Underaker.

Blankets and Carpets &c.

SIZE OF ORIGINAL $7\frac{3}{4}'' \times 6\frac{1}{4}''$ *See page* 20

SIZE OF ORIGINAL $2\frac{3}{8}'' \times 3\frac{3}{8}''$ *See page* 20

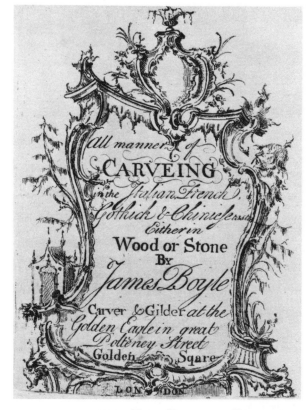

SIZE OF ORIGINAL $5\frac{1}{4}'' \times 3\frac{7}{8}''$ *See page* 23

John Boothby
Upholsterer, and Sworn-Appraiser,
At the Golden Head in Norfolk Street, in the Strand
LONDON.
Makes & Sells all Sorts of Upholstery Goods,
Cabinets, Chairs, and Looking Glasses, &c.
Also Funerals perform'd Publick or Private.

J. Hulme Delin.

SIZE OF ORIGINAL 8¾″ × 6⅜″

See page 23

BELCHIER, JOHN, Cabinet-maker, at *Ye Sun* on the South side of St. Paul's, near Doctors Commons.   1741 (1)
Alternatively described as on the south side of St. Paul's, right against the clock.   1750 (1)
The earliest mention of John Belchier occurs in *The Purefoy Letters*, by G. Eland, for furniture supplied to Shalstone Manor in 1735 (23).
John Belchier died in 1753 and he was succeeded at the above address by Thomas Atkinson (*q.v.*).

(Plates, pages 6, 236, 237)

BELL, DANIEL, Cabinet-maker, in St. Martin's Lane.   1728–34 (5)
From the various accounts given in the London papers between 15th and 20th of October, 1728, of the extensive damage done to his premises by a fire, which broke out at a currier's in Rose Street at the back of St. Martin's Lane, it would appear that Daniel Bell's business was pretty extensive. One paper stated that "he employed several scores of workpeople" and the loss of his stock and the timber stacked in his yard amounted to "some thousands of pounds." A day or two later, however, he was able to announce that he had taken a house and workshop opposite to his old premises. This would have placed him just below Newport Street on the west side of St. Martin's Lane.
Writing in 1928 Mr. E. F. Strange instances a bill rendered by BELL & MOORE and receipted by Thomas Moore "for Daniel Bell and self" dated 20th December, 1734, but no address is given of this partnership.
It seems very possible that Daniel Bell was the originator of the business in St. Paul's Churchyard which continued to be carried on by members of the Bell family during the latter half of the eighteenth century.

BELL, HENRY, Cabinet-maker, at *The White Swan* against the South Gate in St. Paul's Churchyard.   *c.* 1740 (1)
The above address is identical with that of Coxed, and later on of Coxed and Woster (*q.v.*) who occupied it from about the year 1700 until 1736, when the death of Woster is recorded and presumably Henry Bell took over the business. (His connection, if any, with Daniel Bell (above) can only be a matter for conjecture.) Within a few years he was succeeded by his widow Elizabeth (*q.v.*) (1). Henry Bell achieved a finely designed trade-card which was a great advance on the crude wood-cut used by his predecessors and that he continued to keep abreast of his times we see from the footnote on his card: "N.B. Old Glasses (*i.e.* mirrors) hand worked & made up Fashionable."   (1)

(Plate, page 6)

BELL, ELIZABETH, Cabinet-maker, at *The White Swan*, against the South Gate in St. Paul's Churchyard.   *c.* 1750 (1)
Successor to Henry Bell—see above. This card is identical with that of Henry Bell save for the alteration of the first name. Later she took her son into partnership—see below.

BELL, ELIZABETH, & SON, Cabinet-makers, at *The White Swan*, against the South Gate in St. Paul's Churchyard.   *c.* 1760 (1)
This card is identical with that of Elizabeth Bell except for the interpolation of the words "& SON." It was found pasted on the bottom of a drawer in a small walnut knee-hole writing table.

BELL, PHILIP, Cabinet-maker and Upholder, at *The White Swan*, against the
South Gate in St. Paul's Churchyard.   1768–74 (1) (2)

One may assume that Philip was the "Son" in the firm Elizabeth Bell & Son, but
he has departed from the distinguished design of his parents' card and commissioned Matthias Darly to produce one in the more fashionable Chinese-
Chippendale manner. The old sign of *The White Swan* is now obscured by a
tangle of bulrushes. Darly it was who executed most of the plates for Chippendale's *Director*. With the suppression of the old signboards and the introduction
of street-numbering at this period, *The White Swan* now became No. 18, St. Paul's
Churchyard, which we can identify from Horwood's Plan of London (1799) as
a little to the east of Paul's Chain facing the south door of the Cathedral. According
to the London directories William Henshaw, cabinet-maker (*q.v.*) was at No. 18,
St. Paul's Churchyard from 1768–72, and two years later Henry Kettle's
name (see Plate, page 255) is given there. On Kettle's trade-card he claims to
be "successor to Philip Bell" although his address is then stated to be No. 23 in
St. Paul's Churchyard and the directories give him at this number until 1796 (2).
Henshaw's card of an earlier date was issued from *The Cabinet and Chair* on the
south side of St. Paul's Churchyard. (1)
For earlier records of this long-established business see under COXED & WOSTER.

(Plates, pages 6, 252, 253)

BELL, ROBERT, Upholsterer, No. 29, Minories.   1803 (19)

BELLETT, JOHN, Upholder, No. 12, St. Mary Axe.   1779–92 (2)

BENNETT, JOSEPH, Cabinet and Chair maker, No. 164, Tottenham Court Road.
                                                                      1817 (2)

BENNETT, SAMUEL, Cabinet-maker, at the sign of *The Cabinet* in LOTHBURY.
                                                       1723 (6), deceased 1741

A very fine bureau which contains the label of Samuel Bennett is preserved in the
Minister's study of her Majesty's Legation to the Holy See in Rome.
A walnut bookcase inscribed "Samuel Bennett, London Fleet" in the Donaldson
sale (1925) fetched 1600 guineas. A somewhat similar bookcase is in the Victoria
and Albert Museum.

(Plate, page 233)

BENSON, WILLIAM, Cabinet-maker, Cross Lane, Long Acre. 1755 (17), 1774 (3)

BENT, THOMAS, Bed-joyner, opposite Bridewell Bridge, Fleet Ditch.
                                                     c. 1760 (1), 1749 (4)

A copy of this card in Miss Banks' collection bears the misleading date 1809.
The engraver Brooke worked between 1748–68.

(Plate, page 6)

BERESSELAER, JOHN, Cabinet-maker (deceased), at *The Three Crowns*, in the
Strand against Southampton Street.   1733 (5)

BERNARDEAU, DANIEL, Hardwood turner and oval frame maker.
Late apprentice to Mr. Storer of Snow Hill at *Ye Golden Coffee Mill* in
St. Martin's Court near Leicester Fields.   *c.* 1750 (1)

(Plate, page 11)

SIZE OF ORIGINAL $7\frac{1}{2}$" $\times$ 5"

See pages 25, 26

SIZE OF ORIGINAL $6\frac{5}{8}$" $\times$ $4\frac{1}{8}$"

See page 26

16

ANN BUCK,
at the Queen's-head, near Hatton-Garden, in
HOLBORN:
Buys and Sells Beds, Bedding, Burves Thork
Cane Chairs, Glaſses, China, and all Sorts
of Houſehold Furniture New & Old.

N.B. Quilts, Blankets, Tickens, Harrateens, &Cheneys Sold, Wholeſale,
and Retale

SIZE OF ORIGINAL 6⅜" × 4¾"

See page 26

HENRY BUCK

Removed from the Hand & Crown
at the East end of St Pauls to the
Hand, Crown and Star, on the
South side of St Pauls Church-Yard.
LONDON.
Makes and Sells all ſorts of Chairs
Tables, Cabinet Work, Looking Glaſses,
and Window Blinds. &c.
at Reaſonable Rates.
both for Sea and Land.

SIZE OF ORIGINAL 6¼" × 4"

See page 29

Samuel Burton

UPHOLDER & CABINET-MAKER,

in S. Mary Ax. near Leadenhall Street,

London.

Makes & Sells all sorts of Cabinet & Upholstry Goods, in the genteelest & newest fashion, in silk and Worsted Damask Furniture: Mohair: Morine, and Cotton Ditto, with all sorts of Cheque, Mountateen, &c.a Feather Beds. hair & Flock Mattrasses, Counterpanes, Cotton Quilts, Blankets, &c.a Chests of Drawers, Desk & Book-Cases, Wardrobes, Dining Tables, Card Ditto, and Commode Dressing Tables, Chairs, Looking Glasses, &c.a Turky, Wilton & other Carpets: for Home use or Exportation. Variety of Paper Hangings.

GOODS APPRAISED and FUNERALS FURNISH'D.

SIZE OF ORIGINAL 6⅝" × 5¼"

See page 30

Peter Burchatt

C A R V E R

Chair and Cabinet Maker,

at the Cabinet Warehouse in Fleet Market near Holborn Bridge.

L O N D O N.

Makes and sells all sorts of Looking Glasses, Chairs, & Cabinet Work &c in y.e neatest Manner Wholesale & Retail. Where Gentlemen, Merchants and others may depend upon being supplyed with all sorts of the above mentioned Goods for Exportation at Reasonable Rates.

N.B. Funerals decently Performed. Goods Appraised and the most Money given for Household Furniture.

SIZE OF ORIGINAL 7⅜" × 4¾"

See page 29

18

BERROW, HENRY, Upholder, removed from *The George & Mitre* in King
    Street to *The Crown* in Bow Street.   1714 (5)
    Deceased.   1723 (5)

BERRY, J., Carpet warehouse, No. 131, Fleet Street.   1803 (19)

BEST, WILLIAM, Cabinet-maker, Fleet Ditch.   1722 (6)

BEVAN, EDWARD, Carpenter and blind maker, Air Street, Piccadilly.   1778 (1)
    He was granted a patent for "his new and peculiarly constructed Venetian
    Blinds" for which he charged at the rate of one shilling per sq. ft. The bill dated
    1778 is made out to Sir Humphrey Morice, Comptroller to the Household of
    George II, 1757.

BINNS, —, Cabinet-maker, No. 99, Mount Street, Grosvenor Square.
                                                        1803 (19)

BINNS, JOSEPH, Cabinet-inlayer, Albion Buildings, Bartholomew Close.
                                             1790–93 (2)
    No. 24, Duke Street, Smithfield.   1794–96 (2), 1803 (19)

BIRD, WILLIAM, Turner, at *The Rocking Horse*, just without Newgate.
                                              1724 (6)

BIRKIT, RICHARD, Cabinet-maker, King Street, Golden Square.   1803 (19)

BISSET, JOHN, Cabinet-maker and Undertaker.
    At *Ye Chair & Coffin* in Lower Moorfields.   *c.* 1760 (1)
    Cabinet and upholstery warehouse, Brokers' Row, Moorfields. 1790 (2)

BLACKBORNE, JOHN, Upholster, Cornhill Ward.   1640 (15A)

BLADES, JOHN, Glass manufacturer, No. 5, Ludgate Hill.   1816 (46A)

BLADES, THOMAS, Cabinet-maker, St. James's Market.   1774 (3)
    No. 114, Jermyn Street.   1790–93 (2)

BLADES & PALMER, Upholders, No. 177, Piccadilly.   1803 (19)

BLADWELL, JOHN, Upholsterer, Bow Street, Covent Garden.
                                     1725 (5), 1768 (2)

BLAIKLOCK, M., Cabinet-maker, No. 14, North Audley Street.   (19)

BLAIR, THOMAS, Ivory and hardwood turner, successor to Isaac Barnes (*q.v.*)
    at *The Blue Coat Boy*, No. 446 in the Strand, opposite Buckingham
    Street.   1774 (1)

BLANCH, SAMUEL, Cabinet-maker and Upholsterer, Compton Street, Soho.
                                        1749 (1) (3)

BLANCHARD, SAMUEL, Cabinet-maker, Cornhill.   1705–13 (5)

BLAND, CHARLES, Cabinet-maker (no address).   1672 (8)

BLAXLAND, HENRY, Upholsterer, No. 71, Old Broad Street.
                                    1783–96 (2), 1803 (19)

BLEASE, — (*see* SEDDON & BLEASE), No. 24, Dover Street.   1802–13

BLENNERHASSET, R., Upholder, No. 9, Windmill Street, Finsbury.   1803 (19)

BLISSETT (*see* MACKENZIE & BLISSETT).

BLUDWELL, JOHN, Upholster, Bow Street.   1749 (3)

BLUNDEL, R., Upholsterer, *The Royal Bed*, Paternoster Row.   1710–11 (5)

BLUNT, CHARLES, Upholsterer, Brook Street, near Holborn Bars.   1690 (5)

BLYDE, CHARLES, Cabinet-maker and upholsterer (late foreman to Gally & Baker), at *The Chair and Tea Chest*, in Knaves Acre.   *c.* 1760 (1)

(Plate, page 11)

BODHAM, PHILIP, Upholster, who was partner with the late Mr. John Hibbert [*q.v.*], is now remov'd to the next door at *The Three Chairs*, up the stone steps in Bartholomew Close, West Smithfield.

1720 and 1722 (5)

BODOVINE, RENÉ (*cf.* PAUDEVIN), Upholsterer, King Street.

temp. Charles II

BOGAERT AND CO., Carvers and Gilders, No. 23, Air Street, Piccadilly.

1809–11 (2)

BOLTE, ADRIAN, Cabinet-maker (no address).

Applied for re-appointment to the office of cabinet-maker to the King, a position he had held in the previous reign (State Papers of Charles II).   1660

BOLTER, JAMES, Upholder and Cabinet-maker, No. 45, Bishopsgate Without.

1779 (2)

Dorset Street, Spitalfields.   1792 (2)

BOLTER AND DAWS, Upholders, No. 1, Moorfields.   1774–77 (2)

BOLTON, JOHN, Upholsterer, No. 109, St. Martin's Lane.   1803 (20)

BOMER, ABRAHAM, Looking-glass maker, Bedfordbury, Covent Garden.

1709 (4)

BOND, BENJAMIN, Cabinet and Chair maker, No. 24, Ratcliff Highway.

1790 (2)–1803 (20)

BONELLA, WILLIAM, Cabinet, Chair maker and Upholsterer, No. 107, White Chapel Road.   *c.* 1800 (1)

(Plate, page 11)

BONIFOLD, JOHN, Chair maker (no address).

The account books of the Hospital of Sir John Hawkins, Knight, at Chatham, record the purchase of eight mahogany arm-chairs of Hepplewhite design in 1791 at a cost of £16. In 1944 these chairs fetched £640 at Sotheby's.   1791

BONNELL, THOMAS, Upholder and Cabinet-maker, No. 133, Long Acre.

1749 (3)–1779 (2)

BOODEN, THOMAS, Upholder, Fenchurch Street.   1727 (3)

BOOTH, BENJAMIN, Turner, at *The Rocking Horse* near Serjeant's Inn, Fleet Street.   1749 (1)

David Curto

[Cabi]net-Maker, Undertaker, & Sworn Appraiser:

[at] the Dripping Pan between New

[......] Street & Little Moorgate, in

Moorfields LONDON.

[......] and Sells all Sorts of Household Goods

[New] or Old at very Reasonable Rates.

[f]urnisheth Funerals to any Part of Great

Britain at the Lowest Prices.

See page 33

SIZE OF ORIGINAL 6⅛" × 3½"

CABINET and UPHOLSTERY Work in General Viz.

Chairs, Tables and Glasses of all Sorts, neat Mahogany

Bedsteads & Cloaths Prefses. with the greatest Variety of nice

Tea-Tables, Trays and Chests. done at reasonable Rates by

William Cauty.

At the West End of Somerset House in the Strand,

At the Sign of the Chair and Curtains

LONDON.

See page 34

SIZE OF ORIGINAL 7½" × 5⅝"

See page 35

SIZE OF ORIGINAL $6\frac{1}{2}$" × $4\frac{3}{4}$"

See page 34

SIZE OF ORIGINAL $6\frac{1}{4}$" × $4\frac{3}{4}$"

BOOTHBY, JOHN, Upholsterer and Appraiser, at *The Golden Head* in Norfolk Street in the Strand (deceased). 1747 (1)
(Plate, page 12)

BORNE, ROBERT, Cabinet-maker, over against George Yard in Lombard Street (deceased). 1727 (5)

BOROUGHS, JOHN, *see* JOHN BURROUGH.

BOSTOCK, JAMES, Upholsterer, at *The Two Black and White Balls* in Holbourn Row, Lincoln's Inn Fields. 1727–35 (5)

BOULTON, JOHN, Upholder, No. 48, Threadneedle Street. 1777–94 (2)
A small bow fronted mahogany chest-of-drawers with his label was sold at Sotheby's, 19th November, 1948.

BOUNFALL, A., Japanned Chair manufacturer, Middle Row. 1803 (20)

BOWKER, JOHN, Upholder, 128, Leadenhall Street. 1783–84 (2)
No. 3, Postern Row, Tower Hill. 1790–96 (2)

BOYCE, JOHN, Cabinet-maker, Garlick Hill. 1724 (5)

BOYCE, R., Upholsterer, No. 22, Charlotte Street, Fitzroy Square. 1803 (20)

BOYLE, JAMES, Carver and Gilder at *The Golden Eagle* in Great Pulteney Street, Golden Square in the Italian, French, Gothick and Chinese tastes. 1763 (2)
(Plate, page 11)

BRADBURN, JOHN (or BRADBOURNE), Cabinet-maker to George III, Hemings Row, in St. Martin's Lane. 1758 (49)–1767 (64)
Long Acre. 1774–76 (3)
R. W. Symonds (*Connoisseur*, April, 1938) quotes a legacy in the will of William Vile (*q.v.*) in favour of his "servant" John Bradbourne, who succeeded Vile in his office of cabinet-maker to the throne in 1764, and retained it until he retired in 1776. (64)
He appears to have moved in 1767 from Hemings Row to a house in Long Acre which subsequently became No. 8. (56)
Mr. R. W. Symonds instances a clock case by John Bradburn, cabinet-maker for Queen Charlotte. (51)

BRADFIELD, E., Cabinet and Bedstead manufacturer, No. 169, Tottenham Court Road. 1817 (2)

BRADFORD, JAMES, Japanner and Cabinet-maker, *The Angel*, at the corner of Poppins Alley, Fleet Street. 1714 (5)

BRADFORD, JOHN, Cabinet-maker, in Printing-House-Yard in Black-Friers.
c. 1690 (1)
His label found inside a drawer of a walnut cabinet, reads as follows: "Cabinets, Escreutors, Desks, Tables, Burows, Likewise Glasses, Peirs, Chimney-Glasses, Sconces. And all manner of Cabinet, or Joyner's Work Made or Mended by me JOHN BRADFORD, in Printing-House-Yard in Black-Friers, LONDON."

BRADLEY, FRANCIS, Cabinet-maker, No. 2, Newman Street, Oxford Road.
1803 (19)

BRADSHAW, WILLIAM (address unrecorded). 1736–45 (56)

BRADSHAW, —, Upholster, in Soho Square. 1747 (5)

BRADSHAW, GEORGE SMITH, Upholder and Cabinet-maker, Dean Street, Soho. 1760–84 (2)
     Crown Court, Soho. 1769–93 (2)

     The above two addresses might apply to the same premises though actually Crown Court was not off Dean Street but off Princes Street, near by.

BRADSHAW, GEORGE SMITH, AND SAUNDERS, PAUL, Upholders and Cabinet-makers, Greek Street, Soho. 1756 (5)

     This partnership was dissolved in 1756, Bradshaw continuing in Greek Street and Saunders trading from Soho Square at the corner of Sutton Street. (56)
     John Mayhew (see Mayhew and Ince) was apprenticed to Mr. Bradshaw and was in his service in 1756. (5)

BRADSHAW, MICHAEL, Upholsterer, in Bridge Row. 1763 (2)

BRADSHAW, THOMAS, Upholsterer, No. 10, St. Paul's Church Yard.
1768–74 (2)
     in Gracechurch Street. 1792 (2)

BRADSHAW, THOMAS, Carver and gilder, No. 4, Coventry Street. 1790–93 (2)

BRAITHWAIT, —, Upholder, at *The Ship and Anchor* in Cornhill. 1732 (2)

BRAITHWAIT, WILLIAM, Upholder (address unknown). 1724 (3)
     See also BRATHWAITE.

BRAMANT, WILLIAM, Upholsterer, Strand. 1709 (4)

BRAND, GEORGE, Cabinet-maker, in Petticoat Lane (deceased). 1761 (61)

BRAND, George, Cabinet-maker, No. 37, Houndsditch. 1790–93 (2)

BRATHWAITE, BENJAMIN, Upholder, of Southwark. 1723 (5)

BRATHWAITE, EBENEZER, Upholster, of Cornhill. 1734 (5)

BRATHWAITE, SAMUEL, Upholder and Cabinet-maker, No. 315, High Holborn.
1772–92 (1)
     And No. 145, Cheapside. 1779
     And No. 13, High Holborn. 1781–84

BRETLAND, SAMUEL, Cabinet-maker, at *The Looking Glass*, Church Street, near Cornhill. *c.* 1740 (1)
     Later he was at *The Looking Glass* in Threadneedle Street, near the South Sea House. 1760 (1)

BREWER, WILLOUGHBY, Carver, Gilder and Looking-glass manufacturer, No. 7, Aldersgate Street. 1779 (2)
     No. 67, Red Lion Street. 1792 (2)
     Clerkenwell. 1796 (2)

BRIDGES, CHARLES, Chair maker and Turner to His Majesty, No. 49, Wardour
  Street.   1829 (1)
  Successor to John Gee (*q.v.*) at above.

BRISCOE, —, Upholster, in Old Jury (deceased).   1658 (13)

BRISCOE, RICHARD, Upholsterer, at *The Golden Lion*, corner of Blackmoor
  Street, Drury Lane.   1721 (6)
  In St. Clement Danes.   1727 (5)

BRISSENDER, —, Upholder and Cabinet-maker, No. 203, High Holborn.
                                                                   1780 (1)

BRODSTOCK, WILLIAM, Upholsterer and Cabinet-maker to Charles II.
                                                                   1667 (8)

BROMWELL, JOHN, Upholder, New Palace Yard, Westminster.   1725 (5)

BROMWICH, THOMAS, Paper stainer and Upholsterer, at *The Golden Lyon*
  on Ludgate Hill.   1740–87 (1)
  He supplied "the new furniture wall paper" to Horace Walpole.   1754 (26)
  In 1763 he was appointed "Paper-hanging Maker in Ordinary to the Great
  Wardrobe."
  Master of the Painter–Stainers Co. in 1761. Died 1787.

BROMWICH, THOMAS AND LEIGH, LEONARD, at above.   1758–65 (1)

BROMWICH AND ISHERWOOD, at above.   1766 (1)

BROMWICH, ISHERWOOD AND BRADLEY, at above.   1770–88 (1)

BROOKS, ROBERT, Upholder and Cabinet-maker, 1, Budge Row.
                                                                   1774–93 (2)

BROOKSHAW, GEORGE, Cabinet-maker, No. 48, Great Marlborough Street.
                                                                   1783–86 (56)
  Supplied goods to the Prince of Wales at Carlton House.

BROWN, J., Upholsterer, etc., No. 38, Little Pulteney Street, at the corner of
  Crown Court.   1794 (2)

BROWN, JAMES, Upholsterer and Cabinet-maker, at *The King's Arms* (No. 29)
  the south side of St. Paul's Church Yard.   1768–96 (1, 2)

BROWN, JOHN, Chair maker and Cabinet-maker at *The Three Cover'd Chairs
  and Walnut Tree*, on the East Side of St Paul's Church Yard near the
  School.   1738 (1)
  At John Brown's—At *The Three Chairs and Walnut Tree* in St. Paul's Church
  Yard, near the School, are made and sold Window Blinds of all sorts, painted
  in Wier, Canvas, Cloth and Sassenet, after the best and most lasting manner
  ever yet done so that if ever so dull an dirty they will clean with sope and sand and
  be like new; where may be seen great choice of the same being always about
  them. Likewise at the same place is made the new fashion Walnut Tree Window
  seat cases to slip off and on, very much approved of beyond stuff seats.   1729 (5)
  John Brown would have taken over the shop when William Rodwell (*q.v.*) vacated

BROWN, JOHN—*continued*.

    it. Rodwell was advertising his specialities in window blinds from this shop, then called *The Walnut Tree* in St. Paul's Church Yard in Jan., 1727.   (1)

    It is noticeable that at this early date he was advertising "all sorts of *Windsor* Garden Chairs of all sizes painted green or in the wood."

    In another label of John Brown's (1728) the sign was *Ye Three Chairs and Walnut Tree*.   (1)

    "Remov'd from *The Three Cover'd Chairs and Wall-nut Tree* in St. Paul's Church Yard to the house that was formerly Mr. Robert Garnidge's, and lately *The Crown* Tavern, two doors above the School nearer Cheapside."   1730 (5)

    John Brown is recorded at this address until 1744.

(Plate, page 15)

BROWN, JOHN AND SON, Upholsterer and Cabinet-maker, No. 43, St. Paul's Church Yard.   1763–68 (2)

BROWN, THOMAS, Upholder, No. 41, Cannon Street.   1762–77 (2)

BROWN, W., Chair manufactory, Carlisle Lane, Lambeth.   1803 (20)

BROWN, WILLIAM, Upholder, at *The Cross Keys and Star*, the corner of Spittle Square, Spittlefields.   *c.* 1760 (1)

BROWN AND READ, No. 41, Cannon Street.   1770–83 (2)

BROWN AND RING, No. 45, St. Paul's Church Yard.   1770 (2)

BROWN AND WILSON, Cabinet-makers, in Long Acre.   1763 (2)
    See also WILSON AND BROWN.

BROWNING, —, Upholder and Appraiser, at *The Royal Tent* in Threadneedle Street.   1747 (5)

BROWNING, GEORGE, Upholder, Appraiser and Auctioneer, in the East Pawn,* over the Royal Exchange, up the Great Stair-case in Cornhill.   *c.* 1760 (1)

(Plate, page 15)

BROWNING, GEORGE, Upholder, No. 30, Cornhill.   1783 (2)

BRUCE, DAVID, Cabinet-maker and Upholder, No. 113, Aldersgate Street.   1803–17 (20)

    Miss Jourdain records that he supplied the chairs for the Governor's Room in the Bank of England.   1809

BRUCE AND ROBINSON, Cabinet-makers and Upholsterers, No. 29, Little Queen Street, Lincoln's Inn Fields.   1794 (2)
    See ROBINSON at same address.

BUCK, ANN (widow of Henry Buck) (*q.v.*), Dealer in furniture, etc., at *The Queen's Head* in Holborn, near Hatton Garden.

    Her signature is on a receipted bill of Henry Buck's with date 1741. She advertised the sale of "Buck's Views," a well-known series of topographical engravings by S. and N. Buck, from the above address.   1748 (5)

(Plate, page 16)

* Pawn = a corridor on the first floor.

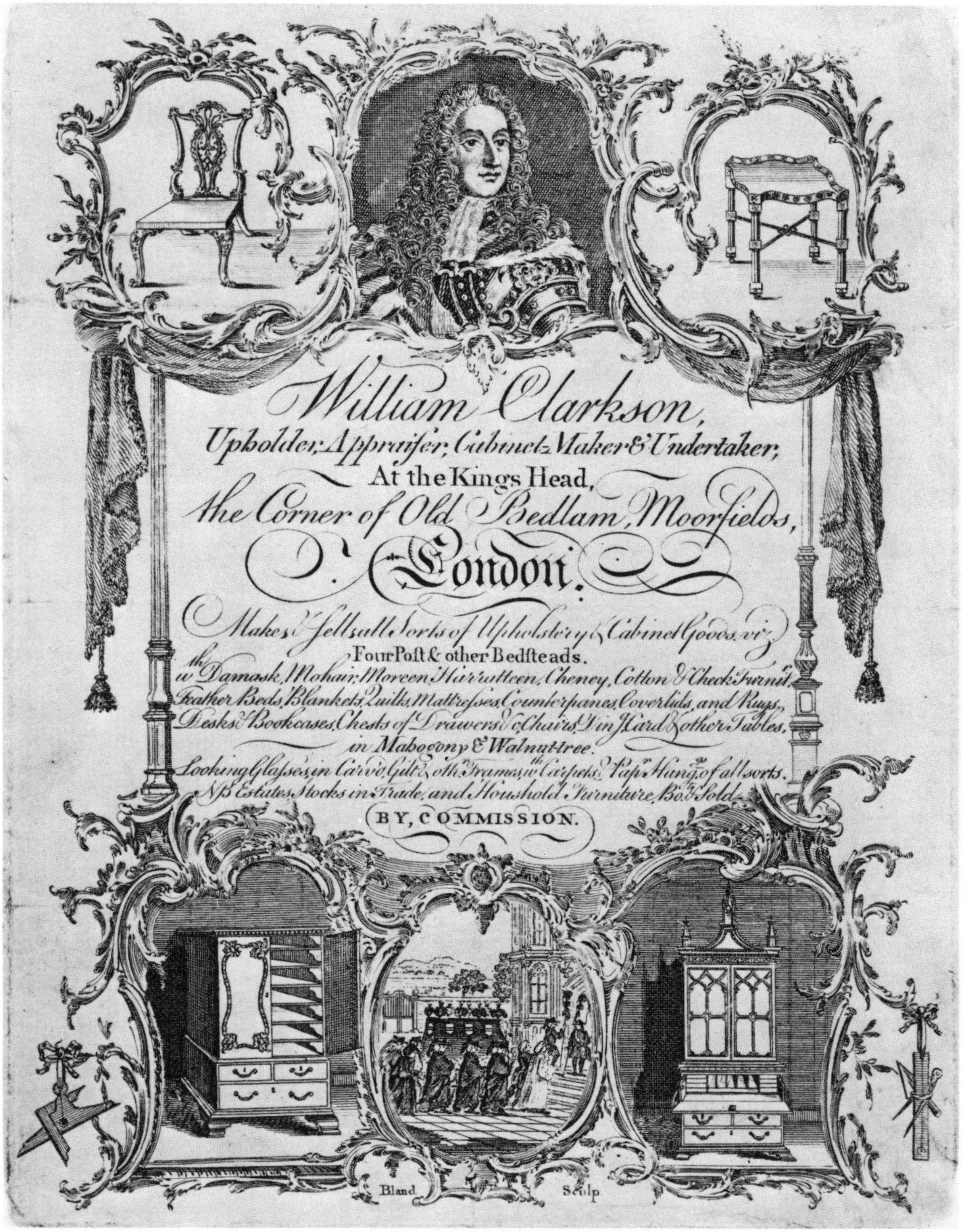

SIZE OF ORIGINAL 7$\frac{3}{8}$" × 5$\frac{7}{8}$"

See page 37

T. HOMAS CLOAKE,
UPHOLDER, CABINET-MAKER,
AND
APPRAISER,

At No 4, the GOLDEN-LION, in Lower-Moorfields,
near Old Bethleham, LONDON.

BUYS and fells all Sorts of Houfhold Goods, as Defks and Book-
Cafes, Buroes and Double Chefts of Drawers, Dreffing Chefts
and Tables, Three Drawer Dreffing Tables, Breakfaft, Dining,
Card, Turn Over, and Tea Tables, Tea Boards, and Tea Chefts;
Chairs in Mahogany, Walnut-Tree, Beach, &c. Looking, Chimney,
and Sconce Glaffes, in French, Carved, Pediment, and Gilt Mahogany
and Walnut-Tree Frames; Dreffing, Swinging, and Hanging Glaffes,
in Mahogany and Walnut-Tree Frames; Harrateen, Cheney, Linfeys,
and Checks of all Colours, in Whole and Half Teafters; Feather Beds
of all Sorts, with Blankets, Quilts, Coverlids, and Rugs; Settee,
Buroe, Chefts of Drawers, Four Pofts, and Turn up Bedfteads;
Carpets, and Floor Cloths; with all other Sorts of Upholftry.
Potage, Coffee, and Chocolate Pots, Sauce Pans, and Stew Pans;
Tea Kettles, Brafs Candlefticks, Peftles, Mortars, and Warming Pans,
Brafs and Steel Stoves, Bath Stoves, Shovels, Tongs, Pokers, &c.
Blowing Stoves, Kitchen Grates, and Fenders; with all other Furni-
ture, both New and Old.
Moft Money for all Sorts of Houfhold Goods.
N. B. Funerals Furnifhed.

SIZE OF ORIGINAL $6\frac{1}{4}'' \times 3\frac{7}{8}''$

See page 38

James Comery
Cabinet Maker and Broker
at ye Golden Eagle in Caftle Street. behind Long Acre
LONDON

Appraifeth Buyeth & felleth all manner of Houfehold Goods
at Reafonable Rates

SIZE OF ORIGINAL $6\frac{3}{8}'' \times 4\frac{3}{4}''$

See page 39

BUCK, HENRY, Cabinet and Chair maker, at *The Hand, Crown and Star*, on the south side of St. Paul's Church Yard, removed from *The Hand and Crown*, at the *East* End of St. Paul's.   1741–50 (1)
Previously Henry Buck had been in partnership with Richard Farmer at *The Hand and Crown*, where Farmer remained until his death in 1747.

(Plate, page 16)

See also FARMER AND BUCK, 1723–41.   (5)

BUCK AND FARMER, Two bills in these names for chairs supplied to Sir Richard Hoare dated   1732 and 1733 (1)
No address on billhead.
See also RICHARD FARMER and FARMER AND BUCK.

BUCK, JOHN, a Cabinet-maker of this name subscribed to Chippendale's *Director*.   1755 (18)

BUCKINGHAM, H., Japanned chair manufactory, Old Street, near the Mint.
1803 (20)

BUCKLE, OSWALD, JUNIOR, Upholsterer, at *The Chair Royal*, Bury Street, St. James's.   1725 (6)

BUDD, —, Upholster, at *The Rising Sun*, Chancery Lane.   1716–19 (5)

BUHL FACTORY, owned by L. C. Le Gaigneur, No. 19, Queen Street, Edgware Road.   1815 (46A)

BULLOCK, G., Cabinet-maker (address unrecorded).   *c.* 1810
Referred to in Maria Edgeworth's letters.

BUNCE, WILLIAM, Upholsterer, No. 8, Russell Street, Covent Garden.
1803 (20)

BUNDOCK, WILLIAM, Upholsterer, No. 53, Great Russell Street. 1808–14 (2)
cf. W. E. CALDECOTT.

BURBEROW, MATTHEW, Carver and Gilder, No. 32, Chandos Street.
c. 1800 (1)
58, Oakley Street, Lambeth.   1827 (2)

BURBURY, —, Cabinet-maker, George Street, Oxford Road.   1803 (20)

BURCHAM, PETER, Carver, Chair and Cabinet-maker, at the Cabinet Warehouse in Fleet Market.   1755 (1)
near Holborn Bridge.   1763 (2)

(Plate, page 17)

BURFORD, JOHN, Carver and Gilder, on the Pavement, St. Martin's Lane.
1763 (2)

BURFORD, WILLIAM, member of the Joiners' Company, Broadway, Westminster.   1792 (2)

BURNETT, GILBERT, Upholsterer, No. 16, Strand.   1774 (2)
Apprenticed to Thomas Burnett.   1753 (14)

BURNETT, THOMAS, Upholsterer, at *The King's Arms*, against the New Church in the Strand. 1747–66 (2, 5)

In the years 1764–66 Mr. Burnett supplied furniture to Lord Leigh for Stoneleigh Abbey to the extent of between £3,000–£4,000.
See also CHILLINGWORTH AND BURNETT, 1724–40.

BURNETT, THOMAS AND GILBERT, Upholsterers and Cabinet-makers, at above. 1765 (1)–1772 (2)

Supplied writing tables to Lord Braybrooke at Audley End. 1765 (1)

BURNLEY, WILLIAM, Upholder, Bartholomew Close. 1711–13 (5)

BURROUGH, JOHN, Cabinet-maker, at *Ye Looking Glass*, Cornhill.
1662–*c.* 1690 (1)

An account made out to "Mr. Clayton and Mr. Morris" for a "large cabinett £56 18s. od." and other items is dated June 17, 1662. The former was knighted Sir Robert Clayton in 1671, made Lord Mayor 1679 (*see D.N.B.*) and the latter John Morris (Alderman), with whom Clayton was in partnership, "money scriveners" at the Flying Horse in Cornhill.
John Burrough, in partnership with William Farnborough (*q.v.*) was cabinet-maker to Charles II and William and Mary. 1677–*c.* 1690 (49)
A later tenant at the above address was James Hudgebout (*q.v.*) in 1704.

BURTON, SAMUEL, Upholder and cabinet-maker, in St. Mary Ax* near Leadenhall Street. T.C^d. (1)
13, Houndsditch. 1768–83 (2)
8, Houndsditch. 1784–93 (2)

(Plate, page 17)

BUSHNELL, JOHN, Cabinet-maker and Upholder, No. 1, Bishopsgate Within.
1772–92 (2)

BUTLER, THOMAS, Upholder, Cabinet-maker and Chair Manufacturer, Nos. 13 and 14, Catherine Street. 1804 (1)
8 doors from the Strand. 1790 (2)–1803 (20)

"Patent bedstead maker to the King and Queen and Royal Family."

(Plate, page 18)

BUTLER AND KEPPEL, at above address. 1790–93 (2)

CADDEY, JOHN, Cabinet and Looking-glass maker at *The Cabinet*, in King Street, the corner of Guildhall Yard and also in Wood Street.
1724–27 (5)

CAINCROSS, WILLIAM, Cabinet-maker, No. 11, Hollen [*sic*] Street, Soho.
1803 (20)

CALCOT, ARTHUR, Upholsterer, New Street South, St. Martin's Lane.
1709 (4)

CALCOTT, —, Upholder, upon the Pavement, St. Martin's Lane. 1722 (5)

* St. Mary Axe joins Houndsditch.

John Coxed,

AT the *Swan* in St. *Paul's* Church-Yard, *London*, makes and fells Cabinets, Book-Cases, Chefts of Drawers Scrutores, and Looking-g, *&c* of all forts.

Printed in Bow Church-Yard, Printer of all forts of Advertisements.

SIZE OF ORIGINAL 5″ × 3½″   *See pages* 40, 229

G. Coxed and T. Wofter.

AT the White Swan in St. *Paul's* Church-Yard, *London*; makes and fells Cabinets, Book-Cafes, Chefts of Drawers, Scrutores, and Looking-glaffes of all forts at reafonable Rates.

Cluer, in Bow Church-yard, Printer of all forts of Advertifements.

SIZE OF ORIGINAL 5″ × 3½″   *See pages* 40, 43, 230, 231

Jᵒ COCKERILL,
PAINTED
& JAPAND
Chair Manufacturer,
Nᵒˢ 1 & 3, Curtain Road, Worship Street, Finsbury Square,
And Nᵒ 203, Oxford Street, near Orchard Street.
ELEGANT JAPAND CARD; TABLES & BED-CORNISHES.
The greatest variety of Drawing-Room Japand Chairs in Colours, or
Black & Gold in the most Superb style.
Likewise all sorts of Japand Bed-Room Chairs
to match Bed-Furniture, Paper Hangings, &c.)
— in the Newest & most Elegant Taste.——
And on MORE REASONABLE TERMS than any
other Warehouse or Manufactory, in London.

SIZE OF ORIGINAL 3⅛″ × 4½″   *See page 38*

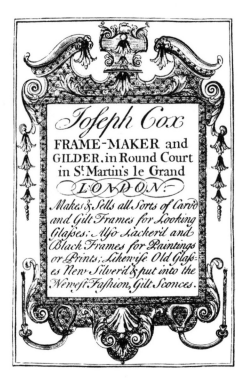

Joseph Cox
FRAME-MAKER and
GILDER, in Round Court
in Sᵗ Martin's le Grand
LONDON.
Makes & Sells all Sorts of Carv'd
and Gilt Frames for Looking
Glasses: Also Lacker'd and
Black Frames for Paintings
or Prints; Likewise Old Glass-
es New Silver'd & put into the
Newest Fashion, Gilt Sconces.

XXXIII

SIZE OF ORIGINAL 5⅝″ × 3⅝″   *See page 40*

CRIBB
Glass & Picture Frame
Maker,
CARVER GILDER &
Printseller,
Nᵒ 288
near Great Turn-stile
HOLBORN.
Old Frames new Gilt, &
Glasses new Silvered.
Pictures Cleaned,
Lined & Repaired.

Venetian Window Blinds,
Paper Hanging &c.

Neele Sculpt 352 Strand

SIZE OF ORIGINAL 4⅝″ × 3″   *See page 43*

CROSS,
Cabinet Maker,
Upholder,
Auctioneer &
APPRAISER.
Funerals Furnish'd

57 Barbican.

SIZE OF ORIGINAL 3½″ × 2¼″   *See page 44*

CALDECOTT, W. E., Upholsterer and Cabinet-maker, No. 53, Great Russell Street, Bloomsbury, opposite the British Museum.   1817–39 (1, 2)
Successor to Mr. W. BURDOCK (*q.v.*).

CALDWALL'S carpet and bedding warehouse, above Gray's Inn Gate in Holborn.
"Persons residing at the Court End of Town may likewise be served at his warehouse in Piccadilly, the corner of Albemarle Street."   1759 (1)

CALLOWAY, FELIX, Upholsterer, in New Bond Street.   1749 (3)

CALLOWAY HENRY, Upholsterer, in New Bond Street.

CALLOWAY, JOHN, Upholsterer, Hanover Square.   1727–34 (1, 3)
No. 64, New Bond Street.   1790–1817 (2, 20)

CALVERT, —, Upholsterer, at *The Raven* in Cornhill.   1693 (5)

CALVERT, JOHN, Turner, No. 189, Fleet Street.   1793 (1, 2)

CAMPBELL, —, Upholster, within 3 doors of *The Dog and Duck*, on the south side of New Bond Street, near Hanover Square.   1726 (5)

CAMPBELL, GEORGE, Upholder.   1764 (1)
Grosvenor Street.   1774 (3)
See also WILLIAM CAMPBELL.

CAMPBELL, JOHN, Upholder and Cabinet warehouse, No. 140, High Holborn.   1774–94 (2)

CAMPBELL, ROBERT, Cabinet-maker and Upholsterer to the Prince of Wales, Little Marylebone Street, Golden Square.   1774–93 (2)
He is reputed to have worked under Henry Holland, the architect, at Carlton House.
Sheraton, in his *Drawing Book*, says that he made a speciality of library steps.
He took out a patent for convertible Library Steps "first made for the King" in 1774.

CAMPBELL AND SON, Cabinet-makers and Upholsterers, No. 34, Little Marylebone Street.   1791–96 (2)

CAMPBELL, WILLIAM, Upholder (*cf.* George Campbell), Grosvenor Street.   1727–49 (5)

CAMPFIELD, RICHMOND, Upholder, King Street, St. James's.   1712–24 (5, 3)

CAPLE, ROB, Cabinet-maker, Edward Street, Carnaby Market.   1749 (3)

CARKEET, W., Upholsterer, No. 17, Tavistock Street, Covent Garden.   1817 (1)
The present site of the offices of *Country Life*.

CARTO, DAVID, Cabinet-maker and Undertaker, at *The Dripping Pan*, between New Broad Street and Little Moorgate in Moorfields.   1745 (1)
(Plate, page 21)

CARTO, NICHOLAS, Cabinet-maker, at *The King's Arms*, over against Bride Lane, Fleet Street.   1725 (5)

CASBERT, JOHN, Upholsterer and Cabinet-maker (address unrecorded).

1660–75 (8)

"Rich bed of Crimson Velvett lyned with Scarlett Satten and trymed with gold and silver lace . . . at Hampton Court £30."

CASEMENT, WILLIAM, A designer and probably also a maker of furniture.

c. 1750

He was responsible for two plates in *The Cabinet Maker's Book of Prices* (*c.* 1760). The name occurs also as one of the subscribers to the first edition of Sheraton's *Drawing Book* (1791).   (62)

A large dining table bearing his label is now in use at Clarence House.

CASIMIR, JOSIAH, Upholsterer, in Nag's Head Court, Gracechurch Street.

1714–24 (5, 3)

CATIGNOU, JAMES, Cabinet-maker (address unrecorded).

temp. William and Mary (8)

CAUTY, WILLIAM, Cabinet-maker and Upholsterer, at the sign of *The Chair and Curtains* at the West End of Somerset House in the Strand.

1757 (1)

in King Street, St. James's Street.   1774 (3)

"N.B. Bedsteads, Sophas and Chairs finished so that no vermin of any Denomination can possibly exist in either by a new and infallible method never before found out and done no where else but at the above shop."

(Label in mahogany chest of drawers.)

1780 (4)

(Plate, page 21)

CHALLEN, WILLIAM, Fancy chair maker "from London."   1797 (55)

CHAMBERLAIN, JOHN, Cabinet-maker, the corner of Crown Court in Knaves Acre.   deceased 1743 (61)

CHAMBERS, RICHARD, Upholder, in Throgmorton Street. 1727 (5)–1734 (3)

CHAMBERS, SAMUEL, Upholder, Milk Street.   1724–34 (3)

CHAMBERS, TRISTRAM, Upholsterer, in Cary Street, near Lincoln's Inn Play House.   1749 (1, 3)

(Plate, page 22)

CHANNON, GEORGE, Cabinet-maker, St. Martin's Lane.   1749 (3)

CHANNON, JOHN, Cabinet-maker, on the west side of St. Martin's Lane.

1760 (6)

CHANNON, SENR. AND JUNR., subscribed to Chippendale's *Director*, 2nd edition.   1754 (18)

CHANNON, T., Cabinet-maker (no recorded address).

A label inscribed "T. Channon fecit 1740" appears on one of a pair of fine early Georgian mahogany bookcases at Powderham Castle. Reported by Mr. Ralph Edwards.   1740 (1)

CHAPMAN, —, Upholder, in Coleman Street. 1748 (5)

CHAPMAN, THOMAS, Cabinet-maker, in Old Bedlam, near Moorfields.
 c. 1760 (1)
 No. 17, Old Bethlem. 1770–79 (2)
(Plate, page 22)

CHAPMAN, WILLIAM, Upholsterer, No. 43, Coleman Street. 1792 (2)

CHARLETON, CHARLES, Wholesale Upholsterer, No. 9, Friday Street.
 1744–77 (2)

CHARLTON, SAMUEL, Upholster, Glasshouse Street. 1749 (3)

CHARRINGTON AND HENNING, Cabinet-makers and Upholsterers, No. 23,
 Leicester Square. 1790–93 (2)

CHAUNORE [sic], — (? CHANNON), a Cabinet warehouse, upon The Pavement
 (St. Martin's Lane). 1743 (5)

CHEMIN (see DU CHEMIN), Carver and Gilder.

CHENERY, WILLIAM, Upholder and Cabinet-maker (successor to Mr. Thos.
 Phipps) (q.v.), No. 81, Leadenhall Street. 1784 (1)

CHESSEY, —, see PITT AND CHESSEY.

CHESSON, WILLIAM, Upholsterer, at *The Three Chairs*, Grocers' Alley in the
 Poultry. 1744 (33)–1747 (5)
 No. 157, Fenchurch Street. 1753–74 (2)

CHESSON AND BATHURST, Upholders, No. 157, Fenchurch Street. 1768–74 (2)
 Succeeded by Taylor and Wright (q.v.).

CHESTER, NICHOLAS, Cabinet maker, No. 9, Butcher Row, Ratcliff Cross.
 1768–84 (2)

CHESTER, NICHOLAS AND SON, Butcher Row, Ratcliffe Highway.
 1790–93 (2)

CHILLINGWORTH, RICHD., AND BURNETT, THOS., Upholsters and Appraisers,
 at *The King's Arms*, against the New Church* in the Strand. c. 1740 (1)
 formerly at *The King's Arms* near Harp Alley, Fleet Ditch. 1724 (6)
 They were succeeded by Thos. and Gilbert Burnett (q.v.) 1747–74.

CHIPCHASE, ROBERT, Upholder, Beak Street. 1774 (2)
 See also LAMBERT AND TURNER, 1790.

CHIPCHASE AND LAMBERT, Upholders, Warwick Street, Golden Square.
 1783–90 (2)
 See also LAMBERT AND TURNER.

CHIPCHASE, ROBERT, AND SON, Upholder, No. 39, Dover Street, Piccadilly.
 1790–96 (2)

CHIPCHASE, R. AND H., Upholsterers, No. 39, Dover Street, Piccadilly.
 1803 (20)

* The "New Church" was St. Mary-le-Strand, completed in 1717.

CHIPPENDALE, THOMAS, SENIOR, *b.* 1718, *d.* 1779.
 Conduit Court, Long Acre.   1749 (48)
 Somerset Court, Strand.   1752 (48)
 At the sign of *The Chair* (later Nos. 60–62), St. Martin's Lane.
                                                            1754–79 (5)

(Plates, pages 248–251)

So much careful research has been devoted by writers on Georgian cabinet-makers to the work of Thomas Chippendale, his parentage and place of birth discussed and so many of his patrons identified that repetition here is superfluous. It may perhaps be pointed out that the more recent of these investigations have been directed to the consideration of what share in the designs which appear in *The Gentleman and Cabinet Maker's Director* (1754) should be attributed to Chippendale himself and how much was due to his draughtsmen Matthias Lock (*q.v.*) and Henry Copland. It should be noted however that the majority of the plates bear the inscription "T. Chippendale, *inv: et del:*" However that may be, it is now generally agreed that the publication of the *Director* gave a prominence to Chippendale's work beyond that of his contemporaries, some of whom were in no way inferior to him either in design or craftsmanship.

Although many of Chippendale's accounts are still preserved in the houses of his wealthy customers, none, so far as I am aware, have come to light which bear a printed heading with his address. Neither did he ever issue a trade-card, which is greatly to be regretted. Identification of his premises, therefore, rests upon the evidence of Rate Books and similar records. It is curious, too, that his name does not appear in the Royal Household accounts nor in any of the London directories of his period. It has escaped general notice that he adopted *The Chair* as his shop sign though this figures in an advertisement of the second edition of the *Director* which appeared in the *Whitehall Evening Post*, 4th December, 1756:

"All commissions for Household Furniture to be sent to the Cabinet and Upholstery Warehouse at *The Chair* in St. Martin's Lane will be most punctually observed and executed in the greatest taste and on the most reasonable terms. By the Publick's most humble servants

                          T. Chippendale
                          J. Rannie."

James Rannie (*q.v.*), a man of means, had been taken into partnership about the year 1755. Some five years after Rannie's death in 1766 he was succeeded by Thomas Haig (1771) who is said to have been Rannie's clerk, which lends colour to the idea that Rannie's role was that of a business manager.

CHIPPENDALE, THOMAS, JUNIOR, *b.* 1749, *d.* 1822.
 60, St. Martin's Lane, near Long Acre.   1779–1814 (19)
 57, Haymarket.   1814–21 (2)   42, Jermyn Street.   1821 (46)

After his father's death in 1779 he was in partnership with Thomas Haig, and the name of the firm appears in the directories as Chippendale and Haig until the latter retired from business in 1796. He supplied much of the furniture at Harewood House in 1797. In the issue of the *Director* in 1805 Chippendale is entered as "upholsterer and cabinet maker to the Duke of Gloucester" at No. 60, St. Martin's Lane. In 1814 he took premises at No. 57, Haymarket, where he

CHIPPENDALE, THOMAS, JUNIOR—*continued*.

is described in the 1817 Directory as upholsterer and undertaker, and seven years later, in 1821, he is found at No. 42, Jermyn Street. His death is recorded in 1822.

Between the years 1784 and 1801 he exhibited pictures at the Royal Academy. He became bankrupt in 1804, when his entire stock was sold by auction (see Whitley's *Artists and Their Friends*, II, 262).

An extremely rare small quarto *Book of Designs*, by Thomas Chippendale, junior, is preserved in the Victoria and Albert Museum.

CHIPPENDALE AND HAIG (*see* above).
No. 60, St. Martin's Lane. 1771–96 (46)
It was during this partnership that the dispute arose over their charge for furnishing Garrick's house in the Adelphi.

CHIPPENDALE AND PEART (*see* JOHN PEART).
No. 60, St. Martin's Lane. 1795–96 (4)

CHIPPENDALE AND RANNIE (*see* JAMES RANNIE).
No. 60, St. Martin's Lane. *c.* 1755–66 (5)

CHIVERS, NOAH, Upholder and Cabinet-maker, 290, High Holborn. 1774 (2)
No. 308, High Holborn. 1777
No. 307, High Holborn. 1783–93

CHRISTIE, JOHN, Chair maker, No. 4, Warwick Street, Golden Square.
1803 (20)

CHUPAIN, ELIJAH, Chair and Cabinet-maker, over against the sign of *The Crown* in King Street, Bloomsbury. 1739 (5)

CLARIDGE, R., Upholsterer, No. 185, Oxford Street. 1803 (20)

CLARK, —, Upholsterer, at *The Lyon and Lamb*, James Street, Covent Garden. 1707–48 (5)

CLARK, JAMES, Upholster, at *The Three Black Lyons* in Paternoster Row.
1723 (5)–32 (6)

CLARK, JOHN, Joiner, at *The Crown and Cabinet*, by Fleet Ditch, near Holborn Bridge. 1724 (6)

CLARKE, JOHN, Upholsterer, No. 1, Castle Street, Long Acre. 1803 (20)

CLARKE, WILLIAM, Upholsterer, next Bedford House in the Strand.
1690 (5)

CLARKSON, WILLIAM, Upholder and Cabinet-maker, at *The King's Head* at corner of Old Bedlam, Moorfields. 1790 (1)
(Plate, page 27)

CLAXTON, WILLIAM, Upholsterer, at *The Golden Lyon* in Fleet Ditch.
1711 (5)
"On Shrove Tuesday, a son of Mr. Claxton, an upholsterer at the Ditch-Side, standing to see a cock thrown at, was killed by a cat-stick* that happen'd to hit him under the ear."—*Weekly Packet*, 22nd February, 1718.
* The stick used in the game of tip-cat.

CLAY, HENRY, Japanner in Ordinary to His Majesty and H.R.H. Prince of Wales, Bedford Street, Strand.

> A bill in the "Strawberry Hill Accounts" (dated 1778) reads: "Writing table of Clay's ware" designed and decorated by Paul Sandby.
>> 18, King Street, Covent Garden.
>> Windsor Royal Archives.   1795
> "Clay died worth £80,000 made entirely out of his papier mâché enterprise."   (30)

CLAYFORD, J., Upholsterer, No. 31, Bartlett's Buildings, Holborn. 1803 (20)

CLEEVE, GEORGE, Cabinet-maker, at *The Chair* in Castle Street, near Long Acre.   1788 (1)

CLELAND, A., Cabinet-maker, No. 14, Charles Street, Middlesex Hospital.
                                                                           1803 (20)

CLEMAPON, GEORGE, Cabinet-maker, Mugwell Street, Cripplegate.

> A "George Siddon" [*sic*], i.e. George Seddon (*q.v.*) was apprenticed to him and the premium paid was £16.   1743 (14)

CLIFTON, WILLIAM, Upholsterer, Great St. Helen's, near Bishopsgate.
                                                                           1729 (5)

CLOAKE, THOMAS, Upholder and Cabinet-maker, at *The Golden Lion*, No. 4, Lower Moorfields, near Old Bethleham.   1774 (1)
Nos. 4, 5 and 6, Broker's Row, Moorfields.   1790–1803 (2, 20)
(Plate, page 28)

COBB, JOHN, Upholsterer and Cabinet-maker, No. 72, the corner house of St. Martin's Lane and Long Acre.   1749 (2)–1778 (3)

> He was in partnership with William Vile (*q.v.*) at this address trading as Vile and Cobb between 1750 and 1765. Vile retired in 1765 and died in 1767. Cobb carried on the business until his death in 1778.   (49)
> Cobb enjoyed the patronage of George III and the noble owners of some of the finest houses of his time. J. T. Smith in his *Nollekens* recounts anecdotes of his pompous behaviour and comments on his tendency to elaborate costume.   (30)
> Horace Walpole, in his *Description of Strawberry Hill*, refers to the furniture which Mr. Cobb made for the bed in the Holbein Chamber as "of purple cloth lined with white satin, a plume of white and purple feathers on the centre of the tester."   (27)
> *See* VILE AND COBB.
> Cobb and Vile rank pre-eminently in the trade, and as such have received full recognition at the hands of all the authorities who have written on eighteenth-century cabinet-making.
> *See also* VILE, STRICKLAND AND HALLETT.

COCKERILL, EDWARD, Japanned Chair manufacturer, Nos. 1–3, Curtain Road, Finsbury Square and 203, Oxford Street.   1797 (1)–1803 (20)

COCKERILL, JAMES, Painted and japanned chair manufacturer, at above.
                                                                       1790–94 (20)

(Plate, page 32)

COLE, GEORGE, Upholder, Golden Square. 1747 (3)–1774 (5)

COLE, JAMES, Upholder, James Street, Golden Square. 1774 (3)

COLEMAN, —, Cabinet-maker, Curzon Street, Mayfair. 1803

COLEMAN, ROBERT, Cabinet-maker and Undertaker of funerals, at *Ye King's Arms*, Houndsditch. 1726 (6)

COLEMAN, THOMAS, Upholsterer, at *The Ship* on London Bridge. (1)
His card bears engraved date 1734.

COLLINS, MATTHEW, Upholsterer, at *Ye Half Moon*, Cheapside, corner of Soper Lane. *c.* 1669 (35)

COLLINS, WILLIAM, Cabinet-maker, Tothill Fields. *d.* 1793
The elaborate carved and gilded settee forming part of the "Dolphin" or "Fish" set of furniture, presented to Greenwich Hospital in 1813, has been attributed to him mainly perhaps because the name of William Collins appears on the base of the torchère which accompanies it.

COLLIP, JOHN, Upholsterer, No. 122, Great Portland Street. 1803 (20)
John Street, Oxford Road. 1803 (20)

COMERY, JAMES, Cabinet-maker and broker, at *Ye Golden Eagle* in Castle Street. 1749, (1,3)
Behind Long Acre. 1770
(Plate, page 28)

CONSTABLE, JOHN, Upholder, No. 14, Cullum Street, Fenchurch Street. 1783 (2)
A Henry Constable subscribed to Chippendale's *Director*, 2nd edition, 1755.

COOKE, JACOB, Upholsterer, at *The Three Chairs*, on Little Tower Hill. 1749 (5)

COOKE, JOSHUA, Upholder, No. 3, Broker's Row, Moorfields. 1770–77 (2)

COOKE, THOMAS AND JOSHUA, Upholsterers, Holborn Hill. 1755–68 (2)

COOKE, WILLIAM, (?) Upholsterer, at *The Two Trees*, the lower end of Devonshire Street, near St. George's Chapel, sale of upholstered goods. 1712 (5)

CONWAY, JOHN, *see* FLETCHER AND CONWAY.

COOKMAN, —, Upholsterer, in Ashen-tree Court in White-Fryers. 1689 (5)

COOPER, JOHN, Cabinet-maker, No. 3, St. Michael's Alley, Cornhill. 1784–96 (2)

COOPER, JOSEPH, Wood and Ivory turner, at *The Crown and Bowl*, facing St. Sepulchre's Church on Snow Hill. *c.* 1760
(Plate, page 41)

COOPER, JOSEPH, Upholder and Cabinet-maker, No. 37, Bishopsgate Within. 1790–96 (2)

COPE AND GRAY, Upholders, No. 10, King Street, Bloomsbury.   1803 (20)

COPLAND, HENRY, Furniture designer, Gutter Lane, Cheapside.
1746, *d.* 1752 (51)

Published *A New Book of Ornaments.* (1746)

COPLAND, HENRY, AND MATTHIAS LOCK, at *Ye Swan*, Tottenham Court Road.   1752 (47)

R. W. Symonds, in his *Chippendale, Furniture Designer*, has pointed out that Lock, and his collaborator H. Copland, were in Chippendale's employ at the time when the first edition of the *Director* appeared in 1754, and they were undoubtedly responsible for many of the plates. Books of designs for mirrors and ornaments were produced by Lock between 1740 and 1769. Copland's name is found on engravings of bookplates, invitation cards and trade-cards as early as 1738. See *Creators of the Chippendale Style*, by Kimball and Donnell; and *English Furniture Designers*, by Constance Simon.

CORDY, WILLIAM, Carver and Gilder, No. 24, Cannon Street, London Stone. Bride Lane, Blackfriars.   1790–93 (1, 2)

CORK, WILLIAM, Cabinet-maker, Warwick Street, Golden Square.
1803 (20)

COTTER, WILLIAM, Cabinet-maker, No. 24, Burr Street, Wapping. 1803 (20)

COTTON, THOMAS BERNARD, Carver and gilder, No. 42, Fenchurch Street.
1777–94 (2)

COURTHORP, WILLIAM, Upholder, at *The Rose* and at *The Star*, in Paternoster Row.   1724–30 (5)
in Newgate Street.   1734 (5)

COWPER, JOHN, Upholsterer, at *The Three Blackbirds*, in Cornhill.   1693 (5)

COWPER, JOSEPH, Upholsterer, Cornhill.   1728–31 (5)

COWPER, DANIEL, Upholsterer, Cornhill.

COX, JOHN, Upholsterer, at *The Iron Balcony* in Drury Lane next door to the Lord Craven's.   1718 (5)
under the Piazza, Covent Garden.   1736–49 (2, 5)

COX, JOSEPH, Frame maker and Gilder, Round Court, St. Martin's le Grand.
c. 1760 (1)

(Plate, page 32)

COX, STEPHEN, Upholsterer, Nos. 10 and 11, Great Portland Street.
1803 (20)

COXED, JOHN, Cabinet-maker, at *The Swan*, in St. Paul's Church Yard.
c. 1700 (1)

(Plates, pages 31, 229)

COXED, G., AND WOSTER, THOMAS, Cabinet-makers, at *The White Swan*, against the South Gate in St. Paul's Church Yard.   *c.* 1710–36 (1)

During the last few years some very distinctive bureau-bookcases by this firm

1

Joseph Cooper
Turner.

at the Crown & Bowl facing St Sepulchres Church on Snow-hill

London

Makes & sells variety of Cruett Frames Coffee Mills,
Powder Boxes, Tea Boards, Dressing Boxes & Tea Chests of the
most Curious English & Foreign Woods. with all manner of
Ivory, Lignum &c. Tunbridge Ware. also Ivory Leg.ns & Fant ridge Toys
By Wholesale for Exportation
NB: The best Bowling Green Bowls & Billiard Balls Turnd to the
greatest exactnes

SIZE OF ORIGINAL 6¼" × 4¾"   See page 39

Gerard Crawley
Turner
At the Coffee Mill & Nimble Ninepence
In Cornhill London

Makes & sells variety of Tea Chests Maho-
gany Cruets Tea Boards Voiders Tables &c.
Matting and Floor Cloths All Sorts of
Coffee & other Mills Nine Pin and other
Bowls Salvers Cruets Ladles Bottle and
Ink Stands Sand & Washball Boxes Lignum
Vitæ Tunbridge & all other Turnery Wares
Leghorn & Straw Hats
By Wholesale for Exportation

The Nimble
NINE PENCE

SIZE OF ORIGINAL 5¾" × 3¾"   See page 43

Will.ᵐ Darby,

Upholsterer, Appraiser & Undertaker,

At the Bear & Crown, in Aldermanbury near y.ᵉ Church,

London

Makes & Sells all sorts of Upholstery & Cabinet Goods,
viz, Four Post & other Bedsteads.

In Damask, Mohair, Moreen, Harratteen, Cheney, Cotton & Check Furniture,
Feather Beds, Blankets, Quilts, Mattresses, Counterpanes, Coverlids & Rugs,
Chairs, Dining Card & other Tables, Chests of Drawers & Bureaus,
in Mahogony & Walnut-tree.

Tea Boards, Tea Chests &c. Looking Glasses in Carv'd, Gilt & oth.ʳ Frames,
Wilton & other Carpets, Wind.ᵂ Blinds and Paper Hangings of all sorts,

N.B. Funerals Furnish'd.

SIZE OF ORIGINAL 7⅛″ × 5⅝″

See page 47

COXED, G., AND WOSTER, THOMAS—*continued*.

have appeared in the sale-rooms. They were of an unusual character, being made of mulberry and burr elm inlaid with lines of pewter.

Thomas Woster was employed by Mr. Henry Hoare in 1723 to supply some of the furniture for his new house at Stourhead, which latter has recently been taken over by the National Trust.

The records of *The Swan* in St. Paul's Church Yard go back to the middle of the sixteenth century, when it was a bookseller's shop, and a bookseller's it remained until the end of the seventeenth century when it became an upholsterer's. For the next hundred years a long succession of cabinet makers occupied it:

Mr. Hayes, Upholsterer.	1694 (33)
John Coxed, Cabinet-maker.	c. 1700 (1)
G. Coxed and T. Woster, Cabinet-makers.	c. 1715–36 (1)
Woster died in 1736.	(5)
Henry Bell, Cabinet-maker.	c. 1740
Elizabeth Bell, widow of above.	c. 1750
Elizabeth Bell and Son (the son may be Philip Bell, see below)	c. 1760
W. Henshaw, Cabinet-maker.	1763–72
Philip Bell, Cabinet-maker.	1768–74
Henshaw and Kettle, Cabinet-makers.	1774
Henry Kettle (successor to Philip Bell).	1777–96

The White Swan appears to have become numbered 18 in St. Paul's Church Yard but for a period from about 1770 Philip Bell and Kettle seem to have occupied No. 23, and Kettle stayed on there until 1796, thus extending the period of the firm to one of a hundred years.

(Plates, pages 31, 230, 231)

CRACKERODE, JOHN, Cabinet-maker, at *The Tea Table*, Henrietta Street, Covent Garden. 1722 (5)–1724 (6)

CRAGG, JAMES, Cabinet and Chair maker, No. 188, Tottenham Court Road. 1817 (2)

CRAKE, —, Carver and gilder, No. 21, South Molton Street, Oxford Road. c. 1800 (1)

CRAKE, JOHN, Painter and Gilder, No. 18, Quebec Street and 258, Oxford Street. 1807 (2)

CRAWFORD, WILLIAM, Cabinet-maker, No. 228, High Holborn. 1774–83 (2)

CRAWLEY, GERARD, Turner and small furniture maker, at the sign of *The Coffee Mill and Nimble Ninepence*, adjoining St. Michael's Church in Cornhill. 1768 (1)

(Plate, page 41)

CRIBB, ROBERT, Carver and Gilder, No. 288, Holborn, near Great Turnstile. 1790–1827 (1, 2)

A frame maker of the name of Cribb was employed by Sir Joshua Reynolds.

(Plate, page 32)

CRICHTON, DAVID, Cabinet-maker, No. 28, King Street, Soho. 1774 (3)

CRICHTON, WILLIAM, Upholsterer, No. 28, King Street, Soho.   1803 (20)

CROMPTON, BENJAMIN AND SON, Upholders and Paperhanging makers, No. 23, Cockspur Street, facing the end of Suffolk Street.   1769–90 (1)
1772–96 (2)

Formerly the firm was:
CROMPTON, B. E., AND SPINNAGE, at the end of Suffolk Street, Charing Cross.
1753–70
or Cockspur Street, Charing Cross.   c. 1769 (1)
also in Charles Street, St. James's Square.   1753
See also SPINNAGE AND HOWARD.

CROMPTON AND HODGSON, from Messrs. Crompton and Spinnage at Charing Cross, Paper stainers, in Castle Street, the corner of Bear Street, near Leicester Square.   c. 1770 (1)

CROOK, BENJAMIN, Cabinet-maker, at *Ye George and White Lyon*, on ye South Side of St. Paul's Church Yard.   c. 1730–48 (1)
(Plates, pages 238, 239)

CROSS, EDWARD, Cabinet-maker and upholder, No. 57, Barbican. 1808–11 (1)
No. 123, Aldersgate Street.   1811–25 (2)
(Plate, page 32)

CROW, AUGUSTIN, Upholsterer in Bartholomew Close, near Smithfield, sale of stock. Successor to Alderman Crow, lately deceased.   1689 (5)

CROW, WILLIAM, Alderman of the City of London.   1659 (21)
Upholsterer, in Saint Bartholomew's (Bartholomew Close).   died 1668
No fewer than ten mentions between 1660 and 1668 are found in Pepys' *Diary* recounting his various visits to Crow's the upholsterer. Those in 1668 all relate to some tapestry hangings for his bed. On 15th October "out by coach . . . and then to Alderman Crow's to see variety of hangings, and were mightily pleased therewith, and spent the whole afternoon thereon; and at last I think we shall pitch upon the best suit of Apostles, where three pieces for my room will come to almost £80." The following day having taken his wife and "Deb" they decide "upon buying his second suit of Apostles which comes to £83; and this we think the best for us having now the whole suit to answer any other rooms or service." These tapestries would probably have been taken from Raphael's cartoons of the Acts of the Apostles, originally produced at Mortlake and subsequently recopied. (*See* Introduction, p. ix.)

CROXFORD, FRANCIS, Chair and Cabinet-maker.
"Eminent in his profession for his many new and beautiful designs, etc." 1733 (5)
Address not recorded.

CRUMP, JAMES, Cabinet-maker, King Street, Westminster.   1749 (3)

CULLEN, JAMES, Upholder and Cabinet-maker, 56, Greek Street, Soho.
1765–79 (2)
He supplied a cabinet for Blair Castle, Perthshire, in 1771.

CURE, GEORGE, Upholsterer, Haymarket.   1709 (4)

THE·LACE·CHAMBER

James Danser

Iborn Turner

At the Elephant and Star,
The Corner of Bow Church Yard

CHEAPSIDE LONDON.

Sells Variety of Cane Heads, in
Gold, Silver and other Metals.
Also, Canes and Sticks Mounted

In the Neatest Manner.

SIZE OF ORIGINAL $5\frac{1}{2}'' \times 3\frac{1}{4}''$

See page 47

Dalziel

CABINET MAKER,

At the Chair,

The Corner of Wych Street
facing Drury Lane

LONDON.

Makes & Sells all Sorts of
Mahogany Cisterns & Pails

SIZE OF ORIGINAL $5\frac{7}{8}'' \times 4\frac{1}{4}''$

See page 47

Du Chemin
Carver and Gilder in General.
N.º 3 Great Russ.l Street, Bloomsbury,
LONDON.
Pictures Carefully Cleand & Repaird & Prints
Neatly Fram'd & Glaz'd.

SIZE OF ORIGINAL
3″ × 4⅜″
See page 50

Benj.ⁿ Dell,
Bedstead-Maker,
next Door to the Sash, middle Moorfields,
Makes & Sells all Sorts of Four Post,
Turnup & Stand.g Bedsteads.
Desk & Table Bedst.ds of all sorts.
Mahogony, Wainscot Beach &c.
Wholesale & Retail at y.e most reasonable
—— RATES. ——
NB Bedsteads Dyed, in y.e neatest manner.

SIZE OF ORIGINAL
5⅝″ × 4⅞″
See page 48

CURE, GEORGE, Upholsterer, at *The Three Golden Chairs*, in the Haymarket.
1721–died 1759 (3, 5, 6)

CUSTANCE, J. M., Cabinet-maker, No. 74, Long Acre.
No. 41, Brewer Street, Golden Square. 1790–93 (1)

DAGUERRE, DOMINIQUE, Cabinet-maker, Sloane Street, Chelsea.
1789–95 (50)
He supplied furniture to Carlton House for the Prince of Wales.

DALE, —, Upholsterer, near Mr. Button's Coffee House, over the corner of
the Piazza, Covent Garden. 1714 (5)
An item of news in the *York Mercury* of 12th Decr., 1720, announced "Mr. Dale,
an upholsterer of Covent Garden has purchased the estate which belonged to the
late Viscount Bolingbroke for £50,000."

DALE, GEORGE, Upholder and Cabinet-maker (deceased), near Slaughter's
Coffee House, the Upper End of St. Martin's Lane. 1747 (5)

DALZEEL, WILLIAM, Cabinet-maker, No. 4, Chapel Street, Bedford Row.
1803 (20)
No. 24, Great James Street, Bedford Row. 1817 (2)
The name of Dalziel, cabinet-maker, of Great James Street occurs in a correspondence with the Royal Society of Arts which took place in 1817 in connection
with mahogany.

DALZIEL, —, Cabinet-maker, at *The Chair*, the corner of Wych Street facing
Drury Lane. *c.* 1770 (1)
(Plate, page 45)

DANIEL, THOMAS, Cabinet-maker, Long Acre. 1709 (4)

DANIEL, WILLIAM, Wholesale Upholder, Great Eastcheap. 1763 (2)

DANIELL, —, Clock case, Cabinet and Chair maker, No. 1, St. James's
Street, Clerkenwell. *c.* 1800 (1)

DANSER, JAMES, Turner, at *The Elephant and Star*, corner of Bow Church
Yard, Cheapside. *c.* 1760 (1)
(Plate, page 45)

DANSON, MYLES, Cabinet-maker, King Street, Golden Square. 1774 (3)
Norfolk Street. 1790–93 (2)

DARBY, THOMAS, Cabinet-maker, next door to the Castle Tavern, in Fleet
Street. 1698 (5)
Upholder, Princes Street, Stocks Market. 1727 (3)
Upholder, Blackfriars. 1734 (3)

DARBY, WILLIAM, Upholsterer, at *The Bear and Crown* (No. 12) Aldermanbury, near ye Church. *c.* 1760 (1), 1770 (2)
(Plate, page 42)

DARE, GEORGE, Turnery and Tunbridge wares, No. 4, Carey Lane, Foster
Lane. *c.* 1780 (1)

DARKE, RICHARD, Upholsterer, Bedford Street, Covent Garden.
1755 (18), 1768 (2)

DAVIES, JAMES, Cabinet-maker, No. 13, Great Carter Lane, Doctors'
Commons.   1790 (2)

DAVIS, —, Cabinet-maker, at *The Hen and Chickens* in Great Queen Street.
1710 (5)

DAVIS, J., Upholsterer, next door but one to *The Golden Sugar Loaf*, on the
Terrace in St. Martin's Lane.   1705 (5)

DAVIS, N., Upholsterer, No. 16, Giltspur Street, Smithfield.   1803 (20)

DAVIS, S., Upholsterer, No. 2, Little St. Martin's Lane.   1803 (20)

DAVIS AND ELLIOTT, Upholders, No. 97, New Bond Street.   1783 (2)
See also CHARLES ELLIOTT AND CO.

DAWES, MARK, Upholder, No. 1, Broker Row, Moorfields.   1779 (2)
86, Little Tower Hill.   1792–96 (2)

DAWES, THOMAS, Cabinet-maker and Upholder, 27, Dean Street, Soho.
1783–96 (2)
No. 69, Dean Street, and No. 48, Conduit Street.   1803 (19)

DAWS, —, Upholsterer, inventor of "recumbent easy chairs," No. 17,
Margaret Street, Cavendish Square.   1825–39 (1, 2)

DAWS, JUNIOR, Cabinet-maker, Dean Street, Soho.   1803 (19)

DAWSON, THOMAS, Cabinet-maker and Upholsterer, No. 26, Oxford Street.
1755 (18), 1793 (2)

DAY, JAMES, Upholder, Fleet Street.   1727 (3)

DEACON, SAMUEL, Cabinet-maker, No. 22, Wardour Street, Soho. 1803 (19)

DEEBLE, JOHN, Upholder, No. 85, Cannon Street.   1783–93 (2)

DEEBLE, JOHN THURSTON, No. 82, Cannon Street.   1794–96 (2)

DEEKER, —, Maker of backgammon and billiards tables, Berwick Street,
Soho.   1780 (1)

DELAFIELD, ERASMUS, AND MATTHEWS, TIMOTHY, Upholsterers "at *The
Royal Bed & Rising Sun*," by Fleet Ditch.   1723 (6), 1742 (5)
Delafield retired from partnership in 1750.
See also MATTHEWS AND DELAFIELD, 1748.

DELL, BENJAMIN, Bedstead maker, Punch Bowl Alley, Lower Moorfields,
next door to *The Sash* in Middle*, Moorfields.   1763–92 (1)
Member of Upholders' Co.: Christopher's Alley, Moorfields. "Makes and Sells
all sorts of Four Post, Turn-up and Standing Bedsteads, Desk and Table
Bedstds. of all sorts in mahogany, wainscot, beach, etc. N.B. Bedsteads Dyed
in ye neatest manner."

(Plate, page 46)

DERBISHIRE, JOHN, Cabinet-maker, No. 145, Whitecross Street.   1803 (20)
* The Sash was a glazier's sign in Moorfields.

DERIGNEE (or DEVIGNEE), ROBERT, Carver and Gilder (address unrecorded).
Supplied a number of frames to Kensington Palace. 1691 (8)

DESBOIS, LAZAIRE, Cabinet-maker, at *The Clock case and Cabinet*, Compton
Street. 1723 (6)

DESCHAMPS, FRANCIS, Upholder, No. 23, Wardour Street. 1774–93 (2, 3)

DESCHAMPS, PETER, Upholder, Greek Street, Soho. 1747 (5)
Compton Street. 1749 (3)

DEVENISH, JOSEPH, Upholder, of St. Paul's, Covent Garden. 1712 (5)

DEVENISH, THOMAS, Upholder and Cabinet-maker, No. 33, Villiers Street,
Strand. 1770–96 (2),

DICKSON, —, Upholsterer, Castle Street, Long Acre. 1803 (20)

DINGLE, —, Cabinet and Chair maker, No. 9, Great Pulteney Street.
1803 (20)

DINGWALL, ALEXANDER, Upholder and Cabinet-maker, Leicester Fields,
Charing Cross. 1749 (3), 1774 (3)

DIXON, GEORGE, Cabinet maker, at *The Four Coffins*, Warwick Street,
Golden Square. 1748 (5)

DIXON, THOMAS, Upholder, Bartholomew Close. 1712–24 (3)

DOBINSON, ARTHUR, Upholsterer, at *The Bed*, on London Bridge. 1724 (6)

DOBYNS, THOMAS, Upholder, George Street, Hanover Square.
1734–49 (3), deceased 1765

DOLLETT, GEORGE, Upholsterer and Cabinet-maker, No. 48, Minories.
1789 (1), 1803 (20)

DOMINIQUE, JEAN, Gilder and Founder, ormolu worker, in Marshall Street.
1783–95 (8, 50)

DONALDSON AND APPLETREE, Chair and Cabinet-makers, No. 8, Denmark
Street, Soho. 1803–17 (2)

DORREL, THOMAS, Upholder, Yates Court, Clements Lane. 1724–49 (3)

DOUSE, DANIEL, Turner, at *The Blue Ball and Star*, Snow Hill. 1724 (6)

DOWLING, JOHN, Upholder and Cabinet-maker, No. 24, Portpool (or
Pierpool) Lane, Hatton Garden. 1772–93 (2)

DRAPER, —, Chairmaker and Japanner, Queen Street, Southwark. 1803 (20)

DRAPER, THOMAS, Cabinet-maker and Upholsterer, No. 25, Brokers Row,
Moorfields. 1790 (2)–1803 (20)
At *The Key and Plough*, the corner of Doggets Court, in Lower Moor-
fields. (1)

DRURY, THOMAS, Upholder, No. 21, St. Paul's Church Yard. 1777 (2)
Cabinet-maker, No. 33, Red Lion Street, Bloomsbury. 1790–93 (2)

DRURY, THOMAS, AND SON, Carpet warehouse, No. 2, Little Piazza, Covent Garden.   1802–24 (2)

DUBOURDIEU, A., AND CLARK, Z., Upholsterers, at *The Three Chairs*, in Cannon Street, near the London Stone.   *c.* 1740 (1)

DUCHEMIN, J., No. 4, Long Acre.   1817 (2)

DUCHEMIN, PETER, Carver, Gilder and Looking-glass manufacturer, No. 3, Great Russell Street, Bloomsbury.   *c.* 1790 (1)

(Plate, page 46)

No. 4, Long Acre.   1802–14 (2)

DUFFOUR, —, Carver gilder and original maker of papier-mâché at the *Golden Head*, in Berwick Street, Soho.   *c.* 1760 (1)

He was succeeded by RENÉ STONE (*q.v.*) at this address.

(Plate, page 51)

DUNCH, —, Upholsterer, No. 12, Shepherd Street, New Bond Street.   1803 (19)

DUNCOMBE, RICHARD, Upholsterer and Cabinet-maker, Bedford Court, Covent Garden.   1774–79 (2)

DUNTON, —, "an eminent upholsterer," in King Street, Covent Garden.   1764 (5)

DUNTON, JOHN, Upholsterer, at *The Wheatsheaf*, Bedford Street, Covent Garden.   1723 (6)

DURAND, G., Carver and Gilder, No. 8, Catherine Street, Strand. *c.* 1780 (1)

DUTHOIT, JAMES, Upholder and Cabinet-maker, No. 9, Old Broad Street.   1790–96 (2)

No. 1, Budge Row.   1803 (20)
Watling Street.   1817 (2)

EARL, JOHN, Joiner, at *The Cabinet*, Maid Lane, Southwark.   1721 (6)

EARL, THOMAS, Turner, at *The Walnut Tree*, Long Acre.   1722 (6)

EAST, JOHN, Upholder, Gracechurch Street.   1727 (3)

EASTOP, —, Upholster, Bow Street.   1749 (3)

ECKHARDT, ANTHONY G., Cabinet-maker, address unrecorded.   1771 (49)

Invented a portable table, now in the Victoria and Albert Museum.

EDMONDS, JOHN, Cabinet-maker and Upholsterer, No. 6, Old Compton Street.   1803 (20), 1802–17 (2)

He is referred to in *Nollekens and His Times*.

EDSON, JOHN, Upholder and Chair maker, No. 28, Berwick Street.   1794–96 (2)

No. 74, Titchfield Street, Fitzroy Square.   1817 (2)

See page 50

SIZE OF ORIGINAL 5″ × 3⅞″

See page 53

SIZE OF ORIGINAL 6¼″ × 3¾″

52

FALL
Nº 5
at the Blue Curtain in
ST. PAULS-CHURCH-YARD
London.

Makes and sells all sorts of Beds and Bedding,
Mohair, Silk, worsted, and mixt Damasks,
And all Kind of Upholder's Goods
Great Choice of English, French, & Turkey Carpets.
Screens of every kind.
Rich Carved Sconces, Tables, & Picture Frames.
Brass Lanthorns and Arms, with
All manner of Glass, Appraised and
N.B. Goods Appraised and
Funerals Performed
at Reasonable Rates,
Estates BOUGHT & SOLD by Commission.

SIZE OF ORIGINAL 7″ × 6″

See page 54

Thoˢ. Field.
CARVER
In King street
Stᵗ Anns Soho.
LONDON
NB Next door to
the Plaisterʳˢ
Head

SIZE OF ORIGINAL 6¾″ × 4½″

See page 58

EDWARDS, OLIVER, Upholder, Bartholomew Close. 1724–34 (3)

EDWARDS, THOMAS, Cabinet-maker, Chandos Street. 1749 (3)

EELING, —, Cabinet-maker, in Star Court, Butcher Row, near Temple Bar. 1747 (5)

ELLIOT, RICHARD, Carver and Gilder, at *The Golden Head*, Ye corner of Queen Street, Cheapside. (1)

(Plate, page 51)

ELLIOTT, JOHN, Cabinet-maker, of London. Died 1729

ELLIOTT, JOHN, Upholder, Poland Street. 1749 (2)
Late of Clements Lane. Died 1768

ELLIOTT, CHARLES, Upholder to his Majesty, Patentee of Fracture bedstead, No. 98, New Bond Street. 1803 (20), 1784–1808 (2)
Successors to DAVIS AND ELLIOTT and followed by:

ELLIOTT AND FRANCIS, Upholders, No. 104, New Bond Street. 1809–46 (2)
See also W. FRANCIS at same address.

ELLIOTT, WILLIAM, Upholder, No. 2, Clements Lane, Lombard Street. 1768–74 (2)

ELLIOTT, WILLIAM, AND RUTT, Cabinet-makers, No. 2, Clements Lane, Lombard Street. *c.* 1800 (1)

The Elliotts were an old cabinet-making family probably dating back to one William Elliott of Shenley, Herts (1655–1730). His brother John was working in London and died in 1729. The one who is best known was Charles Elliott of New Bond Street whose name occurs in the Royal Household Accounts between 1784 and 1810. This Charles supplied much fine furniture to William Tufnell at Langleys, Essex, which was the subject of a well illustrated article in *Country Life*, 7 August, 1942. *See also* Davis and Elliott (*supra*).*

ELLIS, WILLIAM, Cabinet-maker and Upholder, No. 126, Fenchurch Street. 1774–93 (2)

ELWARD AND MARSH, Upholsterers, No. 13, Mount Street, Grosvenor Square. 1790–93 (2)
See also WILLIAM MARSH.

ELWARD, MARSH AND BAILEY, Upholsterers, No. 13, Mount Street, Grosvenor Square. 1794 (2)

ELWARD, MARSH AND TATHAM, No. 13, Mount Street, Grosvenor Square. 1802 (2), 1803 (20)

Supplied a set of 36 japanned chairs in the small Banqueting Room at the Royal Pavilion, Brighton, in 1802. *See also* Tatham and Bailey, *c.* 1810.

EMANUEL, —, *see* TOUN AND EMANUEL.

ENGLAND, THOMAS, Cane chair maker, James Street. 1709 (4)

* I am indebted to Mr. W. T. T. Elliott for much information relating to his family.

ENGLAND, THOMAS, Cabinet-maker, Newport Street, Leicester Fields.
1727–28 (5)

ENGLEHEART, —, Cabinet-maker, No. 40, Castle Street, Oxford Market.
1803 (20)

EPWORTH, J., Cabinet-maker, No. 12, Little Saint Martin's Lane. 1794–96 (2)

EVANS, —, Upholsterer, No. 1, Budge Row.   1803 (20)

EVANS, PHINEAS, Cabinet-maker, at *The Fleece*, in St. Paul's Church Yard.
1744–47 (5)

EVANS, WILLIAM, Upholder and Carpet warehouseman, No. 3, Talbot Court, Gracechurch Street.   1772–79 (5)

EVATT, RICHARD, Upholsterer, at *The Turk's Head*, Bedford Street, Covent Garden.   1744–56 (5)

EVERSLEY, W., Cabinet-maker, No. 2, French Alley, Goswell Street. 1780 (1)

EYRE, JAMES AND THOMAS, Upholsterers, No. 356, Oxford Street, near the Pantheon.   1783–1814 (1, 20)

EYRE, SIR SIMON, Upholsterer, founder of Leaden Hall, Mayor of London (Registers of St. Mary Woolnoth).   1445 (65)

EYRE AND LARGE, Upholsterers and Cabinet-makers, No. 226, Piccadilly, opposite *The Black Bear* Inn.   1790–95 (1, 2)

FAIRBANK, JOHN, Cabinet-maker, Orange Street.   1749 (3)

FALCK, JOACHIM, Cabinet-maker, at St. Saviour's Dockhead, Southwark. (1)

FALL, JONATHAN, Upholsterer (successor to J. Iliffe, *q.v.*), at *The Blue Curtain*, No. 5, St. Paul's Church Yard.   1765–70 (1, 2)
previously (1763) at Trump Street, Cheapside.
(Plate, page 52)
A member of the Upholders Company on Mile End Green.   1770–92

FANSHAW, EDWARD, Upholder, Bread Street.   1705–07 (9)
"Mr. Fenshaw [*sic*], a relation of the Lord of that name [?Featherstonehaugh] an upholsterer in Bread St., taking a walk about Islington ... died very suddenly."
1717 (5)

FARLAM, JONATHAN, Cabinet-maker, Round Court, Strand.   1774 (3)

FARMBOROUGH, WILLIAM, Cabinet-maker, at *Ye Looking Glass* on Cornhill, in partnership with John Burrough (*q.v.*)   1672 (49)–90 (64)
Supplied several pieces of elaborate furniture for Windsor (*cf.* J. Hudgebout.

FARMBROUGH, WILLIAM, Cabinet-maker, North Audley Street.
1749 (3)–55 (18)

FARMER, RICHARD, Upholder, Holborn Hill.   1724–34 (3)

FARMER AND BUCK, Chairmakers, at above.   1723 (5)–c. 1740 (1)
Henry Buck (*q.v.*) left the partnership about 1740 and set up at *The Hand, Crown and Star* on the *south* side of St. Paul's churchyard. Richard Farmer remaining at the old address. *See* BUCK AND FARMER, *also* ANN BUCK.

Richard Fletcher

Picture Frame Maker Carver *and* Gilder

Removd from No. 143 Fleet Street, to the Golden Head
No. 50, the Corner of Tower Royal Watling Street.

LONDON.

Makes & Sells all Sorts of Carved Brackets, Sconce, Picture and
Chimney Frames, Walnuttree & Mahogony Ditto, with all manner
of black Peartree & Deal Frames, for Maps, Prints or Drawings.
Pictures carefully Cleand, & broken Paintings Mended: with
Carvers & Gilders work, in all its various branches expediti-
ously done after the neatest & newest Taste, at the lowest Prices.
NB. Prints, &c, Pasted Framed and Glazed very reasonable.
I always keep by me Peartree & Deal Mouldings
fit for Picture frames of any Breadth, ready
to make up at a shortest warning, or Sold
as they are for Town   or Country.

SIZE OF ORIGINAL 6¾″ × 5″   *See page* 58

Lock.ⁿ Foulger,
CHAIR-MAKER,
At Wallam Green.
Makes all Sorts of Windsor Chairs,
Garden Seats, Rural Settees &c.
Wholesale & Retail.

SIZE OF ORIGINAL 3¾ × 5¾″   *See page* 59

See page 60

SIZE OF ORIGINAL 7" × 5⅛"

See page 59

SIZE OF ORIGINAL 8⅝" × 6¼"

FARMER, RICHARD, Chair and Cabinet-maker, at *The Hand and Crown*, the East end of St. Paul's Church Yard, near the School.

1744 (1), died 1747 (5)

FARNWORTH, SAMUEL, Carver and Gilder, The Pavement, near Finsbury Square. 179– (1)

FARQUHARSON, WILLIAM, Cabinet-maker and Upholsterer, Villiers Street, No. 3 York Buildings, Strand. 1774 (3)–79 (2)

FARRER, —, Upholsterer, Princes Street, Leicester Square. 1803 (20)

FARRIER, JOHN, Cabinet-maker, Gerrard Street, Soho. 1783 (2)

FAUCON, JAMES, (address not recorded). Sale of Stock. 1731 (5)
"Goods of the noted Mr. James Faucon [sold] at Surnam's great house in Soho Sq." *Daily Post*, 19th Feb., 1731
The goods were "several dozen of the newest fashioned wallnut tree chairs covered with velvet, Damask and black Spanish leather," etc. etc., various types of chairs, settees, chairbeds.

FAULCONER, ALEXANDER, Cabinet-maker, Whitcomb Street. 1774 (3)

FAULKNER, J., Cabinet and Chair maker, No. 17, Suffolk Place, Hackney Road. *c.* 1800 (1)

FAUSET, NATHANIEL, Upholsterer, Strand. 1709 (4)

FAWLEY AND WARD, Japanned Chair maker, No. 43, Wardour Street. 1803 (20)

FELLIOT, NICHOLAS, Cabinet-maker, Long Acre. 1709 (4)

FELLOWS, ROBERT, Carver and Gilder, No. 22, Warwick Street, Golden Square. 1790–94 (1, 2)

FENLYSON, JAMES, Cabinet-maker, St. Martin's Street, Leicester Fields. 1774 (3)

FENTHAM, THOMAS, Carver and Glass grinder, No. 52, Strand, opposite Old Round Court. 1774 (1)–1796 (2)
No. 136, Strand. 1802–11 (2)

FENTON, WILLIAM, Cabinet-maker, Suffolk Street, Haymarket. 1749 (3)

FENWICK, EDWARD, Upholsterer, St. Mary Woolchurch Haw. 1678–1708

FERGUSON, WILLIAM, Cabinet-maker, No. 10, Manchester Street. 1803 (20)

FERRERS, THOMAS, Upholsterer, at *The Sun*, Fleet Street. 1706–1714 (5, 38)
See also WOODROSE, Upholsterer, at this address in 1702.

FEWELL, JAMES, Cabinet-maker, Carnaby Street. 1749 (3)

FIDOE, THOMAS, Upholder, at *The Three Golden Chairs*, over against the Saddlers' Hall in Cheapside. 1711 (3)–1731 (5)

FIELD, JAMES, Cabinet-maker, at *Ye Desk and Bookcase*, Aldermanbury. 1726 (6)

FIELD, THOMAS, Carver, next door to *The Plaster Head*, in King Street, St. Ann's, Soho. (1)

(Plate, page 52)

FIELDER, —, Chair maker, No. 8, Princes Street. 1803 (20)

FIFIELD, WILLIAM, Upholsterer, over against the George Inn in Piccadilly. 1714 (5)

FINER, WILLIAM AND JAMES, Upholders, No. 19, Leadenhall Street. 1790–96 (2)

FINER, WILLIAM, Cabinet-maker and Upholsterer, No. 21, Camomile Street, Bishopsgate Street. 1803 (20)–17 (2)

FINLAYSON, JAMES, Chair maker, Midford Place, Tottenham Court Road. 1794 (2)–1803 (20)

FINSTWAITE, CHRISTOPHER, Upholsterer, next the King's Arms Tavern, at the West End of St. Paul's. 1715 (5)

FIPPS, JOHN, Upholster, Petty France. 1749 (3)

FIRMIN AND SUTTON, Upholders, High Holborn. 1768 (2)

FISH, JOHN, Cabinet-maker, Long Acre. 1749 (3)

FISH, THOMAS, Upholsterer, No. 168, Borough High Street. 1783 (2)

FISHER, JOSEPH, Upholsterer and Appraiser, in the open part of Tooley Street, near the Ram's Head Tavern in Southwark. 1724 (5)

FISHER, JOSEPH, Upholsterer and Cabinet-maker, at *The Black Lyon*, in Houndsditch, near Aldgate Church. *c.* 1740 (1)

FITCHET, JOHN, Upholder, Bartholomew Close. 1727 (5)

FLEMING, WILLIAM AND FREDERICK, Upholders and Cabinet-makers, No. 4, Chandos Street, Covent Garden. 1779–96 (2)

FLEMING AND SHEPPARD, Upholders and Cabinet-makers, No 4, Chandos Street, Covent Garden. 1803 (20)

FLETCHER, —, Upholster, in Cornhill. 1657 (13)

FLETCHER, JOHN, Upholder, No. 8, Houndsditch. 1790–96 (2)

FLETCHER, JOSEPH, Leather gilder and Upholsterer, at *The King's Arms*, St. Paul's Church Yard. 1716 (33)–1732 (5) (died)

FLETCHER, JOSEPH, AND JOHN CONWAY, Leather gilders and Screen makers to H.M. King George, at *Ye King's Arms*, the second Leather Guilders-shop from ye end of Ludgate Street, ye south side of St. Paul's Church Yard. 1732 (5)

On Mr. Fletcher's death in 1732 John Conway carried on the business under his own name. 1734–39 (1)

FLETCHER, RICHARD, Carver and Gilder, at *The Golden Head*, No. 50, the corner of Tower Royal, Watling Street. *c.* 1770 (1)

(Plate, page 55)

Removed from No. 143 Fleet Street. *c.* 1770 (1)

FLEURIOT, —, Upholsterer, No. 7, Great Tower Street.   1803 (20)

FLINT AND McLELLAN, Upholsterers, No. 114, Great Russell Street.
                                                             1803 (20)

FLINT AND THOMAS, Upholsterers and Cabinet-makers, No. 13, Greek
    Street, Soho.   1796 (2)–1803 (20)

FLINTHAM, ROBERT, Cabinet-maker, Heydon Street, Westminster.   1749 (3)

FLINTOFF, WILLIAM, Upholsterer and Feather-bed maker, No. 67, Smithfield.
                                                   1790 (1, 2)–1803 (20)

FLOAT, THOMAS, Gilder, Turner and Frame maker, No. 14, Long Lane,
    West Smithfield.   1747 (5), c. 1770 (1)

FOLGHAM, JOHN, Case and Cabinet-maker, opposite the Castle Inn, Wood
    Street.   c. 1760 (1)
    No. 118, Fetter Lane.   c. 1750 (1), 1777 (2)
    No. 81, Fleet Street.   1779 (1)–1803 (20)
                        (Plate, page 56)

FONTAINE, —, Cabinet-maker and Upholsterer, No. 13, Holborn, opposite
    Middle Row.   (1)
    Upholder, No. 25, Great Russell Street.   1803 (19, 20)

FORBES, WILLIAM, Cabinet-maker, No. 55, Tottenham Court Road.
                                                         1790–93 (2)

FORD, GEORGE AND WILLIAM, Cabinet-makers, No. 12, St. Paul's Church
    Yard.   1777–96 (2)

FORTUNE, TIMOTHY, Upholder, at *The Plough and Harrow*, Witch (Wych)
    Street, behind St. Clement's Church in the Strand.   1721–24 (5)

FOSSETT, —, Upholsterer, Nos. 5 and 6, Leadenhall Street.   1843 (20)

FOUKE, —, Upholsterer, at *The Goat* in Barbican.   1672 (5)

FOULGER, LOCK[N]., Chair maker, "at Wallam Green," makes all sorts of
    Windsor chairs, Garden Seats, Rural Settees, etc.   1773 (1)
                        (Plate, page 55)

FOX, BENJAMIN, Cabinet-maker and Upholsterer, No. 12, Little St. Martin's
    Lane, Long Acre.   1755–93 (2)
    Subscribed to second edition of Chippendale's *Director*.

FOX, EDWARD, Upholsterer and Undertaker, St. James's Street.   1729 (5)
    Conducted the funeral of the Duke of Devonshire at Chatsworth in 1729.
    Upholsterer, Bennet Street, St. James's.   1730 (5)
    Park Place, St. James's.   1731 (5)
    Appointed upholsterer to His Royal Highness the Prince of Wales.
                                                         1731–32 (5)

FOX, JOHN, Upholder, Ludgate Street.   1734 (5)

FOXHALL AND FRYER, Upholsterers, No. 19, Old Cavendish Street. 1803 (20)

FOXHALL, MAR^N., Carver and Gilder, at *The Golden Head* in Great St. Andrew's Street, Seven Dials.   *c.* 1770 (1)

(Plate, page 56)

FRANCE, EDWARD, Upholsterer, No. 101, St. Martin's Lane. 1774 (3)–1777 (2)
Was in partnership with Samuel Beckwith when they supplied much of the fine furniture in Lord Mansfield's house, Kenwood, between 1768 and 1771. The name of the firm appears in the Royal Household bills until the end of the century and their trade-card "France and Beckwith, Upholsterers and Cabinet makers to His Majesty, No. 101 St. Martin's Lane" in the Banks Collection is dated 1803.

FRANCE, WILLIAM, Upholsterer, St. Martin's Lane.   1768 (8)–1786 (49, 61)

FRANCE AND BECKWITH, address see above and also under BECKWITH AND FRANCE.   1768 (56)–1803 (20)

FRANCIS, WILLIAM, Upholsterer and Cabinet-maker. Manufacturer of Buhl to Her Majesty, No. 104, New Bond Street.   1803 (20)–1840 (2)
See also ELLIOTT AND FRANCIS.

FRANCIS, GILBERT AND BONNER, Cabinet warehouse, No. 43, Aldersgate Street.   1790–93 (2)

FRASER AND SCOTT, Cabinet-makers, No. 12, Francis Street, Tottenham Court Road.   1817 (2)

FREELOVE, RICHARD, Upholsterer, Ormond Street.   1728–32 (5)
Queen Square.   1734 (3)

FREELOVE, WILLIAM, Upholder, Lincoln's Inn Fields, near Clare Market.
                                                                1726 (5)

FRENCH, J., Upholder and Cabinet-maker, No. 10, Queen Street, Cheapside.
                                                               c. 1800 (1)

FRIEND, GEORGE, Upholsterer, near the Pump in Watling Street.
                                                               1726–32 (5)

FRYER, FRANCIS, Wholesale Upholsterer, King Street, Cheapside.
                                                               1760–68 (2)

FRYER, ROBERT, Upholder and Cabinet-maker, No. 23, Aldermanbury.
                                                               1772–74 (2)
No. 24, Addle Street.   1790–93 (2)

FRYER, ROBERT AND RALPH, Wholesale Upholsterers, No. 23, King Street, Cheapside.   1768 (2)
23, Aldermanbury.   1770 (2)

FUHRLONG, CHRISTOPHER, Cabinet-maker and Inlayer. Ébéniste to H.R.H. Prince of Wales, No. 24, Tottenham Court Road.   1777–82 (1, 2)

FUHRLONG, CHRISTOPHER, No. 5, Tottenham Court Road, between Percy
Street and Hanway Yard. *c.* 1790 (1)
"Cabinet-maker in the Modern Grecian and Chinese Taste."

FULWOOD, CHARLES, Cabinet-maker, at *The Eagle and Child*, Castle Street,
Leicester Fields. 1723 (6)

FURBER, WILLIAM, Cabinet manufacturer by appointment to Her Majesty.
c. 1840 (1)
No. 122, Great Portland Street. 1814–35 (2)

GABLIN, THOMAS, Upholder, "removed from *The Blackamoor's Head* in
Shandos Street to *Blackamoor's Head* in Bedford Court, Covent Garden."
1710 (5)

GAIGNEUR, LOUIS, Maker of Buhl furniture, No. 19, Queen Street, Edgware
Road. *c.* 1815 (46)

GALE AND SEABROOK, Cabinet-makers and Upholsterers, "at *The Walnut
Tree*, in Houndsditch." 1758 (5)

GALE, JOSEPH, Joiner, at *The Hand, Star and Lock of Hair*, Holborn Bridge.
1725 (6)

GALE, THOMAS AND WILLIAM, Upholders, Catherine Street. 1774 (2)–1777 (3)

GALLAWAY, EDWARD, Upholster, Hog Lane. 1749 (3)

GALLEY, GEORGE, Upholsterer, No. 13, Long Acre. 1763–84 (2)

GALLY AND BAKER, *see* CHARLES BLYDE. *c.* 1750 (1)

GAMIDGE, —, Chair maker, near St. Paul's School. 1715 (5)

GAMLYN, THOMAS, Upholsterer, Bedford Court, Covent Garden.
1725–31 (5)
Supplied furniture for Royal Hospital, Chelsea. 1731

GARBANATTI, JOSEPH, Carver, Gilder and Frame maker, No. 202, High
Holborn. 1808 (1, 2)
No. 404, Strand. 1811–26 (2)
No. 37, Southampton Street. 1827–39 (2)

GARDNER, THOMAS, Upholder, Rood Lane, Fenchurch Street.
1724 (2)–1734 (3)

GARDNER, WILLIAM, Chair maker, at the Sign of *The Cane Chair*, on the
south side of St. Paul's Church. 1709 (5)
"Maketh and selleth cane chairs, couches and cane sashes at reasonable rates of
Dry Wood."

GARTH, JAMES, Upholsterer and Undertaker, Serle Street, Lincoln's Inn.
1769 (1), 1773–84 (2)

GATES, WILLIAM, Cabinet-maker to George III, in Long Acre.
1777 (8)–1783 (52)

GATES, WILLIAM—*continued*.

In 1783 he was in partnership with Benjamin Parran, junior (*q.v.*), and also seems to have had business connection with Charles Elliott (*q.v.*) after the turn of the century.

GEE, JOHN, Turner and Chair maker to His Majesty (George III), No. 49, Wardour Street.   1803 (20)–1817 (2)

Succeeded by Charles BRIDGES (*q.v.*).

GEE AND HOLE, Cabinet-makers, King Street, Holborn.   1817

The name of this firm occurs in correspondence which took place with the Royal Society of Arts on the subject of mahogany in 1817.

GEORGE, REMY, Upholder, Bartholomew Close.   1721 (3)–1727 (5)

GERN, —, Cabinet-maker, Newcastle House, St. John's Square, Clerkenwell.
                                                                          1756 (64)

GIBBONS, —, Upholster, No. 3, Bucklersbury.   1803 (20)

GIBBONS, GRINLING, Wood carver and Designer.

                                                      born 1648, died 1720 (62)

At *The King's Arms* in Bow Street, Covent Garden.   1678–1720
Previously in Belle Sauvage Court, Ludgate Hill.

When first discovered by John Evelyn he was living "in a solitary thatched house near Deptford."
For full particulars of his principal works see *D.N.B.*, etc.

GIBBS, ANTHONY, Upholder, Cornhill.   1718 (7)

GIBSON, —, Upholsterer, at *The King's Arms*, in St. Paul's Church Yard.
                                                                          1736 (2)

GIBSON, —, Upholsterer, Newport Street, St. Ann's, Soho.   *c.* 1780 (1)
                        (Plate, page 65)

GIBSON, GEORGE, Upholstery, cabinet, looking glass and carpet warehouse, No. 53, Ratcliffe Highway.   1790 (1, 2)

GIBSON, JAMES AND JOHN, Upholsterers, James Street, Covent Garden.
                                                                      1746–74 (3, 5)

GIBSON, JOHN, Cabinet and Screen maker, No. 39, Wardour Street. 1817 (2)

GILBERT, —, Upholder to His Majesty (address unrecorded).   1729 (5)

GILBERT, JOHN, Upholder to His Majesty (George II), Great Queen Street.
                                                              1732 (5)–1768 (56)

Supplied richly carved frames and brackets for the Mansion House in 1752, also executed carvings for Lansdowne House, 1768.

GILBERT, JOHN, Carver, Mount Street, Grosvenor Square.   1763 (2)

GILBERT, WILLIAM, Upholstery warehouse, 3 doors below Fetter Lane in Fleet Street.   *c.* 1780 (1)
                        (Plate, page 65)

GILBOA, JOHN, Cabinet-maker, Long Acre.   1709 (4)

GILDING, EDMUND, Cabinet-maker, in Redcross Street.   1742–55 (1)
    Succeeded by his son Francis (*q.v.*).

GILDING, FRANCIS, Upholsterer and Cabinet-maker, No. 113, Aldersgate
    Street, near Charterhouse Square.   1760–90 (1, 2)

GILDING, FRANCIS, AND BANNER, at above, and also at No. 48, Clerkenwell
    Close.   1790–96 (2)

GILL, JOHN, Upholsterer, Maddox Street, Hanover Square.   1747–49 (3, 5)

GILL, GEORGE, AND MAXEY, Upholsterers, No. 121, Upper Thames Street.
                                                   1783 (2)

GILLOW, ROBERT, Cabinet-maker, No. 176, Oxford Road.   (56)
    (Plates, pages 256–259 and see also pages 275–6)
Robert Gillow was the second son of Robert Gillow who founded the firm in
Lancaster about 1731. Robert junior opened the branch of his father's business
in Oxford Street, London, about 1760, and this was carried on by him and his
brothers until 1817. The business continued to bear the name of "Gillow" for
some years after the family had ceased to take active participation in it. Gillows
furnished Streatham Park for Mrs. Piozzi who disputed their account of £2,380
and finally settled with them for £2,070. A gilt carved sofa is now in the Victoria
and Albert Museum. A detailed account of the firm and the various partnerships
is given in *Georgian Cabinet-Makers*, by Edwards and Jourdain.
The earliest entry in the London directories is under the name of:—

GILLOW AND TAYLOR, Cabinet-makers and Upholsters, 176, Oxford Road.
                                                   1771–77 (2)
The name of Taylor disappears after 1777, and in 1779 the style of the firm is:

GILLOW, ROBERT, RICHARD AND THOMAS, No. 176, Oxford Street. 1779–90 (2)
    after that it is:—

GILLOW, ROBERT AND CO., No. 176, Oxford Street.   1790 (2)–1803 (20)
    followed by:—

GILLOW, ROBERT AND GEORGE, No. 176, Oxford Street, until   1817 (2)

GILPIN, JOHN, Upholder, Bedford Street.   1768–83 (2, 3)

GILROY, JOHN, Upholder, Newton Court, Parish of Westminster.
                                                   1774–83 (2, 8)

GLOVER, C., Upholsterer, corner of Albemarle Street, Piccadilly. 1803 (19)

GLOVER, JONATHAN, Upholsterer, corner of Albemarle Street, Piccadilly.
                                                   1777 (1)–1796 (2)

GLOVER AND SONS, Upholsterers, No. 63, Piccadilly.   1790–96 (2)

GLOVER, T., Upholsterer, No. 201, Piccadilly.   1803 (19)

GODDARD, HENRY, Upholsterer, at *The White Lion*, corner of George Alley
    by Fleet Ditch.   1724 (6)–1727 (5)

GODDARD, THOMAS, Upholder, Cornhill.   1727 (3)

GODDARD, THOMAS, Upholsterer, Milk Street.   1734 (3)–1772 (2)

GODFREE, —, Upholsterer and Cabinet-maker, Palace Yard, Westminster.
                          1803 (20)

GODFREY, RICHARD, Upholsterer and Cabinet-maker, New Palace Yard,
     Westminster.   1783–93 (2)
     Union Street, Westminster.   1790–96 (2)

GOFF, WILLIAM, Upholder, Queen Street.   1749 (3)

GOLDSMITH, THOMAS, Cabinet-maker, *Cupid on a Shell Rock*, Greece Court,
     Old Jury, Cheapside.   1694 (33)
     Sold Japan cabinets.

GOLE, CORNELIUS, Cabinet-maker to William III (address unrecorded).
                         c. 1690 (8)

GOMM, WILLIAM, AND SON, Cabinet-makers, Clerkenwell Close.
                         1755–63 (2)
     No. 3, Freeman's Court, Cornhill.   1768 (2)

GOOD, GEORGE, Upholsterer, No. 121, Fleet Street.   1770–79 (2)

GOODCHEAPE, WILLIAM, Cabinet-maker, No. 142, Goswell Road.   1802 (2)
     115, Aldersgate Street.   *c.* 1810 (1)

GOODIAR, —, Upholsterer, at *The Two Green Flower Pots*, Charles Street,
     St. James's Square.   1709 (5)

GOODISON, BENJAMIN, Cabinet-maker, at *The Golden Spread Eagle*, Long
     Acre.   1727–67 (5)

     He was one of the most prominent cabinet-makers of his day and his name is
     frequently met with in the accounts for furniture supplied to the Royal Palaces
     and to many of the nobility. Full details of his work are given in *Georgian Cabinet
     Makers*, by Edwards and Jourdain (1944). Goodison had taken his nephew
     Benjamin Parran (*q.v.*) into partnership and he with Benjamin Goodison junior
     continued to carry on the business after the father's death in 1767 until 1783. (64)

GORDON, —, Upholsterer, Brewer Street, Golden Square.   1747 (5)

GORDON, JOHN, Cabinet-maker, Swallow Street, Argyle Buildings (or
     Argyle Street).   1748 (1)
     In 1748 he was supplying furniture for Blair Castle.

GORDON, JOHN, Cabinet-maker, King Street, Golden Square.   1749 (3)

GORDON, WILLIAM, Cabinet-maker, (?) of Little Argyle Street, Golden Square.
     He subscribed to Chippendale's *Director*.   1754 (18)
     It seems likely that both John and William Gordon were partners in the firm
     of:—

GORDON, WILLIAM, AND TAITT, JOHN, Upholsterers and Cabinet-makers,
     King Street, Golden Square.   1768–70 (2, 58)
     And of Little Argyle Street.   1772–79 (64)

SIZE OF ORIGINAL 4⅞" × 5⅝"

See page 62

SIZE OF ORIGINAL 5⅛" × 4"

See page 62

66

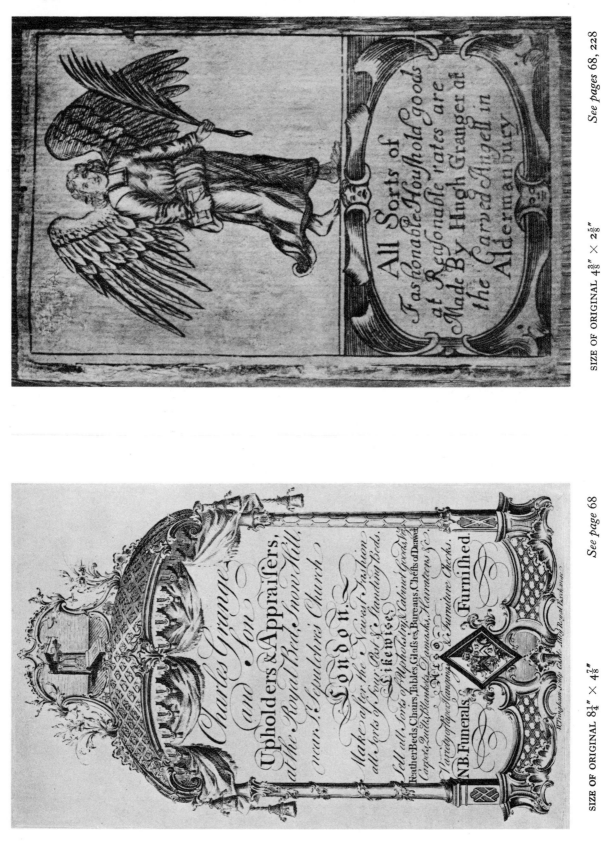

All Sorts of
Fashonable Houshold goods
at Reasonable rates are
Made By Hugh Granger at
the
Carved Angell in
Aldermanbury

See pages 68, 228

SIZE OF ORIGINAL 4⅜″ × 2⅝″

Charles Grange
and Son
Upholders & Apprasers,
at the Royal Bed, Snow Hill,
near S. Sepulchres Church
London.
Make after the Neweſt Fashion
all Sorts of Four Post & Standing Beds.
Likewise
Sell all Sorts of Upholstry & Cabinet Goods.
Feather Beds, Chairs, Tables, Glaſses, Bureaus, Cheſts of Drawers
Carpets, Quilts, Blanketts, Damasks, Harrateens &c.
Variety of Paper Hangings & Furniture Checks.
N.B. Funerals Furniſhed.

See page 68

SIZE OF ORIGINAL 8¼″ × 4⅞″

GORDON, WILLIAM, AND TAITT, JOHN—*continued*.

Shortly after 1779 John Taitt (*q.v.*) moved to Swallow Street and later to Oxford Street where he carried on business until 1799. The firm executed work for Earl Spencer at Althorp between the years 1770 and 1779.

GOSSE, —, Upholster, Queen Street, Westminster. 1747 (5)

GOSSET, GIDEON, Frame maker and Carver, (?) Berwick Street, Soho.

1747 (1, 64), died 1785 (23)

Made frames for Hogarth, Gainsborough and Hoare.

GOSSET, ISAAC, originally a frame maker, but became famous as portraitist wax-modeller. Brother of Gideon (above), and father of Isaac Gosset the bibliographer.

Berwick Street, Soho. 1767–74 (5, 23, 62)

No. 14, Edward Street, Portman Square. 1774, died 1799

GOSSET, JAMES, Wax modeller and Wood carver, Berwick Street, Soho.

1767 (23)

GOUGH, —, Toy and Cabinet-maker, No. 13, Wharton's Court (Holborn).

"Makes Spring Guns and Pistols of various Sizes and Prices likewise all sorts of Mahogany and Kitchen furniture as Chairs, Buroes, Commodes, Bason Stands, Glasses, Chests of Drawers, etc." *c.* 1790 (1)

GOUGH, JAMES, Carver, Gilder and maker of composition ornaments, No. 219, Piccadilly. 1790–93 (2)

GOUGH, JOHN, Maker of chess tables, chess boards and chess men, "at *The Sugar Loaf and Tables*," near Serjeant's Inn, in Chancery Lane.

1686 (5)

GOULD, HENRY, Upholsterer, No. 78, Gracechurch Street. 1783–93 (2)

See WILLIAM GOULD.

GOULD, JOHN, Upholsterer, "at *The Three Nuns*," St. Olave Street, by the Tower. 1725 (6)

GOULD, WILLIAM, Upholsterer and Cabinet-maker, No. 78, Gracechurch Street. 1772–96 (2, 17)

See also HENRY GOULD.

GRAFTON, RAFE, Upholster, in Cornhill. 1640 (13, 17), died 1658

GRAHAM, —, Upholder, St. Martin's Lane. 1803 (18)

See also LITCHFIELD AND GRAHAM.

GRAHAM, JOSEPH, Cabinet-maker, No. 7, St. Paul's Church Yard. 1768–92 (2)

No. 3, St. Paul's Church Yard. 1803–17 (2)

GRAHAM AND LITCHFIELD, Upholders, No. 72, St. Martin's Lane, Charing Cross 1790–1803 (2, 19)

See also LITCHFIELD AND GRAHAM.

GRAHAM AND SON, Carvers and Gilders, No. 18, Greek Street, Soho. 1802 (1)

GRAHAM, W., Upholsterer, No. 48, Threadneedle Street.   1817 (2)

GRAINGER, Mr. (*sic*), Upholsterer, on Snow Hill.   1734 (5)

GRANGE, CHARLES, AND SON, Upholders, at *The Royal Bed*, on Snow Hill, near St. Sepulchre's Church.   *c.* 1760 (1)
"Makes after the Newest Fashion all sorts of Four Post and Standing Beds."
(Plate, page 66)

GRANGE, JAMES, Upholstery warehouse, No. 96, High Holborn. 1768–83 (2)

GRANGE AND MILLS, Upholstery warehouse, No. 96, High Holborn.
1774–79 (2)

GRANGER, HUGH, Cabinet-maker, at *The Carved Angel*, in Aldermanbury.
1692 (1)–1706 (5)

The Angel in Aldermanbury ceased to be a cabinet-maker's shop in 1706, when the stock was sold off, "the house being let to another trade."   (5)
(Plates, pages 66, 228)
A small walnut bureau formerly in the Percival Griffiths collection bears Granger's trade label.

GRAVELY, MICHAEL, Upholster, David Street (Westminster).   1749 (3)

GRAVENOR, JOHN, Upholsterer, at *The Bear and Ragged Staff*, on Cornhill, next to Stocks Market.   1690 (5)
Sale of Furniture Stock at *The Royal Bed and Chair* in Great Rider Street, St. James's.   1730 (5)

GRAVES, I. S., Cabinet-maker and Upholder, No. 54, Bishopsgate Street Within.   1790–93 (1, 2)
(Plate, page 69)

GRAVES, JOHN, Upholsterer, No. 179, Borough.   1794–96 (2)

GRAVES AND SHIPMAN, Cabinet-makers and Upholders, No. 54, Bishopsgate Street Within.   1783–90 (2)

GRAY, WILLIAM, Turner and Cabinet-maker, at *The Golden Cup*, in Addle Street, near Aldermanbury.   *c.* 1750 (1)

GREATHEAD, JOSEPH, Cabinet-maker, in Bucklersbury.   *c.* 1715 (1)

GREAVES, RICHARD, Sedan chair maker, at *The Golden Chair*, in Warwick Lane, by Golden Square.   1746 (24)

GREEN, —, Upholsterer, Bury Street, St. James's.   1725–27 (5)

GREEN, RICHARD, Cabinet-maker, Crown Court (Westminster).   1749 (3)

GREEN, WILLIAM, Upholsterer, Rupert Street.   1749 (3)

GREEN, WILLIAM, Upholder and Cabinet-maker, No. 20, Mortimer Street, Cavendish Square.   1790 (2)–1803 (20)

GREENWOOD, CHARLES, Upholder and Cabinet-maker, No. 5, Rood Lane, opposite the Church.   *c.* 1750 (1, 7)
Fenchurch Street.   1764–79 (2)

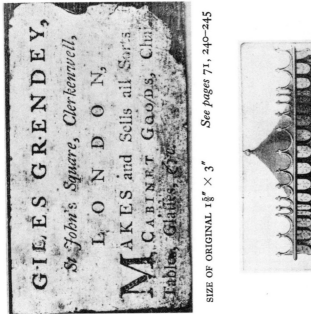

GILES GRENDEY,
St. John's Square, Clerkenwell,
LONDON,
MAKES and Sells all Sorts of CABINET GOODS, Chairs, Tables, Glasses, &c.

SIZE OF ORIGINAL 1⅝" × 3"   See pages 71, 240–245

I.S. GRAVES,
Cabinet-Maker, Upholster, Appraiser, Auctioneer and Undertaker.
No. 54.
Bishopsgate Street within.
London.

SIZE OF ORIGINAL 3½" × 2⅜"   See page 68

William Gumwell
At the Looking Glass ye 3th Side of St. Pauls.
LONDON
Selleth all sorts of Looking Glasses, Sconce Coach Glasses and all sorts of Cabinet and Japand work. Likewise all sorts of the finest & most Fashionable Chairs either matted or Cane'd Blinds for Windows made and Curiously Painted on Canvas Silk or Wire Wholesale or Retale at Reasonable Rates.

See page 72

SIZE OF ORIGINAL 5⅝" × 3⅞"

Hartley
Carver and Gilder
in Newgate Street
№ 108

Performs
all manner of house &
furniture Carving, &c.
Looking Glasses Frames
for Exportation.
Prints and Paintings
framed, Cleaned & Lined.

See page 77

SIZE OF ORIGINAL $5\frac{1}{2}'' \times 3\frac{7}{8}''$

John Hutt

CABINET & CHAIR MAKER.

(Successor to Mr John Arrowsmith)

At the Blue Ball & Artichoke, in Aldersgate Street.

London.

Makes & Sells, all sorts of Comodes, & Book-Cases,
Desks & Book Cases, Library Cases, Chests of Drawers,
Cloaths Presses, Bedsteads, Comode, Dressing & Tea
Tables, & all manner of Chairs & Cabinet work.
Likewise does Upholstery work in the neatest manner.
Also Blinds for Windows & Spring Curtains, Looking
Glasses of all sorts, Coach Glasses, & Lanthorns, Variety
of Gothic & Chinese work in Chairs & Cabinet frames
&c made up and Sold Wholesale and Retail at
very reasonable Rates, & for Exportation.

N.B. Funerals Furnish'd.

See page 77

SIZE OF ORIGINAL $7\frac{1}{8}'' \times 5\frac{5}{8}''$

GREENWOOD AND SENOLS, No. 23, Fenchurch Street. 1781–83 (2)

GREENWOOD, THOMAS, No. 23, Fenchurch Street. 1790–1803 (2)

GRENDEY, GILES, Cabinet-maker and Chair maker, Aylesbury House, St. John's Square, Clerkenwell. 1731 (1)
Various fine pieces of mahogany furniture, lacquered cabinets and chairs are known which bear Grendey's label. A japanned day bed by him is in the Victoria and Albert Museum. Other pieces are in the Metropolitan Museum, New York. He was made liveryman of the Joiners' Company in 1729 and elected Master in 1766. Died in 1780 aged 87. (56)
(Plates, pages 69, 240–245)

GRIFFIN, —, "a noted and wealthy cabinet-maker" in Wardour Street, Soho. died 1731 (5)

GRIFFIN, —, Cabinet-maker to the Royal Household (address unrecorded). 1639 (49)

GRIFFIN, WILLIAM AND THOMAS, Sedan and porters' hall chair and invalid Chair makers, No. 1, Whitcomb Street, Leicester Square. 1802–17 (2)
Savile House, No. 5, Leicester Square. 1823–38 (2)
See HOLMES AND GRIFFIN. 1779–96
When Savile House was burnt down in 1865 it was then in the occupation of the well-known invalid chair makers John Ward and Co., who are still in business in Tottenham Court Road.

GRIFFITH, J., Cabinet-maker, etc., Red Cross Street, Southwark. 1794 (2), 1803 (20)

GRIFFITH, WILLIAM, Upholsterer, Suffolk Street, Haymarket. 1709 (4)

GRIFFITHS, EDWARD, Upholsterer and Cabinet-maker, Dean Street, Soho. 1749 (3)
Probably the same Edward Griffiths who "was an assistant to Benjamin Goodison [*q.v.*] and afterwards set up in business on his own account." (See *Georgian Cabinet Makers*, p. 68.) Between 1746 and 1749 he supplied furniture to the Earl of Cardigan for Longford Castle and Dover Street. (49)

GRIFFITHS, JOHN, Upholsterer, No. 27, Little Alie Street.
(Ayliffe Street, Goodman's Fields.) 1746 (2), 1803 (19)

GRIMES, Jno·, Cabinet-maker, No. 69, Red Lion Street, Clerkenwell. 1803 (20), 1817 (2)

GRONOUS, JAMES, Upholsterer, at *The Black Lion*, Wych Street, Strand. 1724–35 (3, 6)
He has also been recorded under the name of "Mr. Grovehouse."

GROVES, CHARLES, Japanner and Gilder, removed from Long Acre to *Ye Golden Head*, the farther end of Brownlow Street from Drury Lane. *c.* 1750 (1)

GUIBERT, —, No. 179, Borough. 1803 (20)

GUIBERT, (?) PHILIP, Upholsterer, address not recorded.
> He worked at Rousham under the direction of William Kent.   1739
> (Information from Mr. Cottrell-Dorner.)

GUIDOT, —, Upholsterer, at *The Royal Bed*, Marybone Street (Shug Lane), St. James's.   1725 (5)

GUIDOT, ANTHONY, Upholder, Shug Lane, St. James's.   1724–27 (3, 5)

GUIDOT, WILLIAM, Upholsterer at *Ye Three Tents*, near Broad Street Buildings, Moorfields.   (1)

GUIDOT, WILLIAM, Member of Upholders' Company, Dog Row, Bethnal Green.   1792 (2)

GUILLOTIN, —, Upholsterer, next *The Black Lion*, in the Pall Mall, near St. James's.   1691 (5)

GUMLEY, MRS. ELIZABETH, Cabinet-maker and Glass manufacturer, New Exchange, in the Strand.   1694–1729 (56)
> Supplied St. James's Palace (*temp.* George II) in partnership with her son John.

GUMLEY, JOHN, Cabinet-maker and Glass manufacturer, Salisbury Exchange, in the Strand.   1694–1729 (49, 56)
> Also at corner of Norfolk Street, in the Strand.   1714
> He was in partnership with James Moore (*q.v.*) in 1714–26 and later, for a few years, with William Turing. A full account of the firm is given in *Georgian Cabinet Makers*.

GUMLEY, PETER, Cabinet-maker, at *The Cabinet*, near St. Clement's Church, in the Strand.   1674 (5, 33)
> He may have been the husband of Elizabeth and father of John Gumley (*cf.* John Pardoe).

GUMLEY, MRS., AND TURING, WILLIAM, Cabinet-makers, in the Strand.
          1727–29 (49, 57)
> Their accounts for furniture supplied to the Great Wardrobe were questioned by the Comptroller and considerably abated.
> *See also* MOORE AND GUMLEY.

GUNDALL, JAMES, Cabinet-maker, the Paved Court, St. James's.   1749 (3)

GUNTER, —, "An eminent upholsterer in Holborn." *Obit.* notice 1746 (61)

GUNTER, BARBARA, Upholder, Holborn.   1755–60 (2)

GWINNELL, WILLIAM, Cabinet and Looking-glass maker, at *The Looking Glass*, ye South Side of St. Paul's.   1741 (1)
          (Plate, page 69)

GWYN, —, Upholsterer, in St. James's Hay Market.   1747 (5)

HADDOCK, ELKA, Cabinet-maker (address unrecorded).   1739 (49, 61)
> He made a chair for the Society of Dilettanti.

HAIG, ANDREW, Chair and Cabinet-maker, No. 13, Great May's Buildings, in St. Martin's Lane.   1817–27 (2)

HAIG, THOMAS, partner with T. Chippendale, senior, No. 60, St. Martin's Lane. 1771–79 (2, 49, 56)

And with T. Chippendale, junior, under the style of Haig and Chippendale. 1779–96 (56)

Previously to being taken into partnership he acted as clerk to James Rannie—Chippendale's first partner (*q.v.*)

Haig died in 1803 and was buried at St. Martin-in-the-Fields.

HAIG AND CHIPPENDALE (see above). (2)

HAIG AND CO., Upholsterers, No. 60, St. Martin's Lane. 1796 (2)

HAKES, JOHN, JOSEPH AND EDWARD, Upholsterers, at *The Queen's Head*, Upper Shadwell. 1724–26 (6)

HALES, —, Upholsterer, No. 1, Bolt Court, Fleet Street. 1803 (20)

HALFHIDE, THOMAS, Cabinet-maker, Salisbury Court Square, "leaving off trade." 1723 (5)

HALL, EDWARD, Upholsterer, Coventry Court. 1749 (3)

HALL, ELKING[N]., Upholsterer, partner in NASH, HALL AND WHITEHORNE (*q.v.*), at *The Royal Bed* on Holborn Bridge. 1722–49 (3)

HALL, HENRY, Upholsterer, at *The Three Crowns and Dove*, corner of Old Bedlam, Moorfields. *c.* 1760 (1)

Later at *The Three Crowns*, near Old Bedlam. *c.* 1770 (1)

HALL, HENRY, Upholder, No. 1, Moorfields. 1768–72 (2)

HALL, PIERCE, Cabinet and Chair maker, at *The Chair*, in St. John's Street, near Hicks Hall. *c.* 1760 (1) (18)

HALL, ROBERT, Upholsterer, Great St. Helen's, within Bishopsgate. 1717–26 (2, 5)

HALL, WILLIAM, No. 2, Broker Row, Moorfields. 1794–1802 (2)

HALL, WILLIAM AND HERSANT, Cabinet-makers, No. 2, Broker Row, Moorfields. 1803 (1, 2)

Succeeded by HUNTER AND HERSANT (*q.v.*).

HALLETT, WILLIAM, Cabinet-maker, Newport Street. 1732 (64)

Removed to St. Martin's Lane, next door to William Vile (*q.v.*) at the corner of Long Acre. 1752–69 (26, 56, 64), died 1781 (12)

He was esteemed one of the most distinguished cabinet-makers of his day and his work attracted a clientèle from among the wealthy connoisseurs such as the Earl of Leicester and Lord Folkestone, and also drew commendation from Horace Walpole. At the age of 62 he was able to retire from business having previously bought the Cannons estate at Edgware from the Duke of Chandos where he built a new house upon the site. This was inherited by his grandson William who figures with his wife in Gainsborough's well-known picture *The Morning Walk* (1786). William Hallett I married (*en secondes noces*) a daughter

HALLETT, WILLIAM—*continued*.

of James Hallett of Dunmow who, with six other members of the Hallett family, appears in the group painted by Francis Hayman (*c.* 1753). The Dunmow connection lends colour to the supposition that the Halletts were of the same family as the famous goldsmiths of Cheapside who also came from Dunmow (*cf.* Sir James Hallett). I am informed by Mr. R. W. Symonds that he has found reason for thinking that there was a business connection between Hallett and his next-door neighbours, the firm of Cobb and Vile (*q.v.*).

The opening lines of *Elegy Written in an Empty Assembly Room* (1756), by Richard Owen Cambridge:

> In scenes where Hallet's genius has combin'd
> With Bromwich* to amuse and cheer the mind.

HALLIDAY, THOMAS, Cabinet-maker, in Bedfordbury (St. Martin-in-the-Fields).   1774 (3)

HALLOWS, JOHN, Upholsterer, at *The Crown and Sceptre*, in Moorfields.   1760 (1)

HAMBLETON, —, Upholsterer (in partnership with John Howard), at *The Talbot*, in Long Lane, near West Smithfield.   1724–30 (5)
See HOWARD AND HAMBLETON.

HAMILTON, —, Upholsterer, in Whitechapel.   1747 (5)
See William HAMILTON.

HAMILTON, FRANCIS, Upholder, No. 20, Smithfield.   1768–92 (5)
See HAMILTON AND KIRKHAM.

HAMILTON, JOSEPH, Upholder, the corner of Long Lane, West Smithfield.   1743 (5)

HAMILTON, THOMAS, Upholder, of New Bond Street.   1736 (5)

HAMILTON, W., Upholder, No. 76, Wardour Street.   1794 (5)

HAMILTON, WILLIAM, Upholder, No. 54, Whitechapel.   1790–1803 (5) (20)

HAMILTON, WILLIAM AND SON, Upholder, No. 54, Whitechapel.   1760–72 (2)

HAMILTON AND KIRKHAM, Upholders, No. 20, Smithfield.   1783 (2)

HAMMOND, CHRISTOPHER, Frame maker and Gilder, Phoenix Court, Long Acre.   1732 (1)

HANBURY, JOHN, Upholsterer (address unrecorded).   1757 (1)

HARDING, JOHN, Upholder, in the Haymarket.   1747–49 (3, 5)

HARDING, RICHARD, Carver and Gilder to Her Majesty, No. 7, Berwick Street, Soho.   1791 (1)

HARDMAN, JOHN, Upholder, Drury Lane.   1744 (3), 1755 (18)

HARGRAVE, WILLIAM, Upholster, in Newport Street.   1749 (3)
Long Acre.   1752 (5)

---

* Thomas Bromwich, paper stainer (*q.v.*).

Hankins,
UPHOLDER,
CABINET MAKER
and Sworn Appraiser,
At the Royal Bed
in New Bond Street,
HANOVER SQUARE
Makes & Sells all Sorts of
Upholstery Goods, &c
And furnishes Funerals Public or Private
at Reasonable Rates.

SIZE OF ORIGINAL 7⅞″ × 6½″

See page 78

See page 82

SIZE OF ORIGINAL 5″ × 3⅝″

SIZE OF ORIGINAL 4¾″ × 6⅛″
See page 81

SIZE OF ORIGINAL 3″ × 4⅞″
See page 81

SIZE OF ORIGINAL 3⅜″ × 5⅝″
See page 82

HARMAN, Upholster (address unrecorded). 1664–68 (22)

Mr. Pepys visits "Mr. Harman the upholster" on seven occasions. The earliest entry, on 23rd August, 1664: "called at Harman's and there bespoke some chairs," in 1666 he goes to the shop three times during August and September when he is choosing a bed and hangings for "my new closet." Finally, on 19th October, 1668, he sets out from home "by coach with my wife and Deb. and Mr. Harman, the upholster, and carried them to take measure of Mr. Wren's bed at St. James's, I being resolved to have just such another made me."

HARPER AND SHIPTON, Upholstery warehouse, Coventry Street, St. James's, Haymarket. 1768–74 (2)

HARRIOT, WILLIAM, Cabinet-maker, Vine Street. 1774 (3)

HARRIS, —, Upholder and Cabinet-maker, at *The Golden Anchor*, No. 8, Moorfields, near Bedlam Walk between New Broad Street and Old Bedlam. *c.* 1770 (1)

HARRIS, —, Chair maker, Church Street, Lambeth. 1803 (20)

HARRIS, JOHN, AND MOSELEY, RICHARD, Cabinet-makers, opposite East India House, in Leadenhall Street. 1760 (1, 2)

See also RICHARD MOSELEY.

HARRIS, WILLIAM, Upholder, at *The Golden Head*, St. Alban Street, St. James's. 1718–23 (5)

HARRISON, Upholsterer, at *The Cross Keys*, Fleet Ditch. 1748 (5)

HARRISON, WILLIAM, Cabinet-maker, Oxford Road. 1749 (3)

HARRISON, JONATHAN, AND HILL, Upholsterers (address unrecorded). 1732 (1)

HARTLEY, THOMAS, Carver and Gilder, No. 108, Newgate Street, facing Warwick Lane. 1790–94 (1, 2)

(Plate, page 70)

HARTLEY, WILLIAM, Case and Cabinet-maker, No. 78, Newgate Street. 1779–83 (2)

No. 80, Newgate Street. (1)

HARVEY,—, Upholsterer, at *The Cross Keys*, on Ludgate Hill. 1717 (5)

HATCH,—, Cabinet-maker, in High Holborn. 1763 (2)

HATT, JOHN, Cabinet and Chair maker, at *The Blue Ball and Artichoke*, in Aldersgate Street. Successor to John Arrowsmith. 1759–79 (1, 2)

(Plate, page 70)

HAWKINS, —, Cabinet-maker, No. 9, Broad Street, Bloomsbury. 1803

HAWKINS, H., Looking glass and Frame maker, in Compton Street, Soho. *c.* 1760

HAWKINS, JOHN, Upholster, Bond Street. 1749 (3)

HAWKINS, ELIZABETH, (?) widow of foregoing Cabinet-maker and Upholsterer, at *The Royal Bed*, in New Bond Street. 1767 (1)
On the back of the trade card of Hawkins is a bill "Bought of Eliz. Hawkins," dated Nov. 23rd, 1767.

(Plate, page 75)

HAWKINS, WILLIAM, Upholsterer, Bond Street. 1774 (3)

HAWKINS, WILLIAM, Upholder, No. 42, Wigmore Street. 1783 (2)

HAY, —, Cabinet maker, No. 73, Long Acre. 1803 (20)

HAYES, —, Upholsterer, at *The White Swan*, on the South Side of St. Paul's Church Yard. 1694 (33)
He was followed at this address by JOHN COXED (*q.v.*).

HAYS, WILLIAM, Upholder, St. George's Church, Southwark. 1727–34 (3)

HAYWARD, JOHN, Apprenticed to James Smith, (*q.v.*), Cabinet-maker of St. Paul's, Covent Garden. 1744–45 (14)

HAZARD (or HASERT), PETER, Cabinet-maker, at *The Hen and Chickens*, Great Queen Street, St. Giles-in-the-Fields. 1724 (6)
A "Mr. Hazard, cabinet-maker at *The Hen and Chickens* in Lincoln's Inn" was one of the tradesmen involved in the elaborate hoax played upon Hulton the printseller in Pall Mall in 1744.

HAZARD, WILLIAM, Carpenter, at *The Walnut Tree*, in Walnut Tree Yard, Bishopsgate. 1723 (6)

HEAL, JOHN HARRIS, Feather bed and Mattress maker, No. 33, Rathbone Place. 1810–18 (2, 4)

HEAL, FANNY, AND SON, Feather-bed and Mattress-makers, No. 203, Tottenham Court Road. 1818–40

HEAL AND SON, Bedding and Cabinet-makers, No. 196, Tottenham Court Road. 1840

HEARNE, RICHARD AND JOHN, Upholsterers, Nos. 45 and 143, Holborn. 1768–74 (2)

HEARNE, WILLIAM, Upholder, No. 45, Holborn. 1790–93 (2)

HEASMAN, HENRY, Upholsterer, in the Great Piazza, Covent Garden. 1712–34 (3, 5)
"In the Great Piazza in Covent Garden is to be let part of the house Sir Godfrey Kneller lived in: a back house, coach house and stables in parts or together. Inquire of Mr. Heasman, upholsterer, who lives in the house." 1712 (5)

HEATH, A., Cabinet-maker, No. 15, Berwick Street. 1780 (1)

HEATH, JOHN, Upholder, Wych Street. 1724–34 (3)

HEATH, ROBERT, Upholster, Broad Court (Drury Lane). 1749 (3)

HEATH, THOMAS, Upholder and Cabinet-maker, No. 42, Brewer Street, Golden Square. 1790–96 (2)

William Henshaw

CABINET-MAKER.

At the Cabinet and Chair.

On the South Side of St. Paul's Church Yard,

London

Makes and Sells all Sorts of
Glass, Chair, and Cabinet Work,
Where Gentlemen, Merchants, & Others,

may depend upon being serv'd with
the very best Goods, at the most
Reasonable Prices.

See page 81

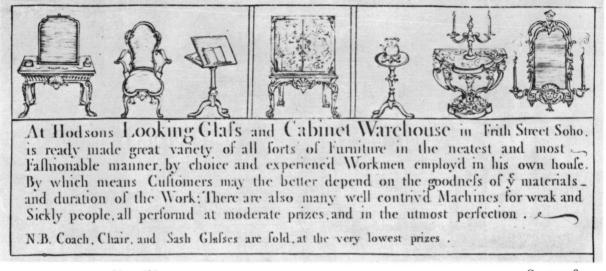

At Hodsons Looking Glass and Cabinet Warehouse in Frith Street Soho. is ready made great variety of all sorts of Furniture in the neatest and most Fashionable manner, by choice and experienc'd Workmen employ'd in his own house. By which means Customers may the better depend on the goodness of $\check{y}$ materials and duration of the Work; There are also many well contriv'd Machines for weak and Sickly people, all perform'd at moderate prizes, and in the utmost perfection.

N.B. Coach, Chair, and Sash Glasses are sold, at the very lowest prizes.

SIZE OF ORIGINAL $2\frac{7}{8}'' \times 6\frac{3}{4}''$

See page 85

Cabcnetts, Looking Glasses, Tables and, stanns, Scretor Chests of Draners, And Curious inlaid Figures for any norke made and Sold By Phillip Hunt at $\check{y}$ Looking Glas & Cabenet at East end of S.t Pauls Church $\check{y}^d$

SIZE OF ORIGINAL $7\frac{3}{8}'' \times 4\frac{1}{2}''$ *See page* 92

HOPE. 36, Rathbone Place Oxford Street. LONDON.

Auctioneer UPHOLSTERER LICENSED & SWORN APPRAISER.

SIZE OF ORIGINAL $7\frac{3}{8}'' \times 4\frac{1}{2}''$ *See page* 86

HEAVEN, JOHN, Joiner and Turner, at *The Floorcloth*, in Bedford Street, facing Bedford Row. *c.* 1760 (1)

HELE, JOHN, Cabinet-maker, at the sign of *The Looking Glass*, in King Street, near Prince's Street, St. Ann's, Soho. died 1746 (5)

HENDEN, ROBERT, Upholsterer, at *The Cock*, Knave's Acre, St. James's. 1726 (6)

HENDERSON, ALEXANDER, Cabinet-maker, Castle Street (Leicester Fields). 1749 (3)

HENNEKIN, GEORGE, Carver and Gilder in general, No. 9, Marylebone Street, Golden Square. 1809 (1)
(Plate, page 76)

HENNEKIN, SIMON, Carver and Gilder, Edward Street, near Broad Street, Golden Square. "Eminent for making laymen for painters, etc." 1763–76 (1, 2)
He compiled "An Album of Original Drawings" of upwards of 400 coats of arms, dated 1776.
(Plate, page 76)

HENNING, DAVID, Upholder, No. 23, Leicester Square. 1794–1817 (2, 20)

HENNING, JOHN, Chair and Cabinet-maker, No. 31, Litchfield Street, Soho. 1790–93 (2)

HENSHAW, WILLIAM, Cabinet-maker and Upholsterer, at *The Cabinet and Chair*, on the South Side of St. Paul's Churchyard. 1755–72 (1, 2, 18)
(Plate, page 79)
In a later trade-card he styles himself "Upholsterer and Cabinet-maker."

HENSHAW, WILLIAM, AND KETTLE, HENRY, Cabinet-makers, No. 18, St. Paul's Church Yard. 1774 (2)
Henry Kettle (*q.v.*) was successor to Philip Bell at No. 23, St. Paul's Church Yard, until 1796.

HEPPEL, JOHN, Upholder, No. 53, Wigmore Street, Cavendish Square. 1794–1803 (2, 20)

HEPPLEWHITE, GEORGE, Furniture designer, Redcross Street, St. Giles's, Cripplegate. died 1786 (49)
The first edition of his book of designs *The Cabinet-makers' and Upholsterers' Guide* was published in 1788—two years after his death—by his widow Alice under the style of A. Hepplewhite and Co.
No pieces of furniture have been identified with the firm and the name of Hepplewhite does not appear in the London directories nor in the *D.N.B.*

HEPWORTH, Cabinet-maker, No. 12, Little St. Martin's Lane. 1803 (20)

HERRING, HENRY, Cabinet-maker and Upholder, No. 13, Lad Lane. 1755–63 (2)
Later Herring, Smith and Slack. 1763–68

HERRING, ROBERT, Upholder and Cabinet-maker, No. 96, Fleet Street, near
Bride Lane. 1774–83 (1, 2, 20)
No. 109, Fleet Street. 1784–1817 (19)

HERRING, ROBERT WILLIAM, No. 109, Fleet Street. 1823–39 (2)

HERVÉ, FRANCIS, Cabriole Chair maker, No. 32, Lower John Street, near
Tottenham Court Road. 1785–96 (2, 56)
He supplied French chairs to Lady Spencer at Althorp and an elaborate con-
vertible set of library steps by him is now in the Victoria and Albert Museum.

HEWITT, NATHANIEL, Upholsterer, at *The Crown and Cushion*, near St.
Thomas's Gate, in the Borough of Southwark (No. 42, Borough).
1768–77 (1, 2)

(Plate, page 84)

HEWLINS, —, Upholsterer, No. 2, Strand. 1803 (20)

HIBBERT, JOHN, Upholder, Bartholomew Close. died 1717 (5)
He was succeeded at this address by his partner Philip Bodham (*q.v.*).

HICKS, JAMES, Cabinet-maker, portable writing desks, dressing cases, etc.,
No. 26, Wigmore Street. 1809–27 (1, 2)
His label was found on a piece of Regency furniture *c.* 1820.

HIDE (*see* Robert Hyde).

HIGGONS, Cabinet-maker, near Gray's Inn. 1699 (5)

HIGGS, THOMAS, Cabinet-maker, Upholsterer and Auctioneer, No. 246,
Roadside, Whitechapel. 1802–39 (1, 2)

(Plate, page 76)

HILKER, ANTHONY, "Cabinet work, carv'd and gilt frames, etc," in Husband
Street in the Gravel Pits, near St. Ann's. 1747–55 (1)

(Plate, page 76)

HILL, THOMAS, Cabinet-maker, of St. Clement Danes. *c.* 1780 (63)
His son Isaac entered St. Paul's School in 1785 and for 36 years he was head-
master of The Mercers' School, 1804–40.

HINTS, FREDERICK, Cabinet-maker, at *The Porcupine*, in Newport Street,
near Leicester Fields. 1738 (5)
Specialised in small pieces of furniture, etc., inlaid with brass and mother-of-
pearl.

HITCHIN, CHARLES, Cabinet-maker, at *The White Hart*, East end of St. Paul's.
1709 (5)

HOBBS, GEORGE, Cabinet-maker, London. 1764 (1)
The sole authority for the above entry is a dated bill for a library table so
inscribed.

See page 86

SIZE OF ORIGINAL 7⅛" × 6¼"

See page 85

SIZE OF ORIGINAL 7⅛" × 4⅞"

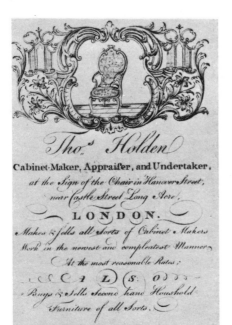

SIZE OF ORIGINAL 3⅜″ × 2⅜″

See page 91

SIZE OF ORIGINAL 6¼″ × 5″   *See page 82*

SIZE OF ORIGINAL 6″ × 4″

See page 85

SIZE OF ORIGINAL 2⅜″ × 3¾″   *See page 86*

HODDER, CHARLES, Upholder and Cabinet-maker, at *The Mahogany Desk and Bookcase*, the corner of Unicorn Yard (No. 100) in Tooley Street, Southwark. 1777 (1, 2)

HODGSON, FRANCIS, Upholsterer, No. 49, Wych Street, Drury Lane. 1790 (2)

HODGSON, GEORGE, Upholsterer and Cabinet-maker, Brook Street, Holborn, near the Sun Tavern. 1745 (61)

HODGSON, WILLIAM, Upholsterer and Cabinet-maker, No. 70, Great Queen Street, Lincoln's Inn Fields. 1783–1803 (2, 20)

HODSON, JOHN, Upholder and Cabinet-maker, at Hodson's Looking Glass and Cabinet Warehouse, in Frith Street, Soho. 1727–44 (1, 3)
> He supplied a tripod table, a fine carved and painted side-table, and a wine-cooler for the Duke of Atholl at Blair Castle in 1738. A bill dated 1744 is receipted by P. Smagget as for "Hodson and Self."

(Plate, page 80)

HODSON, ROBERT, Cabinet-maker, Frith Street, Soho. 1723 (6)

HODSON AND RUDYARD, Upholsterer, in St. Ann's, Soho. 1748 (5)

HOLBART, THOMAS, Upholster, Berwick Street, Soho. 1749 (3)

HOLBERD (or HOLBIRD), JAMES, Upholder, No. 16, Noble Street, Cheapside. 1790–1803 (2, 20)

HOLBIRD, ISAAC, Cabinet manufactory, No. 13, Catharine Street, Strand. 1817 (2)

HOLDEN, SAMUEL, Upholder and Cabinet-maker, No. 9, Aldersgate Street. 1777–79 (1, 2)
No. 37, Charles Street, Westminster. 1792

HOLDEN, THOMAS, Cabinet-maker, etc., "at the sign of *The Chair*," in Hanover Street, near Castle Street, Long Acre. c. 1750 (1)

(Plate, page 84)

HOLINSHADE, —, Cradle-maker, King Street, Drury Lane. 1803 (20)

HOLLAND, HENRY, Architect and Designer of furniture, Hans Place. born 1746, died 1806 (62)
> Much of the furniture at Carlton House and the Royal Pavilion at Brighton was made from his designs.

See TAPWELL AND HOLLAND.

HOLLINSHED, THOMAS, Turner and Cabinet-maker, corner of Great Queen Street, Drury Lane. 1755 (1)

(Plate, page 83)

HOLLINWORTH, W., Upholsterer (address not recorded). 1761 (1)

HOLLIWOOD, —, Bedstead maker, at Fleet Ditch, near Black-Fryers. 1734 (5)

HOLLOWAY, —, Upholsterer, No. 34, Rathbone Place. 1803 (20)

HOLLOWAY, JOHN, Cabinet-maker and Upholsterer, No. 101, Great Saffron Hill.   (1)

HOLMES, ALEXANDER, Cabinet-maker, at *The Unicorn*, No. 15, Brokers Row, Moorfields.   1790–93 (1, 2)

HOLMES, RICHARD, Cabinet-maker and Glass grinder, at *The Tea Chest*, No. 22, in Barbican.   1783 (1, 2)
(Plate, page 84)

HOLMES AND GRIFFIN, Sedan chair makers, Whitcomb Street, Leicester Fields.   1779–96 (2)
See W. AND T. GRIFFIN.   1802–38

HOMERSHAM, THOMAS, Upholder, No. 238, Borough High Street. 1784–96 (2)
No. 245, Borough.   1803 (20)

HOOLE, JOHN, Upholsterer, at *The Rose*, Cornhill.   1690 (33)
Removed to *The Rose*, in Bishopsgate Street.   1693–1710 (5)

HOOPER, JOHN, Cabinet-maker, at *The Blue Boar*, in Cornhill.   1730–44 (33)
After his death in 1744 the business was carried on by his widow, Ann Hooper.

HOPE, THOMAS, Virtuoso and Designer of furniture and decorations, Duchess Street, Cavendish Square.   born 1770 (?), died 1831 (62)
His *Household Furniture and Interior Decoration* (1807), though not very favourably received by the critics, did much to influence the final phases of Regency design. He produced books on architecture and costume.

HOPE, WILLIAM, Upholsterer, etc., No. 36, Rathbone Place, Oxford Street.
1805–39, (1, 5)
(Plate, page 80)

HOPKINS, DAVID, Cabinet-maker, Hart Street.   1749–55 (3, 18)

HOPKINS, WILLIAM, Upholder and Cabinet-maker, at the corner of Rood Lane, No. 15, Fenchurch Street.   1746–74 (1, 2)

HOPLEY, WILLIAM, Upholder, near *The Four Swans*, in Bishopsgate Street.
1732–49 (5)

HORMAN, JOHN, Cabinet-maker and Upholder, No. 49, Essex Street.
1790–93 (2)
No. 48, Essex Street.   1794–96 (2)

HORNE, ABIAL, Cabinet-maker and Glass grinder, No. 19, Well Close Square.
1768–83 (1, 2)
(Plate, page 83)

HORNE, JOHN, Upholder, Brewer Street, St. James's.   1716–27 (5)

HORNER, —, Upholsterer, Queen Street, Westminster.   1712 (5)

HORNER, —, Upholsterer, at the West End of St. Ann's, Soho.   1720 (5)

HORNER, WILLIAM, Upholster, Tothill Street, Westminster.   1749 (3)

See page 91

SIZE OF ORIGINAL $4\frac{3}{4}'' \times 3\frac{3}{4}''$

See page 92

SIZE OF ORIGINAL $8\frac{1}{4}'' \times 6''$

SIZE OF ORIGINAL $3\frac{1}{8}'' \times 4\frac{3}{4}''$ *See page 96*

SIZE OF ORIGINAL $2\frac{7}{8}'' \times 4''$ *See page 96*

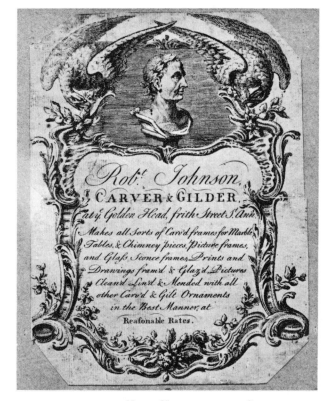

SIZE OF ORIGINAL $7\frac{1}{4}'' \times 5\frac{5}{8}''$ *See page 97*

SIZE OF ORIGINAL $5\frac{3}{4}'' \times 4\frac{1}{4}''$ *See page 98*

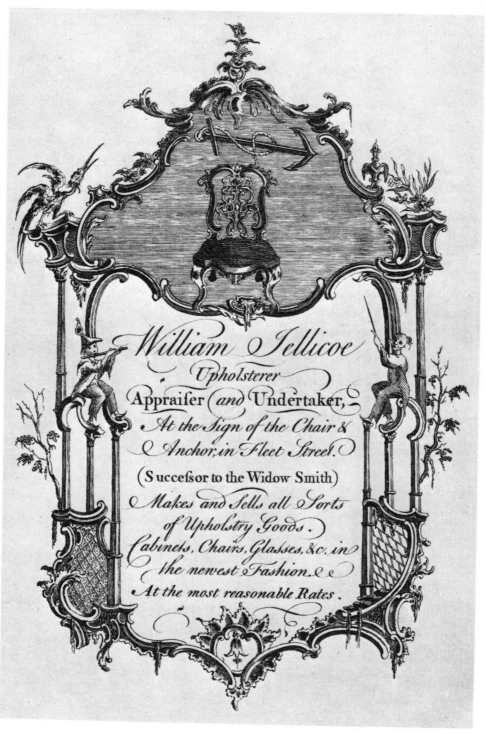

William Jellicoe
Upholsterer
Appraiser (and) Undertaker,
At the Sign of the Chair &
Anchor, in Fleet Street.
(Successor to the Widow Smith)
Makes and Sells all Sorts
of Upholstry Goods.
Cabinets, Chairs, Glasses, &c. in
the newest Fashion.
At the most reasonable Rates.

SIZE OF ORIGINAL 7¼″ × 5″

See page 97

Geo: Kemp
at the Golden Ball Cornhill
London

Maker & Sells all Sorts of Cabinets,
Chairs, Upholstry, Glasses &c: &c Cheap
Library Book Cases, Beaureau Writing
Gabinet Commode Dressing
Dining Tables &c

TABLES:
&c

SIZE OF ORIGINAL 7⅜" × 6⅜"   See page 99

William Kirk
at the Sign of the Golden Chair
the Corner of Salisbury Street in ye Strand
London

Makes & Sells all sorts of Cabinet Work. Chests of
Drawers, Desks, Bookcases, Beaureau, Dining, Card &
Tea Tables, Sconce, Pier and Chimney Glasses, &c.
Feather Beds, Blankets, and Quilts &c.
Blinds for Windows.
All sorts of Goods Apprayed.
Funerals Performed
Either Public or Private to any Part of
England

NB. All sorts of Houshold Goods bought and sold.

SIZE OF ORIGINAL 7⅛" × 4⅜"   See page 101

HORROCKS, ALEXANDER, Upholder and Undertaker, at *The White Bear*, against Gray's Inn Gate, in Holborn. 1724–32 (1, 5)

HORSLEY, —, Chair maker, No. 1, Worship Street, Finsbury. 1803 (20)

HORTON, JOSEPH, Upholsterer, Panton Street. 1709 (4)

HOW, ROBERT, Upholder, Germain [*sic*] Street. 1726–49 (3, 5)

HOW, THOMAS, Upholsterer, of Westminster. *c.* 1720
> Supplied furnishings for Lord Scarsdale's house at Sutton.

HOWARD, *see* SPINNAGE AND HOWARD.

HOWARD, GERARD, Carver and Gilder to the Royal Family (address unrecorded). 1727–35 (49)

HOWARD, JOHN, Upholsterer and Dealer in tapestries and oriental carpets, at *The Talbot*, in Long Lane, near West Smithfield. 1717–32 (1, 62)
> Father of John Howard, the philanthropist and prison reformer. Died in 1742. For a short period he took a Mr. Hambleton (*q.v.*) into partnership.

HOWARD AND HAMBLETON, at above. 1724–30 (5)

HOWCRAFT, THOMAS, Cabinet-maker, at *The India Cabinet*, in Long Acre. 1711 (5)

HOWELL, —, Chair maker, Red Cross Street. 1803 (18)

HUDGEBOUT, JAMES, Glass grinder and Cabinet seller, at *The Looking Glass*, in Cornhill, "selling off stock as he is leaving off trade." 1704 (5)
> *See* JOHN BURROUGH at the same address until about 1690.

HUDSON, —, Upholsterer, in St. James's Street (deceased). 1735 (5)

HUDSON AND CORNEY, Upholders and Cabinet-makers, Nos. 4 and 13, Broad Street, Golden Square. 1790–1809 (1, 2, 20)

(Plate, page 84)

HUDSON, STEPHEN, Carver and Gilder, Titchfield Street, Cavendish Square.
> Supplied pier-glasses for Blickling Hall, Norfolk. *c.* 1770–93 (2)

HUGGETT, —, Chair maker, Borough Road. 1803 (20)

HUGHES, PATRICK, Cabinet-maker and Upholsterer, opposite ye Royal Hospital in ye Market Place, Greenwich. *c.* 1780 (1)

HULBEART, THOMAS, Upholsterer and Cabinet-maker, at *The Ship and Anchor*, over against Gun Yard in Houndsditch.
> "Where you may be furnished with several sorts of lin'd Beds as Velvet, Damask, Mohair and Camblet . . . already standing up with silk quilts suitable. Likewise Screwtores, Tables, Stands, Looking-glasses of Japan or other work as also Tapestry-Hangings of several sorts." 1689 and 1690 (5)

HULETT, PETER, Frame maker and Gilder, in Little Bartholomew Close. *c.* 1750 (1)

(Plate, page 87)

HULL, —, "Eminent cabinet-maker and glass seller of Radcliff Highway with house at Peckham."   deceased 1743 (61)

HUMPHREYS, THOMAS, Upholsterer, in Newgate Street.   1747 (5)

HUMPHRY, WILLIAM, Upholder, in Fetter Lane.   1724–27 (5)

HUMPHRYS, —, Upholsterer, in St. Paul's Church Yard.   1764 (5)

HUNT, —, Upholsterer and Cabinet-maker, in Castle Street, near Cross Lane, Long Acre.   1780 (1)

HUNT, PHILLIP, Cabinet-maker, "at *Ye Looking Glas and Cabenet* at East end of St. Pauls Church Y^d. . . . cabenetts, Looking Glasses, Tables and stanns [*sic*], Scretor Chests of Drawers. And curious inlaid Figures for any worke."   *c.* 1680–1720 (1, 56)

The mirror frame in his trade-card bears the interlaced cypher of William and Mary flanked by lion and unicorn. He was the maker of "The bed with embroidered satin in the state bedroom at Erthig, Denbighshire, which was made for John Mellor, the owner of the house in 1720. This is perhaps the most ornate and splendid specimen of the tester or Duchesse bedstead which survives from the period."*

(Plate, page 80)

HUNTER, WILLIAM, Upholder, in Token House Yard, near ye Royal Exchange.   *c.* 1760 (1)

"Maker after the Newest Fashion all sorts of Four Post and Standing Beds."
A William Hunter subscribed to Chippendale's *Director*.   1755

(Plate, page 87)

HUNTER AND HERSANT, Cabinet-makers and Upholders, No. 2, Lower Moorfields, opposite the Middle Walk.   1808 (1, 2)
Late Hall and Hersant (*q.v.*).

HURST, GEORGE, Carver and Gilder, Little Compton Street, St. Ann's, Soho.   *c.* 1780 (1)

HURST, NICHOLAS, Upholsterer, over against the Rose Tavern in Russell Street, Covent Garden.   1666 (5)
"Who fled from the Plague."

HUTCHINS, —, Upholder, in King Street, Covent Garden.   died 1746 (61)

HUTCHINS, HASSIL, Upholder and Auctioneer, No. 41, King Street.
                                                         1783–90 (2)

HUTT, ELIZABETH, AND SON, Upholders, at *The Blew Curtain*, in St. Paul's Church Yard.   1741 (1)

This bill for "a Dressing Table and Glass £6 6s. od." in the accounts of the Duke of Norfolk, is made out to "Mr. Howard" and dated 1741. Succeeded by John Iliffe (*q.v.*).

* *See* illustration p. 177, *Georgian Cabinet Makers.*

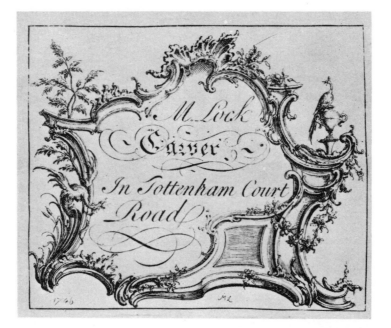

SIZE OF ORIGINAL 3″ × 3⅝″   *See page* 104

SIZE OF ORIGINAL 5⅛″ × 3½″   *See page* 101   SIZE OF ORIGINAL 4¼″ × 3″   *See page* 102

94

Peter Langlois
CABINET-MAKER
in Tottenham Court Road near Windmill Str.
Makes all Sorts of Fine Cabinets and
Commodes made & inlaid in the Politest manner
with Brass & Tortoishell, Likewise all rich Ornamental Clock Cases, and Inlaid work mended
with great Care, Branch Chandelier & Lanthorns
in Brass.
at the Lowest Prices

Pierre Langlois Ebeniste.
dans Tottenham Court Road Proche Windmill Str.
Fait toutes Sortes de Commodes et Secrétaires,
Enseignures, et autres Meubles, Inscrutés de
fleurs en Bois et Marqueteries, garnies
de Bronzes dorées, Boëtes de Pendulles,
en Vert en Ecaille et Marqueteries
garnies de Bronzes, Bras Lustres
Lanternes, racco-   mode les
Vielles Ouverages,
de Marqueteries et
les remet a neuf
le tout à juste
Prix

SIZE OF ORIGINAL $8\frac{5}{8}'' \times 6\frac{1}{8}''$

See page 102

HUTT, JOHN, Upholder, at *The Three Pillows*, over against the South Gate, St. Paul's Church Yard. 1712–21, died 1729 (5, 33)

HUTT, RICHARD, Upholsterer and Cabinet-maker, in St. Paul's Church Yard. 1748 (61)

HYDE (or HIDE), ROBERT, Cabinet-maker, in Maiden Lane, Covent Garden. 1744–49 (3, 5)

IDEN, HENRY, Cabinet-maker, at *The Looking Glass*, in Ludgate Street. 1687 (5)
Removed to Bell Yard, in Carter Lane. 1688 (5)

ILIFFE, JOHN, Upholder, at *The Blue Curtain*, in St. Paul's Church Yard. Successor to Mrs. Elizabeth Hutt (*q.v.*). 1760–65 (1, 2)
Iliffe was followed by Jonathan Fall (*q.v.*).

INCE, —, 23, Holles Street, Cavendish Square. 1803 (20)

INCE, WILLIAM, AND MAYHEW, JOHN, Cabinet-makers and Upholsterers, Broad Street, Golden Square, Soho, also in Marshall Street, Carnaby Market. 1759–1803 (5, 49, 56)
They published an important folio of designs entitled *Universal System of Household Furniture*, which came out in parts between 1759 and 1763. Later their announcements appear under the style of MAYHEW AND INCE (*q.v.*) at the above address and also at Nos. 20 and 47, Marshall Street, Carnaby Market, in the directories until 1811 (2). William Ince was apprenticed to Mr. West, Cabinet-maker (*q.v.*) in King Street, Covent Garden, and John Mayhew served his time with a Mr. Bradshaw of Soho. In January 1759 they advertised that they had taken the house of Mr. Charles Smith (*q.v.*), cabinet-maker and upholsterer, opposite Broad Street in Carnaby Market: from here they issued an invitation to their customers to inspect "an Assortment of French Furniture consign'd from Paris." A remarkable set of twenty-four Board Room chairs were supplied by the firm to the Westminster Fire Office in 1792 where they are still in use. (Reported by Mr. C. Hussey in *Country Life*, 21st Dec., 1951.) A fine bookcase now in the Museum of Decorative Arts at Copenhagen bears this firm's label.
See JOHN MAYHEW, *also* WHITTLE, NORMAN AND MAYHEW.
(Plate, page 106)

INSLEY, W., Sedan chair maker, in Marylebone Street, St. James's. 1780 (1)

IRELAND, —, Upholsterer to their Royal Highnesses, Prince's House, in Leicester Fields. died 1726 (2)

IRELAND, JOHN, Upholstery warehouse, No. 3, Friday Street. 1784 (2)
29, Old Compton Street. 1790–93 (2)

IRELAND, RICHARD, Upholder, Bow Street, Covent Garden. 1770–79 (2)
Presumably he was "Ireland the upholder" who is mentioned in the letters of Edward Gibbon, the historian, as having supplied the white and gold bookcases when Gibbon moved into No. 7, Bentwick Street in 1772. It was in this house that the first three volumes of the history of the Roman Empire were written. (*See* p. x, Introduction.)

ISHERWOOD, JOHN, Decorator and Upholsterer, No. 6, New Bond Street, and later at No. 493, Oxford Street, until 1855.   1840 (2)

ISHERWOOD, N., AND SONS, at above, and later at No. 493, Oxford Street, until 1855.   1836 (2)

ISHERWOOD AND BRADLEY, Upholsterers and Paper-stainers (late partners with Mr. Bromwich, q.v.), *The Golden Lyon*, No. 35, Ludgate Hill.
                    1787–92 (1)

ISSARD, JOHN, Cabinet-maker, in Half Moon Alley, Bishopsgate Street.
                    1765 (7)

IVEY, JOHN, Hardwood and Ivory turner, No. 34, Leather Lane, Holborn.
                    1781 (1)
    Succeeded by M. Ivey at above.   1790 (1)

JACKSON, —, Turner of oval frames, in Tottenham Court Road.   1763 (2)

JACKSON, BENJAMIN, Upholder and Cabinet-maker, New Compton Street, Soho.   c. 1790 (1)
(Plate, page 88)

JACKSON, EPHRAIM, Cabinet-maker, Charles Court, Strand.   1749 (3)

JACKSON, JOHN, Upholder, Broad Court, Drury Lane.   1774 (3)
    No. 25, Drury Lane.   1790 (2)

JACKSON, JOHN, Upholder and Cabinet-maker, No. 9, Aldersgate Street.
                    1783–90 (2)

JACKSON, JOSEPH, Cabinet-maker, No. 5, Bull Head Court, Jewin Street.
                    1755–93 (2)

JACKSON, PETER, Upholster, Cornhill Ward.   1640 (16)

JACKSON, ROBERT, Upholder and Cabinet-maker, Rupert Street.   1774 (3)
    16, Berwick Street.   1790 (2)

JACKSON, THOMAS, Turner at *The Golden Coffee Mill*, in Mutton Lane, near Clerkenwell Green.   c. 1750 (1)

JAMAR, WILLIAM, French Cabinet-maker, No. 29, Wardour Street. 1817 (2)

JAMES, PHILIP, Upholsterer, No. 63, Shoreditch.   1770–94 (2), 1803 (20)

JAQUES, JOHN, Carver and Gilder, removed from No. 301 to No. 14, *The King's Arms*, Holborn, near Gray's Inn Gate.   1784–90 (1)

JAQUES, THOMAS, Hardwood turner and maker of Tunbridge wares, No. 65, Leather Lane, Holborn.   c. 1790 (1)
(Plate, page 88)

JARVIS, SAMUEL, Hardwood turner, at *The Rose and Crown and Fowler*, on Snow Hill.
    An entry in one of his bills reads :—"6 small lignum vitae dishes £0 6s. 0d." 1740
    No. 41, Snow Hill.   1753–84 (1, 2)

JEACOCK, CALEB, Cabinet-maker, 76, Oxford Street, opposite Poland Street. 1755–83 (2, 18)

JELLICOE, WILLIAM, Upholsterer, at the sign of *The Chair and Anchor*, No. 88, in Fleet Street. 1760 (1), 1770–72 (2)
Successor to WIDOW SMITH (*q.v.*).

(Plate, page 89)

JEMMETT, JOHN, Turner, at *The Three Brushes*, Leadenhall Street. 1726 (6)

JENKINS, JOHN, Upholder, "late foreman to Mr. Cobb" (*q.v.*), No. 75, Long Acre. 1774 (2)–1803 (19)

JENKINS AND STRICKLAND, at above. 1780 (2)–1793 (19)
See STRICKLAND AND JENKINS.

JENNENS, C., Carver and Ormolu worker, No. 42, Poland Street. (1)

JENNINGS, JOHN, Upholder, No. 15, Newgate Street. 1790–96 (2)

JENNINGS AND WALKINGTON, Upholders and Cabinet-makers, at *The Vine* in Long Acre. *c.* 1770 (1)

JENSEN, GERREIT, or JOHNSON, GERARD, Cabinet-maker, upon the Pavements in St. Martin's Lane. *c.* 1680, died 1715 (5, 8, 56, 64)
He held warrant of Cabinet-maker to the Crown from the reign of Charles II to Queen Anne. Much of the furniture which can be attributed to him was decorated with lacquer and marquetry and fitted with mirror panels, all of it of the very finest quality. The work of Jensen is fully dealt with in articles by Mr. R. W. Symonds which appeared in *Connoisseur*, May 1935 and July 1937. See also *Georgian Cabinet Makers* (1944) by Edwards and Jourdain, and *Dictionary of English Furniture*.

(Plates, pages 224–227)

JEREMY AND BRAGG, Upholsterers and Cabinet-makers, Southampton Street, Covent Garden. *c.* 1820 (1)

JERMAIN, —, Cabinet-maker, No. 10, Broad Street, Golden Square. 1803 (20)

JOEL, THOMAS, Upholsterer, at *The Angel and Crown*, in Barbican. 1724–27 (5, 6)

JOHNSON, GERARD, Cabinet-maker, west side of St. Martin's Lane. 1709 (4)
See GERREIT JENSEN.

JOHNSON, JOHN, Cabinet-maker, at *The King's Arms*, in Long Acre.
His widow advertised sale of stock. 1695 (5)

JOHNSON, ROBERT, Carver and Gilder, at *Ye Golden Head*, Frith Street, Soho. *c.* 1760

(Plate, page 88)

JOHNSON, ROBERT, Upholder, No. 3, Talbot Court, Grace-church Street. 1765–74 (2)

JOHNSON, THOMAS, Cabinet-maker, Wardour Street. 1749 (3)

JOHNSON, THOMAS, Carver and Gilder, Queen Street, Seven Dials.

    From *The Golden Boy* in Grafton Street, St. Ann's, Soho.   1755–63 (2)
    From the former address he published his first book of designs, *Twelve Girandoles*,
    in 1755. He published *The Book of the Carver* with 53 engraved plates in 1758,
    and *One Hundred and Fifty New Designs* came out in monthly parts between
    1756–58.
    Finely carved mirrors and girandoles by him are to be seen at Corsham Court
    and Hagley Park.

JOHNSON, THOMAS AND GEORGE, Cabinet-makers, No. 34, Carey Street,
    Lincoln's Inn Fields.   1802 (1)

JOHNSTONE, JUPE AND CO., Patentees of the Circular Dining Tables, No. 67,
    Bond Street.   1840 (2)
    See also JUPE, JOHNSTONE AND CO.

JOLIT, FREDERICK, Cabinet-maker, No. 6, Old Broad Street. 1803–17 (19)

JONES, —, Upholsterer, St. James's Street, two doors above St. James's
    Palace.   1717 (5)

JONES, —, Upholder, at *The Blue Anchor*, on Tower Hill.   1731 (5)

JONES, F., AND CO., Sedan chair makers, No. 77, Lower Grosvenor Street.
    1794 (5)

JONES, FRANCIS, Upholder, Bloomsbury.   1719 (7)

JONES, HUGH, Upholder, Peter Street, Westminster.   1727 (5)

JONES, JOHN, Upholsterer, at *The Angel*, Minories.   1708 (5)

JONES, PETER (the late), Upholder and Cabinet-maker, within two doors of
    Durham Yard in the Strand. Sale of stock.   1744 (5)

JONES, SAM, Upholder, at *The Woolpack and Crown*, in the Strand. 1729 (5)

JONES, SAMUEL, Chair and Cabinet-maker, at the sign of *The Three Chairs*,
    facing the South Gate in St. Paul's Church Yard.   1740 (5)

JONES, THOMAS, Cabinet-maker, at *The Seven Stars*, in St. Paul's Church
    Yard, moving to his marble manufactory at Craven House in Wych
    Street.   1724 (5)
    "Leaving off shop-keeping."   1725 (5)

JONES, WILLIAM, Upholder, on Tower Hill.   1734 (5)

JORDAN, JOHN, Chair and Cabinet manufactory, No. 15, Artillery Street,
    Bishopsgate Street.   1790 (2)–1803 (20)

JORDAN, THOMAS, Turner and Cabinet-maker, at *The Rose and Crown*, on
    Snow Hill.   1721 (6), died 1735

JOURET, HENRY, Picture frame maker, Carver and Gilder, at *The Architrave
    Frame* in Grafton Street, Soho.   *c.* 1760 (1)
    At *The Gold Frame*, the Middle of Maiden Lane, Covent Garden.
    c. 1770 (1)

    Trade-card engraved by Matthias Lock.
                (Plate, page 88)

JUPE, JOHNSTONE and Co., Cabinet makers, Upholsterers and Patentees of the circular dining tables. No. 67, New Bond Street. 1835–39 (2)

Robert Jupe took out a patent for an expanding circular dining table in 1835.

JUPP, ELIZABETH AND THOMAS, Frame makers and Gilders, No. 5, Eagle Street, Red Lion Street. 1790–93 (2)

JUPP, STEPHEN, Cabinet-maker, High Holborn. 1715 (5)

KAY, QUENTIN, Upholsterer, No. 14, Ludgate Hill. 1755 (18), 1783–93 (2), 1803 (20)

See SAY AND KAY.

KEEBLE, SAMUEL, Carver and Gilder, No. 11, Old Change. 1781, 1790–92 (2, 15)

KELSALL, THOMAS, Upholder, St. Mary Axe. 1724–34 (3)
In St. Lawrence Lane. 1736 (5)

KELSEY, JOHN, Cabinet-maker, over against *The Bull and Gate*, in Holborn. 1746 (5)

KEMP, GEORGE, Cabinet-maker, at *The Golden Ball*, No. 64, Cornhill. c. 1760 (1), 1772–90 (2)

(Plate, page 90)

KEMP, GEORGE, AND SON, No. 64, Leadenhall Street. 1790–93 (2)

KEMP, MATTHEW, No. 64, Cornhill. 1792–1814 (2, 19)

KEMP AND GOULD, No. 64, Cornhill. 1770 (2)

KENNETT, ROBERT, Upholder and Cabinet-maker, No. 67, New Bond Street. 1779–96 (2)

KENNETT AND VERNON, Upholder and Cabinet-maker, Piccadilly. 1777 (2)

KENT, ABBOT, Upholsterer, Nos. 65 and 67, London Wall. 1792 (2)

KENT, WILLIAM, Architect and Furniture designer, Burlington House, Piccadilly. born 1684, died 1748 (40, 62)

Horace Walpole said "He gave designs for most of the furniture at Houghton as he did for several other houses."

KENT, WILLIAM, Upholder, at *The Black Lion and Tent*, opposite the Church Wall, in Houndsditch. (1)

KENT AND LUCK, Carpet, Upholstery and Cabinet warehouse, Carpenters' Hall. (1, 2, 20)
No. 67, London Wall. 1792–1803
Successors to LUCK AND KENT (*q.v.*).

KENT, TOMKINS, AND WILLIAMS, Carpet, Upholstery and Cabinet warehouse, at above address. 1812–17 (1, 2, 19)

KERBY, —, Cabinet-maker, Sackville Street, Piccadilly. 1763 (2)

KERR, JOHN, Cabinet-maker and Upholsterer, No. 31, Pall Mall.

1790–1803 (2, 19)

KERRINTONE, —, Upholsterer, at *The Boar's Head*, within Aldgate. 1731 (5)

KETTLE, HENRY, Cabinet-maker, successor to Philip Bell (*q.v.*), No. 18, St. Paul's Church Yard (formerly Henshaw and Kettle).   1774 (2)
No. 23, St. Paul's Church Yard   1777–96 (1, 2)

(Plate, page 255)

KIDD, —, Upholsterer and Cabinet-maker, No. 62, New Bond Street.
1803 (20)

KILBURN, —, Upholder, St. John Street.   1763 (7)

KILPIN, WILLIAM, Upholder, in Mark Lane.   1747–55 (5)

KING, —, Upholdster, at *The Black Lyon*, in Cambridge Street, by Broad Street, St. James's.   1727 (5)

KING, JOHN, Chair maker, late of St. Paul's Church Yard. deceased 1703 (5)

KING, JOHN, Upholder and Cabinet-maker, Castle Street, Long Acre.
1790–93 (2)
His bill for furniture supplied to Earl Spencer is quoted in *Dictionary of English Furniture*.

KING, THOMAS, Cabinet-maker and Gilder, in Long Acre.   1742 (5)

KING, WILLIAM HENRY, Cabinet and Case maker, No. 12, Turn-again Lane, Snow Hill.   1790–93 (2)
No. 2, Bartlett's Buildings, Holborn.   1827 (1, 2)

KINGHAM, —, Frame maker to George III, in Long Acre.   1763 (2)
M. Jourdain's article in *Country Life*, 6th Oct., 1950, says that Kingham of Long Acre framed the Raphael cartoons at Hampton Court for George IV at a cost of £500.

KINGSBURY, ye widow, Upholsterer, at *The Three Crowns*, in New Street, Hand Alley (Bishopsgate Street Without).   (1)

KINGSMAN, THOMAS, Upholsterer, Bear Street, Leicester Fields. 1709 (4)

KINGSMAN, —, Upholster, at the sign of *The Red Lamp*, in Broad Street, Golden Square.   deceased 1718 (5)

KINGSNORTH, JOHN, Upholder, No. 57, Friday Street.   1770–83 (2)

KINGSNORTH AND ROWLEY, at above.   1755–68 (2)

KINLOCK, JAMES, Upholder and Cabinet-maker, No. 4, Warwick Street, Golden Square.   1790–93 (2)

KIRBY, RICHARD, Cabinet-maker, Drury Lane.   1749 (3)

KIRK, —, Chair maker, in Holborn.   1743 (5)

KIRK, THOMAS, Cabinet-maker, No. 17, Greek Street, Soho.   1794 (2)

KIRK, WILLIAM, Cabinet-maker, at the sign of *The Golden Chair*, the corner of Salisbury Street, in the Strand.   1749 (1, 3)
Also in Bell Yard, Grace Church Street.

(Plate, page 90)

KIRKWOOD, JOHN, Cabinet-maker, Haydon Street (in the Minories).

1749 (3)

KNAGGS, THOMAS, Cabinet and Chair maker, No. 15, Moor Lane, Fore Street.   1790 (2)

KNAPP, ALEXANDER, Cabinet-maker, in the Strand.   1774 (3)

KNIGHT, JAMES, Cabinet-maker, Long Acre.   1709 (4)

KNIGHT, JAMES, Upholsterer, Queenhithe.   1727 (5)

KNIGHT, THOMAS, Upholder, in Bread Street.   1747 (5)

KNIGHT, WILLIAM, Upholsterer, at *The Crown*, in Leadenhall Street.

1723–25 (6)

KNOWLES, JOHN, Cabinet-maker and Undertaker, at *The Cabinet and Four Coffins*, near the Maypole, in Tooley Street.   1747 (5)

KNOWLES, RICHARD, Cabinet-maker, No. 27, Tottenham Court Road.

1790–93 (2)

KRIPE AND MOWER, Cabinet-makers, Upper Oxford Road.   1803 (20)

LADYMAN, —, Upholder, No. 51, Fleet Market.   1790–93 (2)

LA GRANGE, Upholster (address unrecorded).   1674 (8)

LAMB, —, Cabinet-maker, Nos. 9 and 10, Jervin Street.   1803 (20)

LAMBALL, JACOB, Carpenter, at *The Three Compasses*, in Hyde Street, Bloomsbury Market.   1726–31 (5, 6)

LAMBERT, GEORGE, Sale of tapestries, at *The Rose and Dolphin*, London Wall, over against Little Moorgate.   1727 (5)

LAMBERT AND TURNER, Upholders, Beak Street, Golden Square.

1790–93 (2)

See CHIPCHASE AND LAMBERT, *also* ROBERT CHIPCHASE.

LANCE, GEORGE, Cabinet and Buhl manufacturer, No. 39, Castle Street East, Oxford Market.   1817–27 (1, 2)

LANDALL, THOMAS, Cabinet-maker, Little Argyle Street.   1724–49 (3, 6)

LANDALL AND GORDON, Cabinet and Chair makers, at *Ye Griffin and Chair*, in Little Argyle Street, by Swallow Street.   *c.* 1750 (1)

(Plate, page 93)

LANE, JOHN, Maker of knife cases, etc., No. 44, St. Martin's-Le-Grand.

c. 1790 (49)

Sheraton in his *Drawing Book* (1792) recommends Lane as a maker of knife cases and ladies' travelling workboxes.

LANGDON, JOHN, Cabinet-maker, in the Old Bailey.   1794 (2)

LANGFORD, RICHARD, Cabinet warehouse, No. 27, Brokers Row, Moorfields.
                                                              1790–93 (2)

LANGFORD, THOMAS, Cabinet-maker, Hart Street (Covent Garden).   1749 (3)

LANGHAM, HENRY, Upholsterer, in Lothbury.   1764 (5)

LANGLEY, STEPHEN, Cabinet-maker (address unrecorded).   (1)
    Supplied furniture to Chatsworth.   1735 (1)
                    (From information reported by Miss M. Jourdain.)

LANGLEY, THOMAS, Upholder (address unrecorded).   1667–82 (66)

LANGLOIS, PETER (PIERRE, ELOI), Cabinet-maker, in Tottenham Court Road,
    near Windmill Street. His fine trade-card is worded in French and
    in English.   1763–70 (1, 2)
    "This artist performs all sorts of curious Inlaid Work, particularly Commodes
    in the foreign taste inlaid with Tortoise-shell, Brass, etc." (Mortimer's *Universal
    Director* (1763).) He was born in Paris in 1738 and carried on his business there
    but was not registered as a master *ébéniste* until 1774. From his London address
    he supplied various pieces of furniture to Horace Walpole for the Strawberry
    Hill house in 1763, and he appears to have been patronised extensively by the
    nobility and gentry both here and in France. The wording of his trade-card
    shows that he specialised in ormolu, boulle or "*meubles inserés de fleurs en bois.*"
    (*Country Life*, 9th June, 1945.)
                            (Plate, page 94)

LANGTON, DAVID, Upholder, No. 10, Queen Street, Cheapside.   1770–77 (2)

LANGTON AND BUTLER, as above.   1783 (2)

LA PIERRE, FRANCIS, Upholsterer, Pall Mall.
    He was employed at the Royal Palaces and at Chatsworth in 1697.   (49)
                                                        deceased 1717 (62)

LAPPINGTON, MRS., Upholsterer, over against St. James's Church, in
    Piccadilly.   1720 (5)

LAUDER, DAVID, Cabinet-maker, New Street, Soho.   1774 (3)

LAUDER, JOHN, Cabinet-maker and Upholder, No. 48, Chandos Street.
                                                            1774 (1, 3)
                            (Plate, page 93)

LAW, MAGNUS, Cabinet-maker, Duke's Court, St. Martin's Lane.
                                                            1790–93 (2)

LAWRENCE, JOHN, Upholder, No. 150, Bishopsgate Street Without.
                                                            1768–72 (1)
                            (Plate, page 105)

LAWSON, —, Upholder, next door to *The Royal Oak* in Pall Mall.   1721 (5)

LAWTON, JAMES AND PETER, Cabinet-makers, No. 4, Chandois Street, Covent
    Garden.   1765–74 (2)

LAYCOCK, THOMAS, Cabinet-maker (deceased), in the parish of St. Ann, Blackfriars. 1691 (5)

LEADER, GEORGE, Carver to His Majesty, No. 188, Oxford Street. 1790 (2)

LEEDS, LEVI, Upholster, Marylebone Street. 1749 (3)

LEEMIN, ROBERT, Cabinet-maker (deceased), in Lee Street, by Red Lion Square, Holbourn. 1750 (5)

LE GAGNEUR, *see* BUHL FACTORY, No. 19, Queen Street, Edgeware Road. 1815 (50)

LEGG, ELIZABETH, Haberdasher and Undertaker, (?) widow of Robert Legg, senior, "at *The Legg*," Bloomsbury Market, against the Market House. *c.* 1723 (6)

LEGG, ROBERT, Upholder and Undertaker (son of the late Robert Legg, opposite Bloomsbury Market), at the sign of *Ye Leg*, near Southampton Street, in Holborn. *c.* 1760 (1)

He issued two rather similar trade-cards—one an elaborated form of the earlier which is here illustrated.

(Plate, page 105)

LEGG, SAMUEL, Upholder, No. 51, Snow Hill. 1783 (2)
Johnson's Court, Fleet Street. 1790–93 (2)
No. 71, Fleet Street. 1794–96 (2)

LEGG, SAMUEL, AND SON, Upholders, No. 71, Fleet Street. 1817 (2)

LEIGH, ROBERT, Cabinet-maker, Bedford Street, Covent Garden. 1726 (5)

LEMAYNE, PETER, Cabinet-maker, Mercer's Street (Long Acre). 1749 (3)

LENN, JOHN, Upholsterer, at *The Crown and Cushion*, Conduit Street. *c.* 1724 (6)

LE SAGE, JOHN, Carver and Gilder (address unrecorded).
His name appears on a bill made out to Earl of Bristol. 1690 (1, 49)

LEVIEN, J. M., Cabinet-maker, No. 10, Davies Street, Grosvenor Square. *c.* 1790 (1)

LEWIS, ISRAEL, Upholsterer, No. 151, Fleet Street. 1779–83 (2)

LEWIS, JOSHUA, Upholsterer, at *The Three Tents*, by Fleet Ditch. 1725 (6)
In Fleet Street. 1748 (14)

LEWIS, JOSIAH, Upholder, the corner of Barnaby Street, Tooley Street, Southwark. 1772
Later of Smarden, near Biddenden, Kent.

LEWIS, WILLIAM, Carver and Gilder, No. 15, Great Newport Street, Long Acre. 1790–96 (2)

LIKE AND TURNER, Upholders, No. 47, Frith Street, Soho. 1779–84 (2)

LILLIE AND TUCKER, Upholders and Cabinet-makers, No. 315, High
  Holborn.   1790–93 (2)

LINNELL, JAMES, Wood carver, St. Martin's Lane.   1720 (56)

LINNELL, JOHN, Cabinet-maker, who succeeded William Linnell at No. 28,
  Berkeley Square, worked at Shardeloes, Amersham, between 1763–68.
  He died in 1796.   1763–96 (1, 12)

Many of his designs are now in the Victoria and Albert Museum and articles on
his work by Miss Jourdain appeared in *Country Life*, 19th Feb., 1943, and 9th Dec.,
1949.

LINNELL, WILLIAM, Carver and Cabinet-maker and Upholsterer, No. 28,
  Berkeley Square.   *fl. c.* 1730–63 (1)

Supplied a quantity of furniture to Sir Richard Hoare at Barn Elms from 1739 to
1753. A bill, dated 1752–53, bears comments against certain items: "too much,"
"extravagant charge," etc. He died at his house in Berkeley Square in 1763,
His name appears frequently in bills at Shardeloes, Amersham, between 1749
and 1758 for furniture supplied to Mr. William Drake.

LINTEL, —, Cabinet-maker, "at *The Cabinet*," Stonecutter Street, near
  Fleet Ditch.   1727 (5)

LITCHFIELD AND GRAHAM, Upholders, No. 15, St. Martin's Lane.   1783 (2)
  No. 72, St. Martin's Lane.   1790–93 (2)

See also GRAHAM AND LITCHFIELD. Graham continued in business until 1808.

LITCHFIELD AND MOREL, No. 72, St. Martin's Lane.   1798 (50)

LITTLE, —, Upholsterer, No. 47, Mortimer Street.   1803 (20)

LLOYD, JOHN, Cabinet-maker, Dean's Place (Westminster).   1749 (3)

LOADER, EDWARD, Cabinet-maker and upholstery warehouse, No. 14,
  Broker's Row, Moorfields.   1790–1803 (2, 20)

LOADER, JUNIOR, No. 5, Broker's Row.   1803 (20)

LOADER AND ATKINSON, Upholders, No. 39, Ludgate Hill.   1817 (2)

LOCK, MATTHIAS, Carver and Designer of furniture.   1740–69 (1)
  Nottingham Court, Castle Street, near Long Acre.   1746 (1, 57)
  Near *Ye Swan* in Tottenham Court Road.   1752 (1, 2, 51)

The two cards referred to bear the same engraved date, "1746." The *Dictionary of
English Furniture* gives his address: Queen Street, Seven Dials.   (49)
In *Georgian Cabinet Makers* (Edwards and Jourdain) he is described as "the
pioneer in England of the *rocaille*." He and his collaborator, H. Copland,
published various books of designs in this style, the earliest of which, *A New
Drawing Book of Ornament*, was first issued in 1740. They both worked for Thomas
Chippendale and they may have been responsible for some of the designs which
appeared in his *Director*.   1754 (18)
Albums and sketch books containing Lock's original designs are now in the
Victoria and Albert Museum. *See also* HENRY COPLAND.

(Plate, page 93)

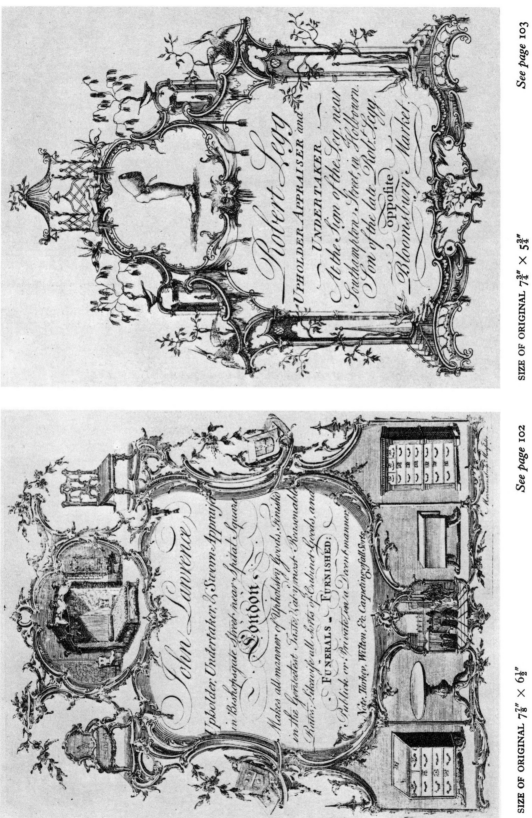

See page 103

SIZE OF ORIGINAL 7¾" × 5¾"

See page 102

SIZE OF ORIGINAL 7⅞" × 6½"

Jno Macklane
Cabinet, Chair Maker, and
UPHOLDER
in little Newport Street
near Leicester Square
London.
N.B. Funerals Perform'd

SIZE OF ORIGINAL 4¾" × 3"
See page 108

SIZE OF ORIGINAL 2⅞" × 4¼" *See pages 95, 114, 200*

Christopher Martin
At the Star in
Hay Market near Mint Street
LONDON.
Makes & sells all sorts of Bedsteads, Tables,
Chests of Drawers, Desks, & all other sorts of
Joyners Goods in Mahogany, Walnut Trees &
Wainscott, at Reasonable Rates.

SIZE OF ORIGINAL 5⅜" × 3⅝"
See page 112

Peter Marchant
Upholder and Appraiser.
at the Royal Bed & Star
Near Fleet Bridge
London.
Makes &c Sells all sorts of Upholsters & Cabinet-Makers Goods.
Funerals Perform'd to any part of Great-Britain.

See page 111

SIZE OF ORIGINAL 2½" × 5¾"

LOCK, MATTHIAS, Carver and Gilder, No. 19, Clerkenwell Green.

1790–94 (2)

LOCKWOOD, STEPHEN, Cabinet and Chair maker, No. 8, Stephen Street, Tottenham Court Road. 1817 (2)

LODWICK, JEREMIAH, Upholsterer, at *The White Lyon*, Houndsditch.

deceased 1731 (5)

LONG, GEORGE, Upholder, No. 13, Great Newport Street. 1803–17 (2, 20)

LONGBOTHAM, HENRY, Carver and Gilder, Snow Fields (Tooley Street).

1790–93 (2)

LONSDALE, EDWARD, Cabinet-maker, No. 12, Princes Street, Cavendish Square. 1790–93 (2)

LONSDALE, WILLIAM, Cabinet-maker, No. 7, Broad Street, Golden Square.

1794–1803 (2, 20)

LOVELL, MICHAEL, Upholder, Gracechurch Street. 1724–27 (3)

LOVELL, RICHARD, Cabinet-maker, Aldermanbury. 1725 (6)

LOWDELL, —, Cabinet-maker, No. 108, Blackman Street, Southwark.

c. 1780 (1)

LOWE, JOHN, Hardwood turner, No. 20, White Cross Street, Cripplegate.

c. 1770 (1)

LOWE, MUSGRAVE, Cabinet-maker, Wardour Street. 1767 (7)

LOWE, PETER, Upholder and Cabinet-maker, Castle Street, Long Acre.

1790–93 (2)

LUCAS, JAMES, Undertaker, Cabinet-maker and Upholsterer, No. 66, Chiswell Street. 1790–93 (1, 2)

LUCK, —, Upholder, at Carpenters' Hall, No. 67, London Wall. 1750 (5)

LUCK AND KENT, Carpet and Upholstery warehouse, Carpenters' Hall, the Corner of the Gateway, No. 67, London Wall. 1781 (1)

See also KENT AND LUCK.

LYALL, GEORGE, Cabinet-maker, No. 243, High Holborn. 1803 (19)

LYATT, —, Cabinet-maker, No. 34, Chiswell Street. 1803 (20)

LYCETT, JOSEPH, Upholsterer, in John Street, Golden Square.

1746–49 (3, 5)

LYNE, F., Cabinet-maker, No. 13, Vere Street, Cavendish Square.

1803 (20)

LYNN, ANDREW, Upholsterer, Great Marlborough Street. 1708 (5)

LYON, GEORGE, Upholsterer, Duke Street, Manchester Square. 1803 (18)

McDONALD, A., Cabinet-maker, in Rose Street, Soho. 1803 (19)

McDOUGALL, Cabinet-maker and Upholsterer, near Durham Yard, in the Strand. 1766 (1)

McDOWELL, —, Chair maker, Tottenham Street, Tottenham Court Road.
1803 (19)

McDOWELL, JOSEPH, Cabinet-maker, Strand. 1774 (3)

MACKAY, JAMES, Upholder, No. 171, Piccadilly. 1763–96 (2)

MACKENZIE AND BLISSETT, Upholders and Cabinet-makers, No. 57, Marylebone Street, Piccadilly. 1790–96 (2)
No. 34, Marylebone Street, Piccadilly. 1790–1803 (19)

MACKLANE, JOHN, Upholder and Cabinet-maker, in Little Newport Street,
near Leicester Square. 1774 (1, 3)
See also JOHN MACLEAN.

(Plate, page 106)

MACKLIN, —, Carver and Gilder, No. 39, Fleet Street, opposite Fetter
Lane. *c.* 1800 (1)

MACLEAN, JOHN, Upholster, in Whitehall. 1749 (3)

MACLEAN, JOHN AND SON, Upholder and Cabinet-maker, on the Upper
Terrace, Tottenham Court Road, and Marylebone Street. 1803 (19)
No. 58, Upper Marylebone Street, near the end of Howland Street,
Portland Place. 1807–14 (1, 2)

A trade-card in the Banks collection, indicates that they specialised in "Elegant
Parisian Furniture," *See* letters to *Country Life*, 16th July and 3rd Sept., 1943,
concerning a writing table and trade-card of this firm.

MACLEAN, WILLIAM, Upholder, No. 58, Upper Marylebone Street.
1817–25 (2)

McNEVIN, ANTHONY, Upholsterer and Cabinet-maker, No. 85, Crown
Court, Dorset Street, Fleet Street. (Successor to Mr. Hill.) *c.* 1827 (1, 2)

MADDOX, RALPH, Carver and Gilder, No. 14, Great Russell Street, Bloomsbury. 1790–94 (2)

MADDOX, RALPH HENRY, Upholsterer and Cabinet-maker, No. 25, Welbeck
Street, Cavendish Square. 1838 (1, 2)

MAIDSTONE, NATHANIEL, Chair maker, St. Lawrence Pountney's Lane.
1718 (2)

MAINWARING, R., *see* ROBERT MANWARING.

MAIRIS, A., Upholsterer and Cabinet-maker, No. 282, High Holborn.
1796 (2)

MALCOLM, MICHAEL, Cabinet-maker, in Panton Street. 1749–56 (2)

MALLET, FRANCIS PETER, Cabinet-maker and Upholsterer, Newcastle House,
No. 48, Clerkenwell Close. 1774–93 (1, 2)

MALTON, THOMAS, senior, Architectural draughtsman, "originally kept an
upholsterer's shop in the Strand" (*Dict. Nat. Biog*). *c.* 1760 (29, 62)

Rob.t Maxwell
Cabinet Maker
Upholsterer,
AND
Undertaker
in great Pultney Street
NEAR
Golden Square

Etch'd by Darly Nr... Strand

See page 114

SIZE OF ORIGINAL 8" × 6"

Charles Mathyson
PICTURE FRAME MAKER
Remov'd from Grafton Street to
Maiden lane facing Bedford Street
Covent Garden,
Makes and Sells all sorts of
Frames for Paintings, Glasses
and Prints in Black or Gold
and all other Ornaments, Carv'd
and Gilt at the lowest Prices.
N.B. Paintings & Prints carefully Clean'd,
Lin'd and Mended in the best Manner.

See page 113

SIZE OF ORIGINAL 8¼" × 6¼"

See page 118

SIZE OF ORIGINAL $6\frac{1}{4}'' \times 5\frac{1}{4}''$

See page 122

SIZE OF ORIGINAL $7'' \times 5\frac{7}{8}''$

MALTON, THOMAS—*continued*.

William Hickey in 1772 took drawing lessons from him and speaks of him as having previously kept a large cabinet-maker's shop in the Strand. His son, Thomas Malton, junior, was the more famous architectural draughtsman whose aquatints of London and Bath topography are highly prized.

MANLOVE, RICHARD, Upholder, near St. Antholin's Church, in Watling Street.   *c.* 1770 (1)

MANN, —, Upholsterer and Cabinet-maker, No. 28, Rood-Lane.   1803 (20)

MANN, ROBERT, Upholder, Little Queen Street, Holborn.   1790–93 (2)

MANWARING, ROBERT, Cabinet and Chair maker, in the Haymarket.
                                                fl. 1760–70 (49, 56)

Published *The Cabinet and Chairmaker's Real Friend and Companion* (from above address) in 1765 and in the following year *The Chairmakers' Guide* appeared, which contained examples of his designs, being upwards of "two hundred New and Genteel Designs, both Decorative and Plain." Previously he had contributed several plates to *One Hundred New and Genteel Designs* published by the Society of Upholsterers and Cabinet-makers.   (49)

MAPLE, JOHN, Furnishing warehouseman, at *The Hen and Chickens*, Nos. 145, 146 and 147, Tottenham Court Road, ten doors from the New Road.   *c.* 1845–53 (1)

MAPLE, JOHN, AND COOK, JAMES, Wholesale drapers and warehousemen, at above address.   1841–*c.* 1845 (1)

The partnership was short lived and Maple soon took over sole control.

MARAM, PHILIP, Upholsterer, Church Lane, Strand.   1709 (4)

MARCHANT, JOHN, Cabinet-maker and Upholsterer, corner of Church Street, Shoreditch.   1814–24 (1, 2)

MARCHANT, JOHN, No. 1, Cloak Lane, Shoreditch.   1827 (2)

See also SABOURIN AND MARCHANT.

MARCHANT, PETER, Upholster and Cabinet-maker, at *The Royal Bed and Star*, near Fleet Bridge.   *c.* 1760 (1)
                        (Plate, page 106)

MAREN, STEPHEN, Carver and Gilder, New Compton Street.   1794 (2)

MARGANIS, —, Cabinet-maker, in the parish of St. Anne's (Soho).   1730 (5)

MARKEY, CORNELIUS, Upholsterer and Cabinet-maker, at the third door from Tooley Street, in Southwark.   1752 (5)

MARKHAM, GREGORY, Upholster, in Little Moorfields.   deceased 1666 (13)

MAROT, DANIEL, Designer of decorations and furniture.
                                        born 1650, died 1712

He is thought to have influenced the work at Hampton Court for William III as he visited London between 1694 and 1698, and took some responsibility for the layout of the gardens there.

MAROT, DANIEL—*continued*.

    In 1712, the year of his death, was published an important volume of 240 designs entitled *Oeuvres du sieur D. Marot*, on the title page of which he is described as "Architecte de Guillaume iii, Roy de la Grande-Bretagne."

MARRIAT, SAMUEL, Upholder, in Thames Street.   1734 (3)

MARSH, WILLIAM, Upholder and Cabinet-maker, No. 13, Mount Street.
                              1778 (2)–1790 (56)

    See ELWARD AND MARSH.   1790–93
    See ELWARD, MARSH AND BAILEY.   1794
    See ELWARD, MARSH AND TATHAM.   1802

MARSH AND TATHAM, *see* TATHAM AND MARSH.   1795

MARSHALL, ALEXANDER, Carver and Gilder, No. 2, Middle Row, Holborn.
                               1790–93 (2)

MARSHALL, JOHN, Upholsterer, near St. James's Church.   1721 (5)

MARSHALL, JOHN, Cabinet-maker and Upholder, in Walkers Court, Knaves Acre, Golden Square.   1749 (3)

MARSHALL, JOHN, Upholder, No. 2, St. Martin's Lane, Charing Cross.
                           1774–77 (2, 3)

MARSHALL, JOHN, Cabinet-maker and Upholsterer, No. 21, Gerrard Street, Soho.   1794–1803 (2, 20)

MARSTON, WILLIAM, Upholder, No. 71, Fleet Street.   1753–84 (2)

MARSTON, WILLIAM, Junior, Upholder, No. 71, Fleet Street.   1792 (2)

MARSTON AND LEGG, Upholders, No. 71, Fleet Street.   1790–93 (2)

MARTIN, ALEXANDER, Cabinet-maker and Upholder, Hedge Lane (now Coventry Street).   1774–93 (2, 3)

MARTIN, BEN, Cabinet-maker, Oxenden Street.   1709 (4)

MARTIN, CHARLES, Cabinet-maker and Inlayer, No. 97, St. John's Street, Smithfield.   1790–96 (2)

MARTIN, CHRISTOPHER, Cabinet-maker, at *The Star*, by Fleet Market, near Fleet Street.   1747 (1, 5)

                  (Plate, page 106)

MARTIN, CORNELIUS, Cabinet-maker, in Dover Street.   1763 (7)

MARTIN, GEORGE, Upholsterer, No. 11, Little Moorfields.   1790 (2)

MARTIN, JAMES, Upholsterer, at *The Crown and Key*, in Drury Lane.
                                 1730 (5)

MARTIN, SAMUEL, Upholder, No. 19, Bucklersbury.   1774 (2)
    No. 32, Walbrook.   1777 (2)

MARTINDALE, NATHAN, Cabinet-maker, Whitcomb Court in Hedge Lane (now Coventry Street).   1755–74 (3, 18)

MARTINDALE, ROBERT, Upholder and Cabinet-maker, No. 14, Brewer Street, Golden Square. 1774–83 (2, 3)

MARTYN, THOMAS, Upholster, in Cornhill. 1665 (13)

MASH, —, "an eminent cabinet-maker of Wardour Street, Soho, died in his house at Chelsea." 1749 (61)

MASKENS, ADRIAN, Carver and Picture frame maker, No. 46, Compton Street, Soho. 1780 (1)

No. 42, Greek Street. 1790–93 (2)

"Three Quarters Kit-Cats and Halflengths may be had in a Minute's Notice for Ready Money."

MASON, CHARLES, Cabinet-maker, by the Steel Yard in Thames Street. 1705 (5)

MASON, DANIEL, Cabinet-maker and Upholsterer, at the corner of Newport Street (Long Acre). 1756 (1)

King Street (Covent Garden). 1749–74 (3)

MASON, EDWARD, Cabinet-maker, Edward Street. 1749 (3)

MASON, JOHN, Cabinet-maker, Bedford Court. 1749 (3)

MASON, RICHARD, Cabinet-maker, No. 119, Aldersgate Street. 1774 (2)

MASON, THOMAS, Upholsterer and Cabinet-maker, No. 59, Princes Street, Leicester Square. 1826 (1)

MASSA, WILLIAM, Carver and Gilder, at *The Golden Head*, near New Inn in Wych Street, Drury Lane. *c.* 1780 (1)

MASSEY, THOMAS, Cabinet-maker, No. 124, Blackman Street, Borough. 1790–93 (2)

MASTERMAN, JOHN, Windsor and Garden Chair maker, Queen Street, Southwark. 1790–96 (2)

MASTERS, CHARLES, Upholsterer, at *The Eagle and Child*, the Ditch Side, near Holborn Bridge. 1725 (6)

MASTERS, WILLIAM, Cabinet-maker, at *The Golden Fleece*, Coventry Street, Piccadilly.

Supplied furniture to Blair Castle, Perthshire. 1746–53 (64)

MASTERS, WILLIAM, Upholster, Princes Street, Wardour Street. 1749 (3)

MATHEWS, LUKE, Upholder, St. Martin's Lane. 1709 (4)

MATHYSON, CHARLES, Carv'd and Gilt picture frame maker, Maiden Lane, facing Bedford Street, Covent Garden. Removed from Grafton Street. *c.* 1770 (1)

(Plate, page 109)

MATTHEWS, JOHN, Carver and Gilder, No. 441, Strand. 1794–96 (2)

MATTHEWS, TIMOTHY, AND DELAFIELD, ERASMUS, Upholsterers, at *Ye Royal Bed and Rising Sun*, near Salisbury Court in Fleet Street.   1748 (1)
Delafield retired from partnership in 1750.
See also DELAFIELD AND MATTHEWS.   1723–42

MATTHEWS, TIMOTHY, as above. In Fleet Street.   1750–65 (2)

MATTHEWS, WILLIAM, Carver and Gilder, No. 46, Rupert Street.
                                                          1790–93 (2)

MAULDEN, JAMES, Upholsterer, at *The King's Arms*, St. Saviour's Dock Head.   1723 (6)

MAULDEN, JAMES, in Tooley Street, Southwark.   1746 (5)

MAXEY, SAMUEL, Upholsterer, No. 60, Aldersgate Street.   1792–1803 (2, 20)

MAXWELL, CHARLES, Upholsterer, at *The Lion and Lamb*, the corner of New Broad Court, in Drury Lane.   1749 (1, 3)

MAXWELL, ROBERT, Cabinet-maker and Upholsterer, in Great Pulteney Street, near Golden Square.   *c.* 1760 (1)
                            (Plate, page 109)

MAYHEW, JOHN, Cabinet-maker and Upholsterer, No. 20, Marshall Street, Carnaby Market.   1774–1811 (2, 3)

MAYHEW, JOHN, AND INCE, WILLIAM, Cabinet-makers and Upholsterers, at above and Broad Street, Golden Square.   1759–1803 (2, 5, 20, 49, 56, 62)
Both partners were married to two sisters on the same day, 20th February, 1762, at St. James's Church, in Piccadilly. John Mayhew was grandfather of Henry Mayhew, author of *London Labour and the London Poor* and one of the founders of *Punch*. John Mayhew died in 1811.
                          Communicated by Mrs. Coumbe (*née* Mayhew).
See INCE AND MAYHEW.   1759–1803

MAYHEW, JOHN, AND INCE, WILLIAM, No. 47, Marshall Street, Carnaby Market.   1802–1809 (2)
See also WHITTLE, NORMAN AND MAYHEW.
                            (Plate, page 106)

MAYLIN, —, Cabinet-maker, in Cannon Street.   1733 (5)

MAYNARD, JOHN, Upholster, Poland Street.   1749 (3)

MAYNARD AND DUNCH, Upholders, Shepherd Street, Bond Street.
                                                          1783–93 (2)

MAYOW, RICHARD, Upholder and Cabinet-maker, No. 46, Crutched Friars.
                                                          1772–74 (2)

MEARS, JOHN, Cabinet-maker, No. 220, The Borough (Southwark).   1783 (2)

MEARS, RICHARD AND CATHERINE, Upholders, Duke Street, St. James's.
                                                          1749–51 (14)

MEDDOM, WILLIAM, Upholsterer, in Lime Street.   1730 (5)

See page 121

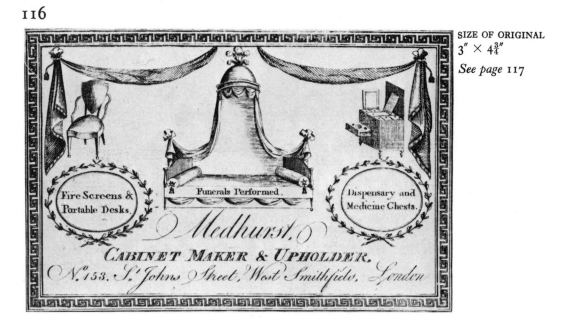

SIZE OF ORIGINAL
3″ × 4¾″
See page 117

SIZE OF ORIGINAL 2⅜″ × 3½″
See page 122

SIZE OF ORIGINAL 3″ × 4¼″
See page 123

MEDHURST, —, Cabinet-maker and Upholder, No. 153, St. John's Street, West Smithfield. *c.* 1790 (1)

(Plate, page 116)

MEEK, —, Chair manufactory, No. 11, Forster Street, Bishopsgate. 1803 (19)

MELLET, —, Cabinet-maker, Knaves Acre, Golden Square. 1749 (3)

MENDEZ, —, Repository for all sorts of Household Furniture, opposite Southampton Street, in the Strand. 1763 (2)

MENZIES, ARCHIBALD, Cabinet-maker, Orange Street. 1774 (3)

MERLE, JOHN, Carver and Gilder, No. 36, Leadenhall Street. 1817–27 (2)

MERLE, THOMAS, Carver and Gilder, at *The Golden Key*, No. 36, Leadenhall Street. 1790–1814 (1)
Successor to Mr. OVERLOVE (*q.v.*).

MERRYFIELD, WILLIAM, Upholster, at *The Three Chairs and Crown*, Fleet Ditch. 1722–60 (2, 6)

MERRYMAN, JOSEPH, AND CO., Cabinet-makers and Upholders, No. 42, Heydon Square, Minories. 1768–77 (2)

MESSENGER, MICHAEL, Cabinet-maker, The Upper Ground, Southwark. 1790 (2)–1793

METCALFE, —, Upholsterer, at *The Helmet*, in Fleet Street. 1692–97 (2, 33)

METCALFE, LASCELS, Upholster, in Gracechurch Street. 1740 (5)

MEYMOTT, THOMAS, Cabinet-maker and Upholder, No. 3, Lower Moorfields) near Old Bethlem. 1799–1814 (1)

MICHELIN, NICHOLAS, Carver and Gilder, No. 26, Wardour Street. 1790 (2)

MICHON, PETER, AND NICHOLAS PIC. 1691 (49)
Supplied furniture to Queen Mary in 1691.

MIDDLETON, CHARLES, Papier mâché manufacturer, in Tottenham Court Road, near Windmill Street 1763 (2)

MIERS, WILLIAM, Ormolu worker and Miniature Frame maker, by Appointment to the Queen, No. 111, Strand. 1802–39 (1)

MILES, —, Upholsterer, at *The White Swan*, in Wych Street. 1688 (5)

MILES, WILLIAM, RICHARD AND JOHN, Wholesale upholders, No. 93, Bishopsgate Within. 1784–93 (2)

MILL, —, Cabinet-maker and Upholsterer, Greek Street, Soho. *c.* 1780 (1)

MILLBOURNE, JAMES, Carver and Gilder, No. 221, Strand. 1793 (2)

MILLER, JOHN, Cabinet-maker, in Drury Lane, opposite Great Queen Street. 1763 (2)

MILLER, WILLIAM, Cabinet-maker, in Oxford Street. 1774 (2)
A William Miller, Cabinet-maker, subscribed to Chippendale's *Director* (1755)

MILLIUM, ANDREW, Upholder, in Fleet Street.   1734 (5)

MILLS, DANIEL, Japanner and Cabinet-maker, at *The Japan Cabinet and Cistern*, in Vine Street, near Hatton Garden.   *c.* 1760 (1)
(Plate, page 110)

MILLS, DANIEL AND JOSEPH, Japanners and Cabinet-makers, at *The Japan Cabinet and Cistern*, in Vine Street, near Hatton Garden.   1768–77 (2)

MILLS, JOHN, Cabinet-maker and Upholder, No. 41, High Holborn.
                                                                    1781–93 (2)
Bedford Row, Brownlow Street, Holborn.   1794–1809, 1803 (2, 19)

MILNER, JAMES, Upholsterer, in King Street, near Guildhall.   1690 (5)

MILNER, MICHAEL AND RICHARD, Cabinet-makers, No. 34, Litchfield Street, Soho.   1790–93 (2)

MILNER, ROBERT, Upholder, in Wood Street.   1727 (3)

MILSON AND WALKER, Upholders, No. 71, Fleet Market.   1790–93 (2)

MINSHALL, JOHN, Carver and Gilder, in Dock Street.   1769 (1)

MINSHALL'S Looking Glass Store, in Hanover Square, opposite to Mr. Goelet's at the sign of *The Golden Key*.   1775 (49)

MOLINE, ROBERT, Cabinet-maker, Charing Cross.   1761 (7)

MOMBRIM, —, Cabinet-maker, No. 40, Windmill Street, Rathbone Place.
                                                                    1803 (19)

MONCUR, JAMES, Cabinet-maker, in Coventry Court (Haymarket).   1749 (3)

MONROE, DAVID, Cabinet-maker, Chandois Street.   1749 (3)
See also MURE AND MONRO.

MONTELLIER, JOSEPH, Cabinet-maker, No. 58, Castle Street, Oxford Street.
                                                                    1790 (2)

MOON, WILLIAM, Chair maker, No. 141, St. John Street, near Smithfield.
                                                                    1794 (1, 2)
"Where the Public may be supplied with all sorts of Mahogany, Walnut Tree, Cherry Tree and Beech Chairs on the lowest Terms of any Man who doth justice to his Customers."

MOOR, —, Cabinet-maker, in Fuller's Rents, Holborn.   1760 (5)

MOOR, JOHN, Upholsterer, Paternoster Row. "Hanged himself."   1721 (5)

MOORE, —, Upholsterer, Leopards Court, Baldwin's Gardens.   1803

MOORE, JAMES, Cabinet-maker, in Short's Gardens, St. Giles'-in-the-Fields.
                                                    c. 1708–26 (2, 19, 56, 64–5)
He was in partnership with John Gumley (*q.v.*) in the Strand until his death in 1726. A full account of the work of Moore and Gumley is given in *Georgian Cabinet Makers*.

MOORE, JAMES, Junior, succeeded his father.   1726–34
Appointed Cabinet-maker to the Prince of Wales in 1732.   (64)

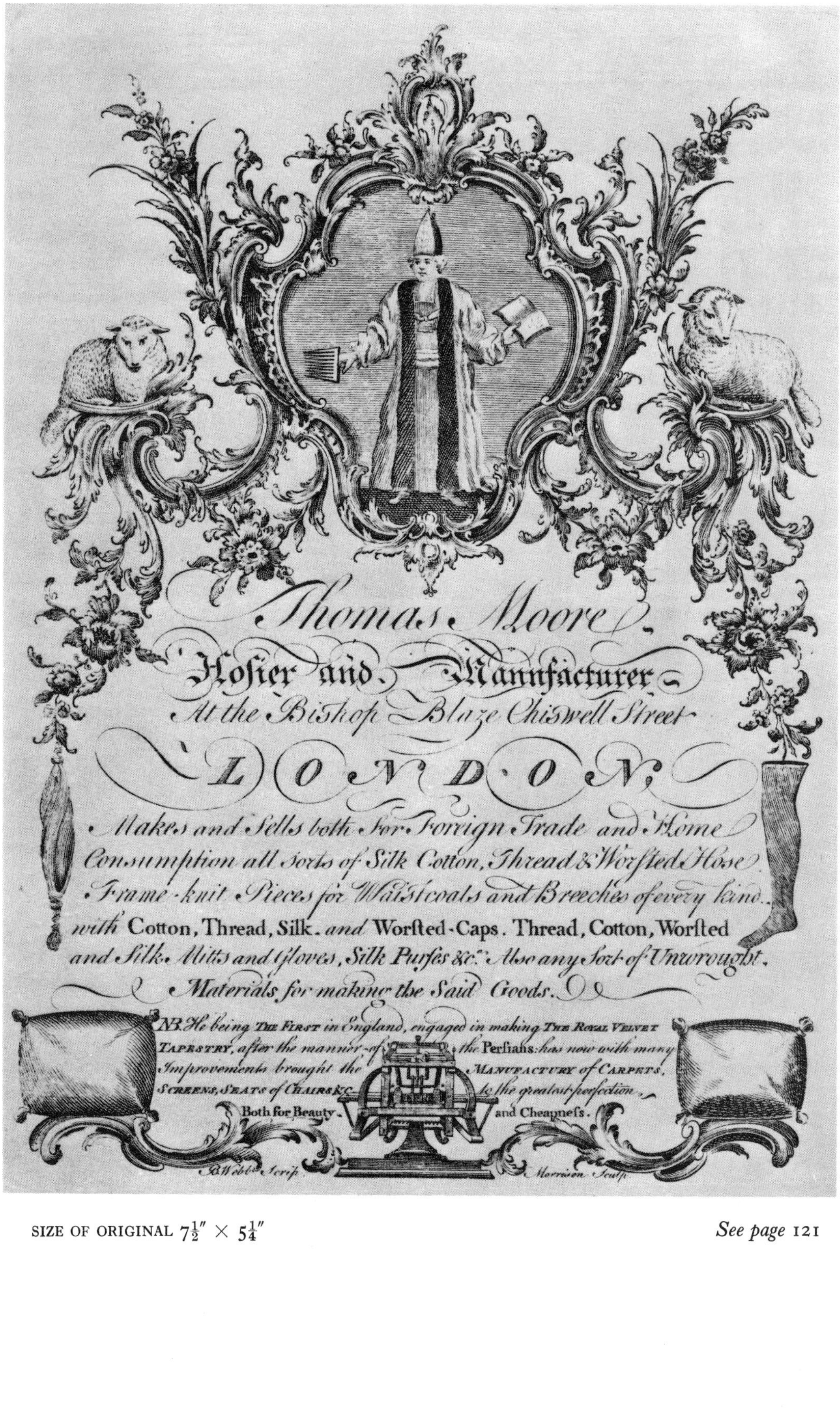

SIZE OF ORIGINAL $7\frac{1}{2}'' \times 5\frac{1}{4}''$

See page 121

THE ROYAL BED

Thoˢ Naſh, Elking.ⁿ Hall, & Richᵈ Whitehorne,
At the ROYAL BED on Holborn Bridge
D.2 -his LONDON.
Make & Sell Fashionable Silk & Stuff Beds, with all other
sorts of Upholsterers Goods. And large Sconces, Pier &
Chimney Glaſses, Dreſsing glaſses, Cheſt of Draws, Buroes, Desk
& Book-cases, Mohogany tables, Card tables, Chairs & Settees,
and all other Sorts of Cabinet Work at Reaſonable Rates.
N.B. All Sorts of Goods Appraiſed.

SIZE OF ORIGINAL 6¼″ × 5⅝″

See page 123

MOORE, JOHN, Upholder, at *The Indian Queen and White Hart* near *The Cock* in Houndsditch. 1721 (6)

MOORE, THOMAS, Cabinet-maker, in St. Martin's Lane. 1734 (1, 5, 64)
He seems to have been in partnership with DANIEL BELL (*q.v.*). died 1738

MOORE, THOMAS, Carpet weaver, at *The Bishop Blaze* (No. 77) in Chiswell Street (Finsbury). 1756–77 (1, 49)
(Plate, page 119)
In 1756 he received a grant from the Royal Society of Arts for excellence in carpet making. He supplied handsome carpets to Horace Walpole and Lord Coventry. A carpet with his name woven in was made for Sion House, dated 1769.

MOORE, THOMAS, Upholder and Cabinet-maker, No. 16, Whitechapel, opposite the Church. 1784 (1, 2)

MOORE AND GUMLEY. *See* JAMES MOORE.

MORANT, GEORGE, Carver, Gilder, Decorator and Upholsterer to His Majesty (William IV), No. 88, New Bond Street. 1814–37 (1, 2)

MORANT, G., AND SON, Interior decorators and Upholsterers, by Appointment to Queen Victoria. 1839 (2)

MOREING, JOHN, Cabinet-maker, Maiden Lane, Covent Garden. 1768

MOREL, NICHOLAS, Upholsterer, in Tenterden Street. 1795 (50)
Great Marlborough Street. 1803
He supplied a set of chairs for Carlton House, 1812.

MOREL, NICHOLAS, Upholsterer, No. 13, Great Marlborough Street. 1802

MOREL, NICHOLAS, AND HUGHES, Upholsterers, No. 13, Great Marlborough Street. 1802–27 (2, 20, 52)

MOREL AND HUGHES, Upholsterers, No. 13, Great Marlborough Street. 1808–27 (2)
In Ackermann's *Repository of Arts* for January–June 1825, are illustrated three chairs made by Morel and Hughes for the Duke of Newcastle.

MOREL AND SEDDON, Upholsterers. Later, Nicholas Morel joined Thomas and George Seddon at No. 16, Lower Grosvenor Street, until 1832. (2)
The firm supplied a set of twenty-four richly carved mahogany chairs to Windsor Castle in 1830.

MORGAN AND SANDERS, Upholsterers and Cabinet-makers, "Trafalgar House," Nos. 16 and 17, Catherine Street, three doors from the Strand. 1803–17 (1, 2, 19)
(Plate, page 115)
A coloured engraving of the interior of their shop appears in Ackermann's *Repository of Arts*, published 1809. The firm took out various patents for extending dining tables and "adaptable" four-post bedsteads.

MORICE, JOHN, Cabinet-maker, at *The Half Moon*, over against Foster Lane, in Cheapside (*see* Captain Morrice below).   1685 (33)

MORIN, —, Carver and Gilder, in Old Belton Street, facing Brownlow Street, St. Giles's.   1748 (5)

MORLAND, JOHN, Upholder, Prince's Street, Leicester Square.   1790–96 (2)

MORLEY, WILLIAM, Cabinet-maker, New Street, Westminster.   1749 (3)

MORRICE, CAPTAIN, Upholsterer (address unrecorded but possibly as John Morice above).   1660–61 (22)

> His name occurs three times in Samuel Pepys' *Diary* in 1660 and 1661, twice as "Captain Morrice" and once as "Mr. Morrice, the upholsterer, came himself today to take notice what furniture we lack for our lodgings at Whitehall."
>
>   22nd June, 1660

MORRIS, —, Upholsterer, in Frith Street, Soho.   1722 (5)

MORRIS, JOHN, Upholder, Kirby Street, Hatton Garden.   1719–27 (3, 5)

MORRIS, JOSHUA, Tapestry worker and Upholsterer, at the *Golden Ball*, in Pall Mall.   1727 (62)

> Joshua Morris was involved in a lawsuit with William Hogarth for attempting to repudiate a commission for a design for tapestry representing "The Element of Earth." The case was decided in Hogarth's favour. (*See Dictionary of National Biography*.)

MORRIS, ROBERT, Upholsterer, at *The Golden Lyon*, near the Stocks in Cornhill.   (64)

> He was appointed the King's Upholsterer at the Restoration.   Jan., 1661

MORRIS, THOMAS AND WILLIAM, Cabinet-makers, No. 15, St. Paul's Church Yard.   1784–90 (2, 20)
No. 26, St. Paul's Church Yard.   1790–1827 (20)

MORRIS AND CUPISS, Cabinet-makers, No. 15, St. Paul's Church Yard.
                                                                    c. 1780 (1)
And at their Manufactory, No. 10, St. Bennet's Hill, Doctors' Commons.   (1)
                        (Plate, page 116)

MORRISON, THOMAS, Upholder, at the corner of Chancery Lane, in Fleet Street.   1748–63 (2, 15)

MORTHOST, PAUL, Cabinet-maker, No. 1, Little Tower Hill.   1790–93 (2)

MORTON, —, Frame maker, to H.R.H. Duke of Gloucester, No. 19, Maddox Street, opposite St. George's Church, Hanover Square.   1826 (1, 2)

MOSELEY, RICHARD, Cabinet-maker, opposite East India House, in Leadenhall Street.   1770 (1, 2)
No. 119, Aldersgate Street.   1770–74 (2)
Cheapside.   1792 (2)
                        (Plate, page 110)

MOSELY AND HARRIS, JOHN, Cabinet-makers, Leadenhall Street.   1759 (61)
   See also HARRIS AND MOSELY.

MOSS, RICHARD, Upholsterer, at *The Three Pillows*, upper end of Broad Street behind the Royal Exchange.   1725–49 (5)

MOTTEUX, PIERRE ANTOINE, Cabinet-maker (address unrecorded).   1711 (5)

MOWBRAY, CHRISTOPHER, Cabinet-maker, in Long Acre.   1774 (3)
   In Porter Street, Newport Market.   1790 (2)

MOWBRAY, PAUL, Upholsterer, Albemarle Street.   1728–49 (3, 5)

MOWYER AND CO., Cabinet-makers, No. 208, Oxford Street.   1803 (20)

MULLIGAN, ROBERT, Bedstead maker, in Mint Street, near St. George's Church, Southwark.   *c.* 1790 (1)
                        (Plate, page 116)

MUNT, GEORGE, Upholder, No. 85, Blackman Street (Southwark).   1783 (2)

MURDOCK, JOHN, Upholsterer, in Blackmoor Street, Clare Market.   1774 (3)

MURE, H., AND MONRO, DAVID, Cabinet-makers, at *The Chair*, Wardour Street, St. Anne's.   1785 (1)
   See also DAVID MONROE.

MURRAY, WILLIAM, Cabinet-maker, The Broadway, Westminster.   1774 (3)

MUSTON, JAMES, Wholesale upholsterer, No. 80, Hatton Garden.   1817 (2)

NAISH, CATHERINE, Chair maker and Cabinet-maker (address unrecorded).
   Cradle maker for the children of King George III.   1766 (1, 8)

NANCOLAS, WILLIAM, Cabinet-maker, Langley Street, Long Acre.   1774 (3)

NASH, THOMAS, Upholder, No. 46, Brewer Street, Golden Square.
                        1790–94 (2)

NASH, THOMAS, Upholsterer, at *The Royal Bed*, on Holborn Bridge.   1722 (5)
   "Whereas by an Act passed the last Session of Parliament no callicoe Furniture can be made up after Christmas next under Penalty of Twenty Pounds:—This is to inform those that have Occasion for Beds of the finest Chince Patterns, callicoe Quilts, Carpets to cover one side of callicoe Gowns to make into Quilts, may be furnished with all sorts by Thomas Nash, upholsterer, at *The Royal Bed* on Holborn Bridge."   (*The Post Boy*, 15th Nov., 1722) (5)

NASH, THOMAS, AND HILL, JOHN, [(?) HALL], Upholsterer, at *The Golden Ball*, New Buildings, by Fleet Bridge.   1724 (6)

NASH, THOMAS, HALL, ELKING^N. AND WHITEHORNE, RICHARD, Upholsterers, at *The Royal Bed* on Holborn Bridge.   1722–49 (1, 5, 6)
                        (Plate, page 120)
   ". . . the Executors and surviving Partner of the late Mr. Thomas Nash, deceased, are now reducing their large and valuable stock of Upholders' and Cabinet Goods by a Hand Sale at their Shop."   (*The Daily Advertiser*, 3rd March, 1749)

NEATE, JOHN, Cabinet-maker, in Charles Court (Hungerford Market).

1774 (3)

NEAVE, JOHN, Cabinet-maker, No. 101, High Holborn.   1768–83 (2)

NEDBY, WILLIAM, Cabinet-maker, No. 75, Lamb's Conduit Street. 1817 (2)

NELSON, S., Carver, Gilder and Upholstery in general, Golden Square. (1)

NEWBURY, FRANCIS, Upholsterer, at *The Blue Boar*, in Moorfields. 1724 (6)

NEWCOMB, —, No. 16, Beak Street.   1803 (19)

NEWCOMB, OLIVER, Upholder and Cabinet-maker, No. 23, Holles Street, Cavendish Square.   1805 (2)

NEWHOUSE, WILLIAM, Cabinet-maker, No. 4, Kirby Street, Hatton Garden.

1817 (2)

NEWMAN, —, Upholsterer, No. 13, St. Catherine's.   1803 (20)

NEWMAN, EDWARD, Carver and Cabinet-maker (address unrecorded).

1749–54 (56)

Master of the Joiners' Company in 1749, and made the Master's Chair which still remains in use.

NEWMAN, JOHN, Chair and Cabinet-maker, at *The Feathers and Ball*, the south side of St. Paul's Church Yard.   1755 (1, 18)

(Plate, page 130)

NEWTON, EDWARD, Upholder, on Dowgate Hill.   1726 (5)

NEWTON, HENRY, Upholster, at *The Three Tents*, the corner of Cullum Street, in Lime Street, near Leadenhall Market.   c. 1760 (1)

(Plate, page 129)

NEWTON, JAMES, Cabinet-maker, Red Lion Court.   1749 (3)

NEWTON, JAMES, Upholder, No. 63, Wardour Street.   1790–1803 (5, 20)

NEWTON, THOMAS, Turner, at the corner of Clifford Street, Saville Row.

1783 (1)

Succeeded by RICHARD TONKINS (*q.v.*).

NEWTON, THOMAS, Cabinet-maker, No. 43, Grafton Street, Tottenham Court Road.   1817 (2)

NICHOLL, JOHN, Carver, John Street, Oxford Market.   1763 (2)

NICHOLL, THOMAS, Upholder and Undertaker, No. 17, Duke Street, West Smithfield.   1724 (1)

NICHOLL, THOMAS, Upholder, in St. Paul's Church Yard.   1724–47 (3, 5)

NICHOLLS, WILLIAM, Carver and Gilder, No. 93, Long Acre. 1770–76 (2, 26)

He was employed by Horace Walpole at Strawberry Hill in 1773 and 1776.

NICHOLS, J., AND RELPH, Cabinet-makers, Well Street, Oxford Street.

1803–17 (2, 20)

See also OSWALD AND NICHOLS.

NICHOLSON, JOHN, Upholder, No. 35, Bishopsgate Within.   *c.* 1790 (1)

NICHOLSON AND BROWN, Upholders, No. 41, Cannon Street.   1774–77 (2)

NIX, GEORGE, Cabinet-maker, King Street, Covent Garden.   1747–49 (3, 5)
"Although of low origin raised himself to eminence in his profession."   (56)

NIXON, JAMES, Cabinet-maker, No. 123, Great Portland Street.   1817 (2)

NIXON, JOHN, Cabinet and Blind maker, No. 34, Cable Street, Well Close
Square.   1790–93 (2)

NOBLE, BARNARD, Upholster and Cabinet-maker, No. 6, Long Acre. 1783 (2)

NODIN, JOHN, Upholder and Cabinet-maker, No. 1, Leadenhall Street.
     1792–96 (2)

NORCOTT, —, Carver and Gilder, No. 17, Drury Court, by the New Church
in the Strand.   1802–27 (1)

NORMAN, SAMUEL, Cabinet-maker.
"At the late Mr. West's house in King Street, Covent Garden."   1758–64 (5)
"Sculptor and carver to their Majesties and surveyor of the curious carvings in
Windsor Castle . . . a sofa and 4 armchairs designed by Robert Adam for Sir
Lawrence Dundas at 19, Arlington Street."   1763 (2)
Norman carried out work under Robert Adam in 1764 at No. 19, Arlington
Street.   (52)
See also WHITTLE, NORMAN AND MAYHEW.

NORRIS, — (NORRICE or NURSE), Frame maker, in Long Acre.
     1669–96 (22, 49)

Mr. Pepys had some prints mounted and in his *Diary*, 30th April, 1669, records
"Thence to the frame makers, one Norris in Long Acre, who showed me several
forms of frames to choose by."
Under the name Norrice he is referred to as "picture-keeper and frame maker to
William and Mary." (Whitley's *Artists and their Friends.*)   (23)

NORRIS, JOHN, Upholstery warehouseman, No. 55, High Holborn, above
Bars.   1803, 1817 (2, 20)

NORRIS, THOMAS, Upholstery warehouseman, No. 55, High Holborn, above
Bars.   1783–96 (1)

NORRIS, WILLIAM, Upholstery warehouseman, No. 4, Coventry Street.
     1783 (2)

NORRIS, WILLIAM, Upholder, No. 16, John Street, Oxford Street.
     1790–93 (2)

NORTH, ROBERT, Upholsterer, in Bartholomew Close.   1724 (6)

NORTH, ROBERT, in Red Lion Street, Holborn.   1735–48 (5)
A long itemised bill (1735) made out to Richard Hoare, Esq., for bedsteads and
hangings for same.   (1)
A similar bill (1748) to Sir Richard Hoare for work done at his house, Barn Elms,
Barnes, receipted by the Executor of Robert North.   1748 (1)

NORTON, EDMOND, Upholsterer, Earl's Court, Drury Lane.   1709 (5)

NORTON, RICHARD, Upholsterer, at *The Golden Anchor*, corner of Stone-cutter Street, Fleet Ditch.   1727 (6)

NORTON, WILLIAM, Upholsterer, of St. Brigid's, Fleet Street.   1712 (5)

NOYES, BENJAMIN, Upholster, in Shire Lane.   1749 (3)

NOYES, WILLIAM, Upholder, in Nicholas Lane, Cannon Street.   1763 (5)

NOYES, WILLIAM, Upholder, No. 61, Cannon Street.   1783–1803 (2, 20)

OAKES, RICHARD, Cabinet and Case maker, No. 86, The bottom of Snow Hill, Holborn Bridge.   1777–84 (1, 2)

OAKLEY, GEORGE, Upholder, No. 22, The south side of St. Paul's Church Yard.   1786 (1), 1790–1808 (2)
"Magazine of General and superb upholstery and cabinet furniture."

OAKLEY, GEORGE, No. 8, Old Bond Street.   1809–14 (2)

OAKLEY, JOHN, Cabinet-maker, No. 13, Dean Street, Soho.   *c.* 1775–93 (2)
He was apprenticed to Abraham Roentgens, the cabinet-maker, at Neuweid, near Cologne in 1766 and did not return to England until about 1772. *See* Miss Jourdain's article on Roentgens, *Connoisseur*, Aug., 1933.   (64)

OAKLEY AND EVANS, Upholders. Manufactory, No. 22, St. Paul's Church Yard. Magazine, No. 8, Old Bond Street.   1817 (2)

OAKLEY AND KETTLE, Upholders, No. 22, St. Paul's Church Yard.   1796 (2)

OAKLEY, SHACKLETON AND EVANS, Upholders. Manufactory, No. 22, St. Paul's Church Yard. Magazine, No. 8, Old Bond Street. 1800–1803 (1, 2, 20)
Shackleton left the firm and joined G. Seddon, his father-in-law, about 1800.

OATS AND SON, Cabinet-makers and Upholsterers, No. 187, Drury Lane.
                                                                 1817 (2)

ODY, JOHN, Liveryman of the Joiners' Company in 1723.   (1)
See OLD AND ODY.

OGBORNE, SIR WILLIAM, late Master Carpenter to the Office of His Majesty's Ordnance.   deceased—sale of stock-in-trade 1735 (5)

OLD, THOMAS, Upholder, No. 14, Fish Street Hill.   1783 (2)

OLD, WILLIAM, Wood turner, at *The Castle*, in St. Paul's Church Yard.
                                                                 1721 (6)
See the WIDOW OLD.

OLD, WILLIAM, AND ODY, JOHN, Cabinet and Chair makers, at *The Castle*, in St. Paul's Church Yard, over against the South Gate of ye Church.
                                                              c. 1720 (1)

(Plates, pages 130, 232)
"Makes and sells all sorts of Cane and Dutch chairs, Chair frames for stuffing and Cane Sashes. And also all sorts of the best Looking-Glasses and Cabinet Work in Japan, Walnut Tree and Wainscot at reasonable Rates."
See also the WIDOW OLD.

OLD, WIDOW, "Entire Stock-in-Trade, goods in the chair and cabinet-making way belonging to the late Widow Old offered for sale at *The Castle*, in St. Paul's Church Yard, facing the south door of St. Paul's."   1738 (5)

See WILLIAM OLD.

OLDFIELD AND TARN, Cabinet-makers, No. 167, Aldersgate Street.
1783–94 (2)

See also TARN AND SON.

OLDNER (or OLDER), GEORGE, Upholder, Bankside, Southwark.   1727 (3)

OLIVE AND ELKINS, Cabinet and Chair makers, Charterhouse Square.
1790–93 (2)

OSBORN, ARTHUR, Upholsterer, at *The Three Chairs*, in Paternoster Row.
1719–36 (3, 5, 6)

OSBORN, JOHN, Upholster, at *The Crown*, the corner of Crown Court, in Old Change.   1723–27 (3, 6)

OSMAN, MARY, Cabinet-maker, No. 57, Ratcliffe Highway.   1790–93 (2)

OSWALD AND NICOLS, Cabinet and Chair makers, No. 75, Wells Street, Oxford Road.   1803 (19)

See also NICHOLS AND RELPH.

OVENSTON, J., Chair maker and Upholsterer, No. 72, Great Titchfield Street.   1827–39 (2)

Successor to John Barker (*q.v.*) at above address.

In the *Life of Thomas Doggett* (founder of Doggett's Coat and Badge race for the Thames Watermen) it is stated that a chair in the hall of the Fishmongers' Company was made by J. Ovenstone from the timbers of Old London Bridge when it was pulled down in 1832.

OVERLEY, WILLIAM, Joiner and Cabinet-maker, at the sign of *The East India House*, in Leadenhall Street.   *c.* 1710–32 (1)

"Makes all sorts of Sea Chests in Deal or Wainscot, Ruff or Smooth, Packing Chests or Cases . . . Presses in Deal and Wainscot and Bedstids, Tables, Desks, Book Cases, Burows and Writing Desks, Letterholes and Draws for Shops."
His card is of great interest because it gives a contemporary view of the Leadenhall Street frontage of East India House as it stood after the ornamented superstructure had been added to it. Pepys in his *Diary* (17th April, 1661) records how he went to inspect it "and I saw the picture of the ships and other things this morning set up before East Indy House which are very well done."
For a few years before 1711 Overley occupied the little shop which stood by the entrance to the East India House (formerly known as Craven House) in Leadenhall Street, but being dispossessed of this he removed to a house four or five doors from his old premises, retaining "The East India House" as his shop sign. A reference to his tenancy is found in *The New Remarks of London . . . collected by the Company of Parish Clerks* (1732) which shows he was still in occupation of the premises at that date.

OVERLEY, WILLIAM—*continued*.

John Stow, in his *Survey of London*, recorded that the original mid-fifteenth-century building had been reconstructed in timber by Alderman Offley, who died in 1594, of which one cannot help remarking the curious resemblance of name to our joiner Overley. The above details have been gathered from the admirable *History of the East India House*, by William Foster, published in 1924.

(Plate, page 133)

OVERLOVE, J., Frame maker and Gilder, at *The Golden Key*, No. 36, Leadenhall Street.   1779 (2)
Succeeded by T. MERLE (*q.v.*).

OVERTON, —, Upholsterer, in Dean Street, near Soho Square.   1705 (5)

OWEN, SAMUEL AND COX, Cabinet-makers and Upholders, No. 54, Broad Street, corner of Berwick Street, Soho.   1790–1808 (1, 19)

OWEN, THOMAS, Cabinet-maker and Glass grinder, near Moorfields. 1736 (5)

OWTREM, WILLIAM, Upholsterer, at *The Clock*, Catherine Street, Strand.
                                                                     1723 (6)

OXENHAM, MARK, Cabinet-maker, Poland Street, Oxford Road.   1749 (3)

OXENHAM, SAM, AND CO., Upholstery and Cabinet warehouse, No. 354, Oxford Street.   1803 and 1806 (1, 19)

"Manufactury for the New Invented Dining Tables and Portable Chairs, etc., etc."

OXENHAM, THOMAS, Mangle and Napkin-press maker, No. 354, Oxford Street, near the Pantheon.   1795 (1)

OXENHAM, THOMAS, AND SONS, Supplied furniture to Sir George Sitwell at Renishaw.   1808 (64)
See Country Life, 26th November, 1938.

PAGE, THOMAS, Cabinet and Knife Case maker, No. 5, Prince's Street, Barbican.   1817 (2)

PAIN, JOHN, Cabinet-maker, at *The Star*, in Lombard Street.   1714 (5)

PALLANT, JAMES, Cabinet-maker, St. James's Walk, Clerkenwell.
                                                                  1790–93 (2)

PALLEDAY, W., Cabinet-maker, at *The Crown*, in Aldermanbury.
A label of this maker has been found inside a Queen Anne walnut bureau.
                                                                 c. 1710 (1)

PALMER, —, Upholder, Queen Street, Cheapside.   1731–32 (5)

PALMER, —, Cabinet-maker, in Masham Street, Westminister.   1746 (5)

PALMER, M., Upholder, Duke Street, Grosvenor Square.   1790–93 (2)

PALMER, MATTHEW, Upholder, High Holborn.   1708 (5)

Henry Newton
UPHOLSTER.
At the Three Tents
the Corner of Cullum-Street in Lime-Street
near Leaden-Hall Market
London
Maketh up & Selleth all Sorts of
—— Upholsterers Goods. ——

Chairs, Cabinet-Work & Glasses, with all Sorts
of Teeks, Feathers, Quilts, Blankets, Coverlids & Rugg.

Household Goods Bought Sold & Appraised.

Likewise Funerals Perform'd.

See page 124

WILLIAM OLD, AND JOHN ODY

At the Castle in St Paul's Church-Yard, (over-against the South-Gate of y.e Church) London.

Makes and Sells all sorts of Cane & Dutch Chairs, Chair Frames for Stuffing and Cane Sashes. And also all sorts of the best Looking-Glass & Cabinet-Work in Japan Walnut-Tree & Wainscot, at reasonable Rates.

See pages 126, 232

SIZE OF ORIGINAL 4⅛" × 2⅝"

John Newman at the Feathers & Ball, on the South-side of St Paul's Church-Yard, London.

Makes & Sells all sorts of Chairs, & Cabinet Work, Looking Glasses, Coach Glasses, Spring Curtains, Window Blinds, & all other Goods in the Cabinet Makers way, after the newest Fashion. Wholesale or Retail at Reasonable Rates.

See page 124

SIZE OF ORIGINAL 6⅜" × 4⅞"

PALMER, WILLIAM, Cabinet-maker and Upholder, No. 50, Fenchurch Street, facing Ironmongers' Hall. 1768–77 (1, 2)

PANER, GEORGE, Upholster, Knaves' Acre, Golden Square. 1749 (3)

PARDOE, JOHN, Cabinet-maker and Upholsterer, at *The Cabinet and Chair*, next to Temple Barr, in ye Strand. Remov'd from agst St. Clement's Church. *c.* 1720 (1, 5), 1748

(Plate, page 133)

"Sale of stock, having left off trade." (1748.) Pardoe's former address, "against St. Clement's Church," may have been identical with the premises occupied by Peter Gumley (*q.v.*) "at the Cabinet near St. Clement's Church" in 1674.

PARKE, REUBEN, Upholsterer, late of St. Clement's parish, now living at the corner of Richbell Court, next *The Hoop and Flask* Tavern in Red Lion Street, Holborn. Is now leaving off trade. 1718 (2)

PARKE, SAMUEL, Cabinet-maker, Piccadilly. 1774 (3)

PARKE AND HENNING, Upholders, No. 20, Piccadilly. 1783 (2)

PARKER, CHARLES, Upholstery and Carpet warehouse, No. 123, High Holborn. 1779–93 (2)

PARKER, ROBINSON, Upholsterer and Cabinet-maker, Wapping New Stairs. 1768 (2)

PARKER, THOMAS, Cabinet-maker, Heming's Row (St. Martin's Lane). 1749 (3)

PARKER, THOMAS, Upholder and Cabinet-maker, No. 22, Judd Street, Brunswick Square. 1817 (2)

PARKER, THOMAS, Buhl manufacturer, No. 22, Warwick Street, Golden Square. 1823 (2)

PARKER, WILLIAM, Clock case maker, Little St. Andrew's Street. deceased 1752 (7)

PARKER AND HARRIS, Carvers, opposite the New Church in the Strand, "likewise in Bond Street, Bath." 1776 (1)

PARKES, NICHOLAS, Upholsterer, Paternoster Row. 1726–31 (5)

PARKES, NICHOLAS, Upholsterer, No. 27, Ivy Lane, Newgate Street. 1768–72 (2)

PARKES, SAMUEL, Upholsterer, at *The Golden Spread Eagle*, in Paternoster Row. 1701–28 (5)

PARKES, THOMAS, Upholder, Fleet Ditch. 1722–34 (3, 6)

PARKINSON, THOMAS, Wholesale Upholsterer, No. 59, Queen Street, Cheapside. 1779–84 (2)

PARKISON, STANFIELD, Cabinet-maker, Little Pulteney Street. 1774 (3)

PARMAN, CHARLES, Carver and Gilder, No. 21, Bedford Row, Bloomsbury. 1790–93 (2)

PARNELL, T. AND J., Cabinet-makers and Upholders, No. 39, High Street, Marylebone. 1817 (2)

PARRAN, BENJAMIN, Cabinet-maker and Upholder, at *The Golden Spread Eagle*, in Long Acre. 1754–83 (3, 49, 57)

On the death of his uncle, Benjamin Goodison, in 1767, Parran continued the business with the son, Benjamin Goodison, and together they continued to supply the Royal Household until 1783, in which year Parran was joined by William Gates (*q.v.*) for a short period.

PARREY, JACOB, Cabinet-maker, in Berwick Street. 1749 (3)

PARRY, MATTHEW, Upholsterer, at *The Three Pillows*, in Watling Street. 1725–29 (5, 6)

PARRY, THOMAS, Upholder, No. 1, Broad Street, Golden Square. 1790–93 (2)

PARTRIDGE, —, Cabinet-maker, in Rupert Street (Haymarket). 1803 (19)

PARTRIDGE, JOHN, Cabinet-maker (?), in Davies Street, Oxford Street. 1792 (2)

PATTERSON, —, Cabinet-maker, at the corner of Spring Garden, over against Charing Cross. 1766 (1)

PATTERSON, JOSEPH, Turner and Chair maker, at *The Crown*, next Her Majesty's Bookbinder in New Bond Street. 1730 (1)

(Plate, page 134)

The bookbinder referred to above was probably John Brindley, who was at *The Kings Arms* in New Bond Street from 1728 to 1758.

PATTISON, —, Cabinet-maker, in Vine Street. 1774 (3)

PATTISON, JAMES, Upholder, in Broad Street (Carnaby Market?). 1749 (3)

PATTISON, JOSEPH, Cabinet-maker, in Holborn, near Hatton Garden. 1756 (5)

PATTISON, JOSEPH, Upholder, in Aldersgate Street. 1770–72 (2)

PATTON AND CO., Chair makers, in Little Rathbone Place. 1803 (19)

PAUDEVIN, JOHN, French Cabinet-maker to Charles II, in Pall Mall. 1677–88 (4, 8)

See also BODOVINE AND POTVIN.

PAUL, C. AND R., Cabinet-makers and Upholders, No. 48, Upper Marylebone Street. 1817 (1, 2)

PAUL, JAMES, Cabinet-maker, No. 27, King Street, Soho. 1790–93 (2)

PAUL, JOHN, Cabinet-maker, in the Strand. 1771 (7)

PAULIN, —, Upholsterer, near Gray's Inn Gate, in Holborn. 1747 (5)

PAVIE, —, Cabinet-maker, in Compton Street, Soho. 1727 (5)

PAYNE, —, Upholsterer, at *The Crown and Cushion*, near Hatton Garden, Holborn. 1747 (5)

John Cardoe

at the Cabinet & Chair,
next to Temple Bar, in ye Strand.
Makes & Sells all sorts of Looking
Glasses, Coach Glasses, Cabinet Work &
Chairs, Beds, & Bedding in all other
sorts of Goods in the Cabinet & Upholstery
way. Likewise Goods Apprais'd and
Funerals Furnish'd.
N.B. Remov'd from agst St Clements Church.

SIZE OF ORIGINAL 6" × 4"   *See page 131*

Will.m Overley Joyner at the Sign of
the East India House in Leaden-hall Street LONDON
Makes all sorts of Tea Chests in Deal or Mahogony
Ryffor Swords Packing Chests or Cafes, and Cafes
of Bottles, & Boxes of all Sizes, Preffes in Deal in
Wainscot, & Right Ash, Tables, Desks, Book Cafes, Bu-
roues & Writing Desks, Letter-boxes, & Draws for Shops
Allfo Counters and all sorts of Joyners worke done
at Reasonable Rates

SIZE OF ORIGINAL 7¼" × 4⅝"   *See pages 127, 128*

133

Joseph Patterson

TURNER, at the CROWN
next Her Majesty's Bookbinder
in New-Bond-Street.

Selleth all Sorts of painted floor-Cloths,
Matting & Hair Cloth, Mops, Brooms, Brushes,
Mahogany Tables & round Tea boards Bellows,
Sieves, Dutch Matted & Wooden Chairs, Walhing
Tubs, Pails, Bowles, Platters, Trays, Shovel, Baskets,
Cradles, fine work Baskets. Likewife neal Leg-
horn Hats. Wooll & Cotton for Quilting Tunbridge
& Lignumvite Ware, And all Sorts of Turners Ware,
by Wholesale & Retale at Reasonable Rates.
Also Pattens and Clogs Made and Sold.

SIZE OF ORIGINAL 5¾″ × 3½″   *See page 132*

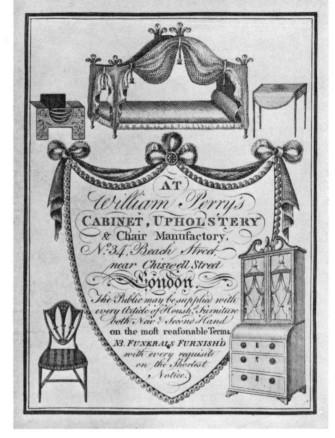

AT
William Perry's
CABINET, UPHOLSTERY
& Chair Manufactory,
Nº 34, Beach Street,
near Chiswell Street
London.
The Public may be supplied with
every Article of Housh. Furniture
both New & Second Hand
on the moft reafonable Terms.
NB. FUNERALS FURNISH'D
with every requisite
on the Shortest
Notice.

SIZE OF ORIGINAL 4⅛″ × 3⅛″   *See page 136*

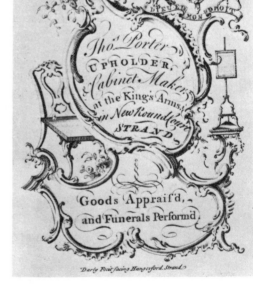

All sorts of Cabinet & Upholsterers Work in General,
LIKEWISE CARVING & GILDING,
in the Neatest Taste,
Goods Apprais'd bought & Sold by Commission
And Funerals Perform'd by
Godwin Prince
At his House
Near Durham Yard in the Strand

SIZE OF ORIGINAL 3⅞″ × 6¼″   *See page 145*

Thos Porter
UPHOLDER,
Cabinet Maker,
at the King's Arms,
in New Round Court
STRAND

Goods Apprais'd,
and Funerals Perform'd

SIZE OF ORIGINAL 4″ × 3″   *See page 141*

PAYNE, BARTHOLOMEW, Upholder, Tottenham Court Road.   1792 (2)

PEACEY, THOMAS, Cabinet-maker, in Cock Lane.   1749 (3)

PEACOCK, JOSIAH, Upholder, in London Wall.   1792 (2)

PEACOCK, ROBERT, Cabinet and Upholstery warehouse, No. 150, Strand.
                                                       1768–74 (2)

PEAKE, THOMAS, Plate case and Cabinet-maker, No. 2, Windsor Court,
    Monkwell Street.   1811–39 (1, 2)

PEARSE AND CHILD, Cabinet-makers, No. 37, Ludgate Street.   1790–96 (2)

PEARSON, THOMAS, Wholesale Upholsterer, No. 25, Clement's Lane.
                                                   1790–1803 (2, 20)

PEART (or PEARETH), JOHN, Member of the Upholders' Company in 1792.
    No. 21, Queen Street, Cheapside.   1783 (2, 4)
    No. 60, St. Martin's Lane.   1783–96
    No. 60, St. Martin's Lane was the address of the Chippendale firm. In the rate
    books of 1795–96 the names Chippendale and Peareth replace the names Haig and
    Chippendale, which had appeared there since 1783. *See* E. J. Layton's *Thomas
    Chippendale*.

PEERMAN, AMBROSE, Upholder, St. Margaret's Hill, Southwark.   1734 (3)

PEIRCE, FRANCIS, Cabinet-maker, Long Acre.   1709 (4)

PEIRSON, THOMAS, Upholder and Mattress maker, No. 14, Cullum Street.
                                                    1796–1803 (2, 20)

PELLETIER, JOHN, Carver and Gilder (address unrecorded).   1690–1710 (56)
    Supplied carved and gilt table and frames at Hampton Court during the reign of
    William III, and he also executed similar work for Duke of Montagu at Boughton.

PEMBROOK (or PEMBROKE), CHRISTOPHER, Upholder, at the sign of *The Bull*
    near Half Moon Street, in the Strand.   1705 (33)
    "Removed from *The Lyon and Bull*, against the New Exchange in the
    Strand, into Buckingham Street, York Buildings."   1731 (5)

PENNOCK, JOSHUA, Cabinet-maker, in White Lion Street, Goodman's Fields.
                                                            1790–93 (2)
    A *Josiah* Pennock, Carver, subscribed to Chippendale's *Director* (1755).

PENSON, STEPHEN, Upholder, in Leicester Fields.   1708–13 (5)

PERIERA, RICHARD, Cabinet-maker, No. 4, Hatton Wall, Hatton Garden.
                                                            1817 (2)

PERKINS, THOMAS, Upholder, at *The Key*, Trinity Minories.   1722 (6)

PERKINS, THOMAS, "a wealthy upholster in Fenchurch Street."
                                                    married 1737 (5)

PERKINS, THOMAS, Upholder, in Castle Street, Long Acre.   1790–93 (2)

PERRIN, HENRY, Dealer in furniture, at *Ye Japan'd Cabinett and Clock*,
    Fleet Ditch-side.   engraved date 1724 (1)

PERRY, ALEXANDER, Cabinet-maker, in Old Bond Street, within three doors of Piccadilly. 1733 (5)

PERRY, JOSHUA, Upholsterer, at *The Royal Bed and Star*, without Bishopsgate Street. 1727 (6)

PERRY, JOSHUA, Upholder, No. 17, Bishopsgate Street Without.

1779–83 (2)

Comparison with the Plans of London by Rocque (1746) and Horwood (1799) show the above two addresses to have been identical.
See also JAMES RODWELL (1756) and PITT AND CHESSEY (1762) at the same address, which was later occupied by Rawlins (1790) (*q.v.*).

PERRY, WILLIAM, Cabinet-maker, No. 34, Beach Street, near Chiswell Street. 1790–93 (1, 2)

(Plate, page 134)

PETTIT, GEORGE, Upholsterer to Her Majesty, No. 48, Brewer Street, Golden Square. 1790–1803 (1, 2)

PHELPS, GEORGE, Carver and Gilder, No. 19, Greek Street, Soho.

1790–93 (2)

PHENE, NICHOLAS, Upholsterer, No. 17, Brokers Row, Moorfields.

	1774–77 (2)
Nos. 18 and 19, Brokers Row.	1779–84 (2)
No. 80, London Wall.	1790–93 (2)
Nos. 18 and 19, Little Moorgate.	1794–1811 (2)

PHENE AND SON, Upholsterers, Little Moorgate. 1811–17 (2)

PHENE, SAMUEL, Upholsterer and Cabinet-maker, at *The Golden Plow*, the corner of Little Moorgate, London Wall. 1756 (1)

PHENE, SAMUEL, AND THOMAS JONES, Upholsterers and Cabinet-makers, at *The Golden Plow*, the corner of Little Moorgate, London Wall.

1763–68 (1, 2)

(Plate, page 139)

PHENE AND WILLIAMSON, Upholsterers, No. 80, London Wall.

1826–39 (2)

PHILL, THOMAS, Upholder, at *The Three Golden Chairs*, in the Strand. 1719 (63)

His rental was £90 at that date.

PHILL, THOMAS, "Upholsterer to Her Late Majesty Queen Anne and also to George I and II." Sale of stock-in-trade. 1728 (5)

PHILLIPS, EDWARD, Upholster, of the Parish of St. Michael, upon Cornhill. 1584 (65)

PHILLIPS, JOHN, Cabinet-maker, at *The Cabinet*, corner of St. Paul's Chain, (on the south side of), St. Paul's Church Yard.   1725 (1, 6)
"Is removed from St. Paul's Church Yard to *The Cabinet*, against St. Peter's Church, in Cornhill, near the Royal Exchange."   1732 (5)

(Plate, page 234)

PHILLIPS, JOHN, Upholstery and carpet warehouse, No. 134, Fenchurch Street.   1781–96 (1, 2), 1803 (20), 1812
"Upholder to the Hon[ble] City of London." Supplied goods to the Mansion House from 1780 to 1787.

Communicated by Mr. H. Clifford-Smith.

PHILLIPS AND SMALL, Upholsterers, Piccadilly.   1783 (2)

PHILLIPSON, NICHOLAS, Upholder, No. 132, New Bond Street.   1790–93 (2)

PHILP, —, Upholsterer and Cabinet-maker, No. 12, Great St. Helen's.
1803 (20)

PHILP, RICHARD, Upholsterer and Cabinet-maker, No. 26, Bishopsgate Within.   1790–93 (2)
No. 29, Bishopsgate Within.   1796

PHIPPS, ROBERT, Upholder and Cabinet-maker, No. 69, Leadenhall Street.
1760–65 (2)

PHIPPS, ROBERT, AND SON, Upholders and Cabinet-makers, No. 69, Leadenhall Street.   1768–72 (2)

PHIPPS AND SHEPHERD, Upholders and Cabinet-makers, No. 69, Leadenhall Street.   1774 (2)

PHIPPS, THOMAS, Upholder and Cabinet-maker, No. 81, Leadenhall Street.
1768–84 (2)

Succeeded by W. CHENERY (*q.v.*).

PIC, NICHOLAS, AND MICHON, PETER, Cabinet-makers (address not recorded).
Supplied furniture to Queen Mary in 1691.   (49)
See also MICHON AND PIC.

PICKHAVEN, RICHARD, Cabinet-maker, St. Martin's Court.   1749 (3)

PICKSTON, THOMAS, Upholsterer, No. 38, King Street, Covent Garden.
1790–94 (2)

PICKSTONE, —, Upholsterer, No. 7, Newcastle Street, Strand.   1803 (20)

PIERCY, —, Carver and Gilder, No. 3, Arthur Street, near the Monument.
c. 1800 (1)

PIGG, RICHARD, Coffer maker to Charles II.   1668 (64)

PIKE, JOHN, Upholder, at *The Three Tents and Lamb*, the corner of Bear Street, near Leicester Fields.   1723–49 (3, 6)

PILTON, THOMAS, Cabinet-maker, Piccadilly.   1774 (3)
    No. 213, Piccadilly.   1790–93 (2)
    No. 214, Piccadilly.   1794–96 (2)

PINCKNEY, WILLIAM, Upholsterer, No. 30, St. Paul's Church Yard. 1770 (2)
    King Street, Golden Square.   1792 (2)

PINDERGATE, DANIEL, Upholder and Cabinet-maker, No. 25, Bow Street,
    Covent Garden.   1790–93 (2)

PISTOR, THOMAS, Cabinet-maker, att *The Cabinett*, on Ludgate Hill.
                                               1699 (1, 5)

    The stock of Mr. Pistor, lately deceased, comprising Fine Japanned and Walnut
    cabinets, scrutores, table stands and mirrors was advertised for sale at very low
    rates in the *Spectator*, 21st March, 1711.   1711 (5)

PITT, —, Upholsterer, at *The Venetian Curtain*, about the middle of London
    Bridge, facing the Chapel House.   1747–49 (5)

PITT, CECIL, Upholster and Cabinet-maker, at *The Rising Sun and Fox*,
    five doors from the corner of New Broad Street, in Moorfields. 1763 (1)
    Upholder, at *The Royal Tent* in Moorfields, four doors from ye corner
    of New Broad Street, and almost facing Bedlam Walk.   *c.* 1765 (1)

                                (Plate, page 139)

    The records of the Upholders' Company show apprentices bound to Cecil Pitt.
                                          1754–75 (5)
    See PITT AND CHESSEY at above address.

PITT, JAMES, Cabinet-maker and Upholder, at *The Easy Chair*, near Bethlem
    Walk, between New Broad Street and Old Bethlem, No. 7, Old Moor
    Fields.   *c.* 1760 (1)

PITT, JOHN, Upholsterer at *The Rising Sun*, in Moorfields.   1714–26 (5)

PITT, JOHN, Upholder, No. 25, New Broad Street.   1783–84 (2)

PITT AND CHESSEY, Upholsterers, at Cecil Pitt's address but with addition
    of "No. 11" in Moorfields. Otherwise their trade-card is identical
    with Cecil Pitt's.   *c.* 1770 (1)
    No. 11, Brokers' Row, Moorfields.   1770–84 (2)
    No. 13, Brokers' Row, Moorfields.   1794–96 (1, 2)

PITT AND CHESSEY, late RODWELL (*q.v.*), at *The Royal Bed and Star*, No. 12,
    Moorfields.   (1)

PITT, CHESSEY AND PITT, Upholders, No. 11, Brokers Row, Moorfields.
                                          1774–79 (2)

PITT, THOMAS, Upholder, No. 26, Addle Street, Aldermanbury.   1779 (2)
    No. 26, Red Cross Street.   1783–93 (2)

PIZZIE, Cabinet-maker and Upholsterer, in Cullum Street.   1803 (20)

See page 138

SIZE OF ORIGINAL 7½″ × 5½″

See page 136

SIZE OF ORIGINAL 7¾″ × 5¼″

SIZE OF ORIGINAL 5⅝″ × 4⅛″   *See page* 146

SIZE OF ORIGINAL 5⅜″ × 7⅞″   *See page* 141

PIZZIE, ALEXANDER, Cabinet-maker and Upholsterer, No. 13, Fenchurch Street. 1790–96 (2)

PLANNER, JOHN, Upholsterer, No. 61, Bartholomew Close. 1768–84 (2)

PLANT, GEORGE, Upholder, at *The Crown and Cushion*, in Prince's Street, opposite the end of Gerrard Street, Soho. deceased 1747 (5)

PLATT, JOHN, Cabinet and Chair maker and Upholsterer, in Bedford Court, Covent Garden. *c.* 1765 (1)

(Plate, page 140)

He is probably the "Mr. Platts" whose name appears in the list of subscribers to Chippendale's *Director* (1755).

PLAXTON, WILLIAM, Cabinet-maker, in Hog Lane (Soho). 1749 (3)

PLUCKROSE, JOSEPH, Upholsterer, at *The Rising Sun*, by Fleet Ditch. 1725–32 (6)

PLUCKROSE, ROBERT, Upholsterer, at *The Sun and Half Moon*, Fleet Ditch. 1720 (5)

On the occasion of a fire which broke out in his warehouse he was summoned to appear before the Lord Mayor on suspicion "that the man had designedly put fire to his own house," it being alleged that the contents were not of the value of £300 though lately insured to the value of £1,000.

Weekly Journal, 4th and 11th June, 1720

PLUNKENETT, THOMAS, Cabinet-maker, High Holborn. 1763 (2)

POCOCKS, —, Cabinet-maker, No. 26, Southampton Street. 1813–17 (1, 2)

An example of "Pococks' patent reclining chair" is illustrated in Ackermann's *Repository of Arts* for January–June 1813.

POLHILL, EDWARD, Upholder, No. 7, Watling Street. 1768–77 (2)

POLHILL, LUCY, Upholder, No. 7, Watling Street. 1783 (2)

PONSONBY, THOMAS, Carver and Gilder, No. 33, Poultney Street, Golden Square. 1794 (2)

POPE AND MACLELLAN, Upholstery and Paper Hanging warehouse, at *The Pope's Head*, the corner of Harvey Court, near Half Moon Street in the Strand. *c.* 1760 (1)

Until 1767 the south end of Bedford Street, Strand, was called Half Moon Street. An advertisement of Samuel Pope's "patent Marbled Papers" appeared in the *Craftsman*, 1734.

(Plate, page 143)

PORTER, J., Cabinet-maker and Upholsterer, No. 166, High Street, Camden Town. *c.* 1800 (1)

PORTER, THOMAS, Upholder and Cabinet-maker, at *The King's Arms*, in New Round Court, Strand. *c.* 1780 (1)

(Plate, page 134)

POTTER, —, Cabinet-maker, in High Holborn.   1737 (5)

POTTER, RICHARD, Cane chair maker, at *The Hen and Chickens*, Aldersgate Street.   1725 (6)

POTTER, STEPHEN, Carver, Gilder and Cabinet-maker, at *The Looking Glass*, in Jewin Street, Aldersgate Street.   *c.* 1760 (1)

POTTS, JOHN, Upholder, at his Paper Hanging warehouse, *The Black Spread Eagle*, King Street, Covent Garden.   *c.* 1760 (1)
(Plate, page 143)

POTTS AND SON, Upholsterers, No. 90, Wardour Street.   1803 (20)

POTTS AND SON, Cabinet-makers, No. 4, Chenies Street, Tottenham Court Road.   1817 (2)

POTVIN, —, French Cabinet-maker to Charles II, Pall Mall.   1677–88 (4, 8)
See also BODOVINE, PAUDEVIN.

POWELL, —, Upholster, at *The Crown and Cushion*, in Prince's Street, facing Gerard Street in Leicester Fields.   1732 (5)

POWELL, BENJAMIN, Upholder, Wardour Street.   1724–31 (3, 5)

POWELL, WILLIAM, Upholster, in St. Giles Fields (trade token).
seventeenth century

POWLE, WILLIAM, Upholder, in Three Kings Court, facing George Yard, in Lombard Street.   1738–46 (5)

POWLE, MRS., Upholder, at above.   *c.* 1760 (?)–65
She was succeeded at above by FRANCIS PYNER (*q.v.*).

PRANKARD, JOHN, Cabinet-maker, at *The Golden Ball*, Aldermanbury.
1725 (6)

PRATT, JOHN, Cabinet-maker, Bedford Court, Covent Garden.   1763 (2)

PRATT, JOHN, Cabinet-maker, No. 4, Earl's Court, Leicester Square.
1790 (2)

PRATT, R., Cabinet-maker and Upholder, No. 29, Greenhill's Rents, St. John Street.   1819 (2)

PRATT, RICHARD, Cabinet-maker, No. 20, Kirby Street, Hatton Garden.
1790–93 (2)

PRATT, THOMAS, Cabinet-maker, Jermyn Street.   1774 (3)

PRATT, THOMAS CHARLES, Fancy Cabinet-maker, No. 9, Coldbath Square, Clerkenwell.   1817 (2)

PRENDERGAST, DANIEL, Upholsterer and Cabinet-maker, No. 25, Bow Street.   1784–93 (32)
Covent Garden.   1790–93 (2)
"An honest cabinet maker" who in 1784 was called in by Edward Gibbon to pack and forward his belongings from Downing Street.   (32)

See page 142

SIZE OF ORIGINAL 7½" × 6"

See page 141

SIZE OF ORIGINAL 7¼" × 5⅜"

See page 146

SIZE OF ORIGINAL $7\frac{3}{8}" \times 5\frac{1}{2}"$

See page 145

SIZE OF ORIGINAL $7\frac{1}{4}" \times 4\frac{7}{8}"$

PRENTICE, WILLIAM, Cabinet-maker, No. 12, Little Wild Street.
1794–1817 (2, 20)

PRESTON, JOHN, Upholder, No. 349, Rotherhithe Street.   1794–1803 (2, 20)

PRICE, —, Upholsterer, in Pall Mall, near St. Alban's Street.   1747 (5)

PRICE, JAMES, Cabinet and Buhl manufacturer, in Castle Street, Long Acre.
1817 (2)

PRICE, JOHN, Upholsterer, at *The Three Chairs and Cabinet*, in Catherine
Street, Strand.   1756 (1, 8)
(Plate, page 144)

PRICE, JOHN, Cabinet and Chair maker, Crown Street, Moorfields.   1817 (2)

PRICE, LEWIS, Upholsterer, No. 5, Brewer Street, Golden Square.
1790–93 (2)

PRICE, RICHARD, Joiner and Upholsterer (address unrecorded).
1670–79 (8)
Supplied chairs and stools for the King's yacht, etc.

PRICE, THOMAS, Cabinet-maker, Redcross Street, Southwark.
1790–1803 (2, 20)

PRIEST, W., Cabinet-maker, Nos. 17 and 24, Water Street, Blackfriars.
c. 1780 (1)
His die is stamped on a "Carlton" writing table possessed by Col. Nichol.

PRIESTLY, WILLIAM, Carver and Gilder, Andrews Hill, Doctors Commons.
1790–93 (2)

PRINCE, GODWIN, Cabinet-maker and Upholsterer, near Durham Yard, in
the Strand.   1749 (1, 2)
(Plate, page 134)

PRINGLE, JOHN AND ROBERT, Cabinet-makers and Upholsterers, No. 126,
Wardour Street, corner of Oxford Street.   1790–1803 (2, 20)

PRITCHARD, JOHN, Upholster, in Long Acre.   1749 (3)

PRITCHARD, WILLIAM, Cabinet-maker, in Philip Lane, Aldermanbury.
c. 1760 (1)
Large trade cards of this maker are in two fine mahogany bureaus supplied to
General Dormer's house at Rousham.

PRUDIE [(?) PURDIE], AND HINCHCLIFF, Cabinet-makers, No. 98, High
Holborn.   1794 (2)

PRYER, CHARLES, Cabinet-maker and Upholsterer, No. 472, Strand, opposite
Craven Street.   1785–97 (1, 2)
And at his Manufactory, in Paradise Row, Chelsea.

PRYER AND SON, Cabinet-makers and Upholsterers, opposite Craven Street,
in the Strand.   1784 (1)
This firm's name appears on an account for billiard cues and balls.

PUCKRIDGE, WILLIAM, Carver and Sign maker, No. 26, Hosier Lane, Smithfield.   *c.* 1760–1809 (1, 2)
(Plate, page 140)

PURDEN, JOHN, Cabinet-maker, etc., opposite Still Alley, in Houndsditch.
c. 1770 (1)

PURDIE, —, Cabinet-maker, No. 98, High Holborn.   1803 (20)
See also PRUDIE AND HINCHCLIFF, at above.

PURDIE, ANDREW, Cabinet-maker, No. 22, Queen's Street, Holborn.
1790–93 (2)

PYKE, MICHAEL, Upholsterer, Coventry Street.   1709 (4)

PYKE, WILLIAM, Upholster, St. Martin's Lane.   1709 (4)

PYNER, FRANCIS, Upholder and Cabinet-maker, at *The Tent*, near George Yard, in Lombard Street.   1765–92 (1, 2)
(Plate, page 144)
Successor to Mrs. Powle, widow of William Powle (*q.v.*) of Three Kings Court, facing George Yard, Lombard Street. Another trade-card gives his address as No. 18, Lombard Street, near George Yard. (*See* below.)

PYNER AND SON, Upholders and Cabinet-makers, No. 37, Lombard Street, near George Yard.   *c.* 1790 (1)

QUARE, DANIEL, Carver and Gilder, No. 78, Houndsditch.   1790–93 (2)
Possibly a descendant of his namesake the famous clockmaker.

QUARTERMAN, THOMAS, Cabinet-maker, in James Street, Grosvenor Square, selling off stock 1759 (5)

QUINO, AUGUSTINUS, Cabinet-maker, Long Acre.   1709 (4)

RABBIT, —, Upholsterer, next door to the coachmaker's in Bishopsgate Street.   1703 (61)

RACKSTRAW, JAMES, Cabinet-maker, in Wardour Street.   1749 (3)

RACKSTROW, BENJAMIN, Cabinet-maker, at *The Crown and Looking Glass*, the lower end of the Paved Stones, in St. Martin's Lane.   *c.* 1720 (1)
(Plate, page 153)

RACKSTROW, BENJAMIN, Cabinet and Picture frame maker, at *Sir Isaac Newton's Head*, the corner of Crane Court, in Fleet Street.
engraved date 1738 (1), 1747 (5)
(Plate, page 154)
B. Rackstrow, Statuary, at *Sir Isaac Newton's Head* in Fleet Street. ". . . he has found out and completed an Apparatus to exhibit that Grand Experiment the Chair of Beatification. . . ."   *Daily Advertiser*, 5th May, 1747 (5)

RADCLYFFE, EDWARD, Carver and Gilder, No. 237, High Holborn, near Little Turnstile, from Brewer Street, Golden Square.   1817–39 (1, 2)

RAGSDALE, RICHARD, Cabinet-maker, Tothill Fields.   1749 (3)

RAMM, WILLIAM, Upholder, No. 14, Brownlow Street, Holborn.
                                                        1790–94 (2)

RAND AND SANDELL, Upholders, No. 1, Compton Street, Soho.   1779 (2)
    No. 101, New Bond Street.   1783

RANDALL, —, Upholsterer, No. 171, Piccadilly.   1803 (20)

RANDALL, JAMES, Upholder, Wardour Street.   1774 (3)

RANDALL, JAMES, King Street, Golden Square.   1790–93 (2)

RANDALL, MATTHEW, Upholder, No. 13, Fenchurch Street.   1783 (2)

RANDALL, WILLIAM, Cabinet-maker, No. 38, Broad Street, Carnaby Market.
                                                           1817 (2)

RANNIE, JAMES, Upholder and Cabinet-maker, No. 60, St. Martin's Lane.
                                                    c. 1755–66 (5)

James Rannie appears to have been a well-to-do business man whom Thomas
Chippendale the elder took into partnership. His name is first met with in the
list of subscribers to the *Director* (1755) and little more is heard of him until the
announcement of his death and the consequent sale. "All the genuine Stock in
Trade of Mr. Chippendale and his late partner Mr. Rannie deceased. . . . The
business to be carried on for the future by Mr. Chippendale on the Premises
upon his own Account."   *Public Advertiser*, 3rd March, 1766.
See also under T. CHIPPENDALE.

RANSHALL, JOHN, Upholder, No. 86, Bishopsgate Without. 1783 and 1784 (2)
    No. 83, Bishopsgate Without.   1790–96 (2)

RATHELL, SAMUEL, Upholder, No. 8, Devonshire Street, Queen Square.
                                                           1790–93 (2)

RAVALD AND HOLMES, Upholders, No. 16, Bedford Street, Covent Garden.
                                                              1794 (2)

RAVALD AND MORLAND, Upholders, No. 13, Princes Street, Soho.
                                                           1783–93 (2)

RAVENHILL, GEORGE, Cabinet-maker, No. 22, St. Paul's Church Yard.
                                                    1783 and 1784 (2)

RAVENHILL, JAMES, Cabinet-maker, No. 22, St. Paul's Church Yard.
                                                           1770–79

RAVENHILL AND SPARROW, Cabinet-makers, No. 87, Bartholomew Close.
                                                           1790–93 (2)

RAVENSCROFT, SAMUEL, Upholster, Alderman of Vintry Ward.
                                                  1640–died 1664 (16)

RAVIS, NATHANIEL, Upholder and Cabinet-maker, No. 6, Three Kings'
    Court, Lombard Street.   1807 (1, 2)
    No. 11, High Street, Borough.   1809

RAWLINGS, EDWARD, Upholder, No. 17, Mount Street. 1790–93 (2)

RAWLINGS, R., Cabinet-maker and Bedstead manufacturer, Theobald's Road. 1794

RAWLINGS, THOMAS, Cabinet and Chair maker, No. 187, Tottenham Court Road. 1817 (2)

RAWLINGS, WILLIAM, Cabinet-maker and Upholder, at *The Royal Bed and Star*, No. 12, Broker's Row, opposite Bedlam Walk, in Moorfields. 1790–93 (1)

Successor to Pitt and Chessey (*q.v.*) at above, and formerly JAMES RODWELL (*q.v.*).

RAY, THOMAS, Upholder, Bartholomew Close, Little Britain. 1724–27 (2, 3), 1734

RAYMENT, WILLIAM, Upholder, No. 137, High Holborn. 1790 (2)

RAYNER, WILLIAM, Upholder, No. 2, Broker's Row, Moorfields. 1779 (2, 21)

READ, JOSEPH, Chair maker and Upholsterer, No. 78, Fleet Market, facing the Dial. 1771 (1)

(Plate, page 153)

His trade-card displays the sign of *The Chair and Crown*.

READY, JOHN, Cabinet-maker, No. 1, Cullum Street, Fenchurch Street. 1790–93 (2)

REASON, THOMAS, Upholsterer, Moor's Yard, St. Martin's Lane. 1709 (4)

REASON, THOMAS, Upholsterer, Frith Street, Soho. 1713 (5)

REASON, WILLIAM, Upholster, Long Acre. 1749, 1752 (3, 8, 56)

Was appointed Royal Upholsterer to George II but was dismissed from his post on account of dishonest practices.

REDNAPP, CHRISTOPHER, Upholsterer, at *The Cock*, in Wych Street. 1697 (5)

REED AND WILSON, Cabinet-makers, No. 22, Princes Street, Leicester Square. 1790 (2)

REEDER, JOSEPH, Upholder, No. 392, Oxford Street. 1790–1803 (2, 20)

REEDER, RICHARD, Upholder, No. 392, Oxford Street. 1783–1803 (2, 20)

REEVE, —, Upholster, in Long Lane. 1668–87 (22)

The entry in Samuel Pepys' *Diary*, 15th Oct., 1668, reads: " . . . after dinner my wife and I and Deb by coach to the upholster's in Long Lane, Alderman Reeve's and then to Alderman Crow's (*q.v.*) to see a variety of hangings."
A MS. survey of London dated 14th March, 1686–87, made by Oliver Mills, twenty years after the Great Fire, reads "I sett out a foundation for Mr. Reeves in Long Lane as described below," Vol. II (1906).

REEVE, HAMBDEN, Upholsterer, Strand. 1709 (4)

REEVE, HAMDEN, Upholsterer, of St. Martin-in-the-Fields. 1712 (5)
> An entry in Lord Chamberlain's Accounts, Record Office Ref. No. 282. Lady Day. 1705 (8)
> "ffor Her Maj^ties Bedchamber at Kensington.
> "ffor a large fine Dimity Bed tick and Bolster covered with White Satin and filled with Seasoned Swans Downe containing ninety pounds of Downe in them £18 10 0.
>> Above supplied by
>> Hamden Reeve
>> craves allowance." deceased 1714 (5)

REID, J. AND W., Cabinet-makers, etc., No. 53, Goodge Street, Tottenham Court Road. 1790–94 (2)

REID, THOMAS, Cabinet-maker, Moorfields. 1779 (7)

REID, WILLIAM, Cabinet-maker, Orange Street. 1774 (3)

REIDER, EDWARD, Upholsterer, No. 392, Oxford Street. 1803 (19)

REILLY, PETER, Upholder, Sharrard Street, Golden Square. 1777 (2)

REYNER, JOHN, Cabinet-maker, No. 404, Oxford Street. 1783 (2)

REYNOLDS, G., Cabinet-maker, etc., in Oxford Road, near Dean Street, Soho Square. 1755 (1, 18)
> (Plate, page 157)

REYNOLDS, JOHN, Upholsterer, at *The Crown and Fox*, in Fleet Street. 1692 (33)

REYNOLDS, JOHN, Cabinet-maker, Redcross Street. 1792 (2)

REYNOLDS, SAMUEL, Cabinet-maker, of St. Martin-in-the-Fields. 1763 (64)
> He was a signatory to the will, made in 1763, of William Vile (*q.v.*) who left him a legacy of £20.
> *See* R. W. Symonds' article on Vile, Cobb and Co., in *Connoisseur*, April 1938.

REYNOLDS, THOMAS, Upholster, Cornhill Ward. 1640 (16)

RHODES, WILLIAM, Upholder and Cabinet-maker, No. 127, Lower Holborn, opposite Fetter Lane. 1779–93 (2)

RHODES, WILLIAM, No. 7, Warwick Court, Holborn. 1803 (20)

RICE, WILLIAM, Carver and Gilder, Ship Alley, Wellclose Square. 1790–93 (2)

RICHARD, WILLIAM, Cabinet and Chair maker, No. 125, Wardour Street, four doors from Oxford Street. 1774, 1793 (1, 2, 3)

RICHARDS, HUGH, Carver and Gilder, No. 279, Strand. 1792–96 (2)

RICHARDS, ROBERT, Upholsterer, at *The Lyon and Lamb*, near the Maypole, in the Strand. 1675 (5)

RICHARDS AND McDONALD, Upholsterers and Cabinet-makers, No. 3, Somerset Street, Portman Square. *c.* 1830 (1)

RICHARDSON, JAMES, Glass and Cabinet-maker, Birchin Lane. 1748 (5)

RICHARDSON, JOSEPH, Upholsterer, at *The Unicorn and Sun*, near Paternoster Row, in Cheapside. 1687 (5)

RICHARDSON, WILLIAM, Upholster, at *The Star in the East*, on Tower Hill. 1735 (5)

RICHARDSON, WILLIAM, Cabinet-maker, No. 10, Newcastle Street, Strand. 1790 (2)
    No. 15, Newcastle Street. 1794–96 (2)

RICHMOND, JOHN, Carver and Gilder, No. 23, Greek Street, Soho. 1790 (2)

RICKARDS, ROBERT, Upholsterer, Brownlow Buildings, in Drury Lane. 1691 (5)

RICKETT, —, Upholder and Cabinet-maker, No. 14, Little Moorgate, Moorfields. *c.* 1820 (1)

RICKETTS, —, Upholstery warehouse, No. 14, Brokers' Row, Moorfields. 1803 (20)

RICKMAN, JOHN, Carver and Gilder, No. 62, Greek Street, Soho. 1790–93 (2)

RIDER AND MILNER, Upholstery warehouse, No. 6, Red Lion Street, Southwark. 1768–70 (2)

RIDGE, JOHN, Upholsterer (address unrecorded). 1685 (5), 1754 (18)

RIDGES, JOHN, Chair maker, near Watling Street. 1729 (5)

RIDGEWAY, THOMAS, Upholder and Cabinet-maker, at *The Easie Chair*, near Gravel Lane, in Houndsditch. 1760–65 (1, 2)
    In Norton Folgate. 1768–72 (2)
    No. 168, Fenchurch Street. 1774–79 (2)

RIDGWAY, WILLIAM, Upholster, the corner of St. Dunstan's Hill, in Tower Street. *c.* 1760 (1)
(Plate, page 157)

RIDSDALE [(?) RIGDALE], RYLEY AND PEARSON, Wholesale upholsterers, No. 25, Clements Lane, Lombard Street. 1781 (2)

RIGDALE, GEORGE, Upholsterer, Clements Lane. 1780 (7)

RIGG, THOMAS, Cabinet-maker, in Peterborough Court, near the Globe Tavern, Fleet Street. 1749 (1)

RIGHTON, RICHARD, Upholder, at *The Artichoke*, in Gracechurch Street. 1725–27 (5, 6)

RILEY, —, Upholsterer, No. 25, Cork Street, Burlington Gardens. 1803 (20)

RILEY, JOHN, Upholsterer, No. 71, Long Acre. 1779–94 (2)

RILEY AND FOWLER, Upholsterers and Cabinet-makers, No. 338, Oxford Street. 1787–96 (1, 2)
    No. 77, Swallow Street. 1803 (20)

RING, —, Cabinet-maker, No. 97, Jermyn Street.   *c.* 1780 (1)

RING, JOHN, Cabinet-maker, No. 43, St. Paul's Church Yard.   1770–72 (2)

RING, PETER, Cabinet-maker, near Portland Chapel, in Portland Street.
                                                                1780 (1)

RIVETT, SAMUEL, Cabinet and Bedstead maker, Crown Street, Middle
   Moorfields.   1790–93 (2)

ROAKE, SAMUEL, Cabinet-maker and Upholsterer, No. 20, Gloucester Street,
   Bloomsbury.   1772 (2)

ROBARTS, W^M AND J^H, Upholsterers, etc., No. 13, Fenchurch Street.
                                                               c. 1800 (1)

ROBBINS, WILLIAM, Upholder and Cabinet-maker, No. 2, Snow Hill.
                                                              1790–93 (2)

ROBERTS, —, Chair maker to His Majesty, Air Street, Piccadilly.
   An attempt at burglary reported   1728 (5)
   Probably RICHARD ROBERTS (*q.v.*).

ROBERTS, —, Upholsterer, at *The Three Chairs*, in St. Bartholomew Close.
                                                                1730 (5)

ROBERTS, JOHN, Cabinet-maker, Cross Lane, Long Acre.   1774 (3)
   A John Roberts, Cabinet-maker (no address) subscribed to Thomas Chippendale's
   Director.   1755 (18)

ROBERTS, RICHARD, Chair maker, (?) of Air Street, Piccadilly.   (56)
   In 1718 he supplied eighteen walnut tree chairs to Hampton Court (*cf.* —. Roberts
   above).   *c.* 1714–29

ROBERTS, RICHARD, "Joiner," at *The Royal Chair*, in Marylebone Street.
                                                                1723 (6)
   It seems probable that he was a son of Thomas Roberts of Air Street, the Royal
   chair maker.

ROBERTS, THOMAS, "Joiner" (Chair and Cabinet-maker), address unrecorded, (?) of Air Street.   *c.* 1688–1714 (49, 56)
   He supplied chairs and an elaborate fire screen for Windsor Castle in 1697 and
   a "Chair of State" for the Coronation of Queen Anne in 1702   (56)
   Probably father of Richard Roberts (of Air Street). Supplied the Royal Palaces
   during the reigns of William and Mary and Queen Anne.   *c.* 1688–1714

ROBERTS, TIMOTHY, Cabinet-maker, in Duckingpond Alley (Clerkenwell).
                                                                1749 (3)

ROBINS, HENRY AND JOHN, Upholders and Auctioneers, Great Piazza,
   Covent Garden.   1790–93 (2)

ROBINS, JOHN, Upholder, No. 28, Chancery Lane.   1779–94 (2)

ROBINS, JOHN, Cabinet-maker and Upholsterer, Warwick House, Beak Street,
   Golden Square.   1803 (20)
   Supplied a library table and other pieces to Sir John Soane in 1804.   1804

ROBINSON, — (*see* Bruce and Robinson), No. 29, Little Queen Street, Holborn.   1794 (2)–1803 (20)

ROBINSON, —, Upholsterer, No. 76, High Street, Marylebone.   1803 (20)

ROBINSON, —, Cabinet-maker, corner of Red Lyon Court, Fleet Street.
1718 (5)

ROBINSON, BENJAMIN, Upholder (address unrecorded).   1724 (3)

ROBINSON, HENRY, Maker of shagreen and mahogany knife cases, tea caddies, etc., No. 11, Angel Court, Snow Hill, removed to No. 18, Cow Lane.
1802 (1)

ROBINSON, J., Bedstead manufactory and furniture warehouse, No. 13, Ratcliff Highway, near Wellclose Square.   *c.* 1790

(Plate, page 157)

ROBINSON, JOHN, Cabinet-maker, Bear Street.   1749 (3)

ROBINSON, JOHN, Cabinet-maker, Barbican.   1790–93 (2)

ROBINSON, JOHN, Upholder and Cabinet-maker, No. 49, Curzon Street, Mayfair.   1817 (2)

ROBINSON, JOHN, Cabinet and Chair maker, Mile End Road.   1817 (2)

ROBINSON, RICHARD, Looking-glass maker, at *The Flower Pot*, in Beaufort Street, Strand.   1697 (5)

ROBINSON, RICHARD, Cabinet-maker, St. Giles, Cripplegate.   1718 (5)

ROBINSON, SAMUEL, Bedstead and Cabinet-maker, at *The Royal Tent*, Redcross Street, Southwark.   1780 (1)

ROBINSON AND BURTON, Japan'd chairs and Sofa manufacturer, No. 203, Oxford Street, near Orchard Street.   1804 (1)

ROCK, JOHN, Upholder, Charles Court, Charing Cross.   1727 (5)

RODWELL, JAMES, Upholsterer and Appraiser, at *The Royal Bed and Star*, the 2nd door from the corner of New Broad Street, facing Bedlam Walk, in Moorfields.   *c.* 1720–62 (1)

(Plate, page 158)

A later and more elaborate card in the Chinese Chippendale style of decoration, with the same address, has a bill on the back "a fine Mahogany double chest of drawers with a table in it" and is dated 1756. Rodwell was still in business in 1762 when an apprentice was bound to him. The business appears to have been taken over subsequently by JOHN BROWN (*q.v.*). Compare also WILLIAM TOMKINS. (15)

RODWELL, WILLIAM, Window blind and Frame maker, at *The Walnut Tree*, south side of St. Paul's Church Yard.   1726 (5)

ROGERS, RICHARD, Upholder, near Great Turnstile, Holborn.   1725 (5)

ROGERS, THOMAS, Upholsterer, at *The Blew Boar*, next door to the White Horse Inn, in Fleet Street.   1675–87 (5)

BENJ: RACKSTROW

At the Crown *and* Looking-Glass *the lower
end of the paved Stones in* St. Martins Lane.

*Makes and Sells all sorts of Cabinet Work, Looking-
Glasses, Coach-glasses, Window Blinds, Picture-
frames &c. after the newest fashion and at the
most Reasonable Rates.*

*He likewise cleans and repairs all sorts of
Cabinet work, Exchanges New Glasses for Old ones
and makes Old ones fashionable.*

*NB. He also cleans Pictures in the best manner
and takes off Bustos, Basso Relievs, and
Figures of any Size, in Wax, Metal, or
Plaister of Paris.*

SIZE OF ORIGINAL $5\frac{3}{4}'' \times 3\frac{7}{8}''$ *See page 146*

London, *July 11* 1771

Bought of JOSEPH READ, Chair-Maker,

and Upholsterer, No. 78,

Facing the DIAL, FLEET-MARKET.

SIZE OF ORIGINAL $2\frac{1}{8}'' \times 6\frac{3}{4}''$ *See page 148*

See page 156

SIZE OF ORIGINAL $6\frac{5}{8}'' \times 4\frac{1}{4}''$

See page 146

SIZE OF ORIGINAL $6\frac{7}{8}'' \times 5\frac{3}{8}''$

ROGERS, THOMAS, Upholster, St. Bartholomew Close. 1726 (5)

ROGERS, WALTER, Cabinet-maker, at *The White Lyon*, in Basinghall Street. Deceased—sale of stock. 1738 (5)

ROGERS, WILLIAM, Upholder, No. 39, Swallow Street, St. James's. 1790–93 (2)

ROGERS, WILLIAM, Upholster, No. 1, Budge Row. 1772–74 (2)

ROGERS AND SOLLY, Upholsterers, No. 1, Budge Row. 1768–70 (2)

ROSE, WILLIAM, Looking-glass and Cabinet-maker, No. 12, Old Street. *c.* 1800 (1)

ROSE, WILLIAM, No. 33, Ironmonger Row, Old Street. 1803 (2)

ROSE, WILLIAM, Upholder, Hampstead. 1734 (3)

ROSELL, PHILLIPE, French polisher, Piccadilly. 1705 (5)

ROSS, DAVID, Carver and Gilder, No. 113, Great Portland Street, Portland Chapel. 1790–93 (1, 2)

(Plate, page 157)

ROSS, DAVID, No. 98, Great Portland Street. 1802 (2)

ROTHERA, J., Cabinet-maker and Upholder, No. 29, Drury Lane. 1817 (2)

ROWBOTHAM, —, Upholsterer, in the Poultry. 1651 (13)

ROWE, CHARLES, Upholder, in the parish of St. Anne's, Soho. 1722 (5)

ROWE, CHARLES, Princes Street, Leicester Square. 1734 (5)

ROWE, JAMES, Upholder, in Broad Street, Westminster. 1727 (3)

ROWELL, WILLIAM, Upholster, Cornhill Ward. 1640 (16)

ROWLEY, EDWARD, Upholsterer, No. 41, Newgate Street. 1768–74 (2)

ROWLEY AND JENNINGS, Upholders, No. 15, Newgate Street. 1783–84 (2)

ROWLING, THOMAS, Carver and Gilder, No. 464, Strand. 1790–1814 (1, 2)

ROWLING AND BROWN, Carvers and Gilders to their R.H. Princess Royal, Augusta and Elizabeth, No. 464, Strand. 1817 (2)

RUCKMAN AND WINTER, Chair manufactory, No. 26, Red Cross Street, Borough. 1803 (20)

RUDGE, THOMAS, Upholder, Houndsditch. 1727 (3)
Hackney. 1734 (3)

RUDYERD, LAUNCELOT, Upholsterer, of St. Anne's, Soho. An apprentice bound to him. 1745 (14)

RUMBALL, THOMAS, Cabinet-maker, No. 29, Minories. 1783–84 (2)
No. 36, Wood Street. 1790–1817 (2)

RUSH, THOMAS, Cabinet-maker, Wardour Street. 1749 (3)

RUSHWORTH, —, Cabinet-maker and Upholsterer, No. 51, George Street, Blackfriars Road. *c.* 1790 (1)

RUSSELL, CHARLES AND THOMAS, Clock case makers, No. 18, Barbican.
1775–1815 (1, 60)

RUSSELL, ISAAC, Cabinet-maker, in Long Acre. 1749–70 (3, 7)

RUSSELL, JAMES, Cabinet and Chair maker, No. 10, Goswell Street Road.
1817 (2)

RUSSELL, JOHN, Cabinet and Chair maker, New Bond Street. 1773–1810 (5)

RUSSELL, JOHN, Cabinet-maker, Panton Street. 1774 (3)

RUSSELL, JOHN, Chair maker to His Majesty, No. 11, Bird Street, Oxford
Road. 1779 (2)
In Great Portland Street, Oxford Road. 1796 (2)

RUSSELL, JOHN, Cabinet-maker and Upholsterer, at *The Ship*, No. 28, the
corner of Bethlem Walk, Moorfields. 1792 (1, 2)

RUSSELL, ROBERT, Cabinet-maker, No. 83, Fleet Market. 1790–93 (2)

RUSSELL, WALTER, Upholder, Strand. 1774 (3)

RUSSELL, WILLIAM, Cabinet and Chair maker (address not recorded), sale
of stock. 1728 (5)

RUSSELL, WILLIAM, Mahogany turner and Cabinet-maker, at his shop in
Bond's Stables, or his house in Fetter Lane. *c.* 1770 (1)
(Plate, page 154)

RUSSELL, WILLIAM, Upholder, No. 75, Strand. 1790–93 (2)

RUSSELL, H., AND BRUCE, Cabinet-makers, No. 67, St. Martin's Lane.
1817 (2)

RUTHERFORD AND WATSON, Cabinet-makers, in Broad Street, St. Giles.
1790–93 (2)

RUTLEDGE, WILLIAM, Upholder and Cabinet-maker, in Conduit Street.
1783–84 (2)
In Mount Street, Grosvenor Square. 1790 (2)
See also VICKERS AND RUTLEDGE.

RUTT, THOMAS, Upholder, No. 2, Clement's Lane. 1783–84 (2)

RYMES, WILLIAM, Cabinet-maker, in Wardour Street. 1749 (3)

SABOURIN, GEORGE, Cabinet-maker, No. 51, Shoreditch. 1805–1807 (2)
No. 39, Paul Street, Finsbury Square. 1817 (2)

SABOURIN AND MARCHANT, Cabinet-makers and Upholsterers, No. 47,
Church Street, Bethnal Green. *c.* 1800 (1)
See also JOHN MARCHANT.

SADGROVE, THOMAS, Cabinet-maker, Mulberry Court, Wilson Street,
Moorfields.
In correspondence with Royal Society of Arts on the subject of the uses of
mahogany. 1817

William Ridgway
Upholfter & Appraifer,
at the Corner of St Dunstanshill
in Tower Street,
L O N D O N.
Makes up & fells all forts of
Upholftry Goods,
in the neatest Manner,
& at the Lowest Prices.

SIZE OF ORIGINAL $5\frac{7}{8}'' \times 4\frac{1}{4}''$ *See page* 150

G. Reynolds
in Crford Road near Dean Street
SOHO SQUARE,
Cabinet Maker, Appraifer Undertaker, &c.
Estates and all forts of
Houshold Furniture bought
or fold by Commiffion,
in TOWN and
COUNTRY

SIZE OF ORIGINAL $5'' \times 3\frac{3}{4}''$ *See page* 149

CHIMNEY   PIECES
Rofs
JOINER, CARVER, GILDER
& PICTURE FRAME MAKER,
At his Composition Ornament
MANUFACTORY,
No 113 Great Portland Street,
PORTLAND CHAPEL.

SIZE OF ORIGINAL $3\frac{1}{8}'' \times 4\frac{7}{8}''$ *See page* 155

J.ROBINSON'S
Bedstead Manufactory,
CARPET BEDDING & FURNITURE WAREHOUSE
No 13,
Ratcliff Highway,
near Wellclose Square,
LONDON.

SIZE OF ORIGINAL $2\frac{3}{4}'' \times 4\frac{3}{8}''$ *See page* 152

158

James Rodwell

Upholster and Sworn Appraiser.

At the Royal Bed & Star the 2.ᵈ Door from the Corner of New Broad Street, faceing Bedlam Walk in Moorfields. LONDON.

Buys, Sells & Appraises all manner of Household Goods, New & Old, as Standing Beds & Bedding, Chests of Drawers, Desk & Book-Cases, Bueroe Desks, Card, Dining, Breakfast & Dressing Tables, (in Mahogeny, Walnut-tree, or Wainscot) Chairs of all Sorts, Settee & Bueroe Bedsteads, Sconces, Pier, Chimney & Dressing Glasses, with all other Sorts of Upholstery, Cabinet & Braizery Goods &c.

SADGROVE, WILLIAM, Cabinet-maker and Upholsterer, No. 18, Brokers Row, Moorfields.   1824 (2)
    Nos. 18–21, Eldon Street, Finsbury Circus.   1832–51 (2)

SAINSBURY, JOSEPH, Upholsterer and Cabinet-maker, No. 167, Tottenham Court Road.   1839 (2)
    No. 182, Tottenham Court Road.   1851 (2)

SALE, JOSEPH, Upholder, St. Martin-in-the-Fields.   1723 (7)

SALLIS, GEORGE, Chair maker, in Bull Head Court, Jewin Street.   1749 (5)

SALMON, —, Chair manufactory, No. 427, Oxford Street.   1803 (20)

SALMON, H., Cabinet-maker and Upholsterer, No. 16, Chapel Street, Bedford Row, Covent Garden.   1794–1817 (2)

SAMBER, SAMUEL, Upholder, in Long Acre.   1749 (3)

SAMMES, JAMES, Upholder, No. 53, Russell Street, Bloomsbury.
                                          1783–1803 (2, 20)

SAMPSON, ABRAHAM, Upholster, in Conduit Street.   1749 (3)

SANDELL, SAMUEL, Upholder, No. 101, New Bond Street.   1783–96 (2)

SANDERS, —, see MORGAN AND SANDERS.

SANDERSON, JOHN, Upholsterer, Haymarket.   1709 (4)

SANDILANDS, —, Cabinet-maker, No. 112, Wapping.   1803 (20)

SANDS, DAVID, Upholder and Cabinet-maker, in Dean Street, Soho. 1749 (3)
    In Greek Street, Soho.   1774 (3)
    In Great Russell Street.   1790–93 (2)

SANDYS, WINDSOR, Upholder, Hoxton Square.   1722–27 (3, 5)
    He was nominated for office of Sheriff in 1722.

SANSOM, —, Turner, No. 20, Prince's Street, Soho.   c. 1780 (1)

SAPP, ROBERT, Cabinet-maker and Upholsterer (address not recorded).
                                           1740 (52)
    Supplied a mahogany writing table and a set of twelve finely carved chairs for the Board Room at the Treasury, after the designs of William Kent in 1740. The above attributions were made by Mr. Clifford-Smith in his *English Furniture Illustrated* (1950) p. 285. A detailed account, dated 1739, has been recorded by Mr. W. A. Thorpe for furniture supplied by "Robt. Sapp, Upholsterer" to the New Treasury for the rooms of Mr. Secretary Stephen Fox.

SARGENT, GEORGE, Pier glass and Cabinet-maker, No. 17, College Hill (Cannon Street).   1790–93 (2)

SAUNDERS, —, Cabinet-maker, New Street, Cloth Fair.   1763 (2)

SAUNDERS, —, Cabinet-maker, No. 158, Aldersgate Street.

SAUNDERS, —, Upholsterer, in Cateaton Street.   1750 (5)

SAUNDERS, JOSEPH, Upholder and Cabinet-maker, No. 42, High Street, Borough.   1783–96 (2)

SAUNDERS, PAUL, Upholster, in Hartshorne Lane, Charing Cross.   1749 (3)

SAUNDERS, PAUL, Upholder and Cabinet-maker.   1756 (5)
In partnership with G. S. Bradshaw (*q.v.*) in Greek Street, Soho, until 1756. He then set up for himself.
In Sutton Street, Soho.   1760 (56)
Great Queen Street, Lincoln's Inn Fields.   1763–68 (2, 7)
Great Russell Street, Bloomsbury.   1770–72 (2)

SAUNDERS, PAUL, AND BRACKEN, Upholders, Charlotte Street, Bloomsbury.
1772–90 (2)

SAUNDERS, THOMAS, Cabinet-maker, in Briton Mews.   1749 (3)

SAVAGE, MRS., Dealer in japanned furniture, at her East India Warehouse, over the New Change, in the Strand.   1732 (5)

SAVILL, THOMAS, Upholsterer, No. 17, Aldgate High Street.
1777–1803 (2, 20)

SAWER, JOHN, Cabinet-maker, in John Street.   1749 (3)

SAY, FRANCIS, Upholsterer, next *The Crown* Tavern (No. 14), on Ludgate Hill.   1745 (1), 1751–63 (33)

(Plate, page 163)

After 1763 he took Mr. Kay (*see* QUENTIN KAY) into partnership (*see* SAY AND KAY)   1765–81 (2)
Freeman of the Upholders' Company in 1745, Junior Warden of the Upholders' Company in 1772, Senior Warden of the Upholders' Company in 1773, Master of the Company in 1774–75. He died at Hadley, Herts, 1778. In the author's collection is a very long and detailed account, dated 7th Jan., 1769, rendered by Francis Say for the funeral of Sir Francis Gosling, the banker, with whose family Say was connected by the marriage of his sister Mary. A short biography of *The Old City Family of Say* was issued by L. G. N. Horton-Smith, F.S.A., in 1948.

SAY, RICHARD, Upholsterer, at the front house, in Racquet Court, in Fleet Street.   1717–34 (3, 5)
Father of Francis Say above. Freeman of the Upholders' Company in 1722, Master of the Upholders' Company in 1744–75. He died in 1762.   (63)

SAY AND KAY, Upholsterers, No. 14, Ludgate Hill.   1765–81 (2)
[FRANCIS SAY AND QUENTIN KAY.]

SCHELTON, —.
"An eminent upholsterer in the Haymarket was lately appointed Beadle to the Company of Upholders."   1734 (5)

SCHOFIELD, —, Cabinet-maker, in Charlotte Street, Rathbone Place. 1803 (20)

SCOTT, JOHN, Leather gilder and Upholsterer, at *The King's Arms*, in Cheapside, over against Bow Church Yard.   1746 (1)

SCOTT, JOHN, Cabinet-maker, etc., No. 52, Berwick Street, Soho.
1794–1817 (2)

SCOTT, THOMAS, Upholder and Cabinet-maker, No. 29, Ludgate Hill.
1783–96 (2)

He was a maker of the ingeniously fitted toilet tables originally designed for a Mr. Rudd and known in the trade as the "Rudd table." *See* Hepplewhite's *Cabinet Makers and Upholsterer's Guide*, published in 1788.

SCRIMSHIRE, RICHARD, Upholder, in Suffolk Street, Cavendish Square.
1792 (2)

SCRIMSHIRE, WILLIAM, Upholder, in Bucklersbury. 1740–44 (2)

SEABROOK, ROBERT, Upholder, in Smithfield. 1724–34 (3)

SEABROOK, SAMUEL, Upholsterer and Cabinet-maker, No. 22, Houndsditch.
1767 (5)

SEAL, —, Upholsterer, in Arlington Street, St. James's. 1725 (5)

SEAL, JOHN, Cabinet-maker, Paulin Street, Hanover Street. 1749 (3)

SEARLE, GEORGE, Upholder, at *The Crown and Cushion*, in the New Road near the Turnpike, Lambeth. (1)

SEATON, —, Carver, Gilder and Upholsterer, No. 40, Oxford Street.
c. 1790 (1)

SEDDON, The firm of. *c.* 1750–1868 (1, 2)

It is beyond the scope of the present work to give more than an outline of this famous firm of cabinet makers that ran continuously through four generations. Within the range of the entries in the London Directories from 1763 to 1868 there are more than twenty variants of the style of the firm and their various addresses. Distinction between the members of the family is not easily made as the two names George and Thomas occur persistently throughout four generations. See also article by the present writer in *Country Life*, 20th January, 1934.

SEDDON, CHARLES, AND CO., Cabinet-maker, Avery Row. 1865 (2)
And No. 58, South Molton Street. 1865 (2)
And No. 70, Grosvenor Square. 1866–68 (2)

SEDDON, GEORGE (born 1727, died 1801), Cabinet-maker, was apprenticed in 1743 to G. Clemapon (*q.v.*). About the year 1750 he set up for himself at London House in Aldersgate Street. (*See Memoir of Thomas Seddon*, the artist, great-grandson of George.) (1, 2, 14, 18, 28, 29, 56)

In 1754 we find his name in the list of subscribers to Thomas Chippendale's *Director*. A disastrous fire broke out in his workshop in 1768 and from the account given in the newspapers we learn that he was then employing eighty cabinet-makers and already being referred to as "one of the most eminent cabinet-makers in London." The entries in directories 1763 until 1770 give him at No. 158, Aldersgate Street and from then until 1784 he appears at No. 151. From then onwards he and his sons, Thomas and George, and his grandsons, also Thomas and George, are always shown as at No. 150, Aldersgate Street.
George Seddon the first died in 1801. Contemporary references to him are found in the *Memoirs of William Hickey* and a vivid account of a visit in 1786 to the

SEDDON, GEORGE—*continued*.

Seddon workshops is given in the diary of a young German lady, Sophie von la Roche, a translation of which was published in 1933 under the title of *Sophie in London*. The work of the Seddon firm has been well described by Ralph Edwards and Margaret Jourdain in their *Georgian Cabinet Makers* and further supplemented by articles contributed by Edwards and the present writer in *Country Life*, 21st Oct., 1933, 20th Jan., 1934, 14th Nov., 1941, and 17th Jan., 1947.

SEDDON, THOMAS AND GEORGE (1765–1805). First in partnership with their father, George Seddon, at No. 151, Aldersgate Street until 1784, and later at No. 150.   1785–1805 (1)

(Plate, page 260)

SEDDON, SONS, AND SHACKLETON, THOMAS (son-in-law of George Seddon, senior) at No. 150, Aldersgate Street.   1790–1800 (2)

Seddon, Sons and Shackleton were the makers of a curious and ingeniously contrived writing table called a "Croft" after the customer who instigated it. This was described and illustrated by the present writer in *Country Life*, 17th Jan., 1947.

SEDDON, GEORGE AND THOMAS, No. 150, Aldersgate Street.   1806–10 (2)

This partnership is generally credited with having made the cradle for Joanna Southcott's "Prince of Peace" in 1814. This is now exhibited in the Peel Park Museum at Salford.

SEDDON, THOMAS AND GEORGE, grandsons of George Seddon, senior, No. 150, Aldersgate Street, Cabinet-makers to Her Majesty.
                                                                  1820–1836 (2)
Calthorp Place, Grays Inn Road.   1836–42 (2)

(Plate, page 260)

SEDDON, JOHN, Furniture broker, No. 38, Cannon Street.   1827 (2)

SEDDON, THOMAS, No. 10, Charterhouse Street.   1790–97 (2)
And No. 24, Dover Street.   1793–1800

SEDDON, THOMAS, Grays Inn Road.   1843–52 (2)
No. 67, New Bond Street.   1854–62 (2)

SEDDON, CHARLES (great-grandson of George Seddon, senior), Avery Row and No. 58, South Molton Street.   1865 (2)

SEDDON AND CO., No. 70, Grosvenor Street and No. 58, South Molton Street.   1865–68 (2)

There are no entries of the firm in the directories later than 1868.

SEDDON AND BLEESE, Upholsterers and Cabinet-makers, No. 24, Dover Street.
                                                             1802–1809 (1, 2)
See THOMAS SEDDON.

SEDDON AND MOREL *see* MOREL AND SEDDON.   (2)

SEMPLE, —, Cabinet-maker, No. 78, Margaret Street, Oxford Street.
                                                               1803 (20)

See page 169

SIZE OF ORIGINAL 7⅞" × 5¼"

See page 160

SIZE OF ORIGINAL 6⅝" × 4¾"

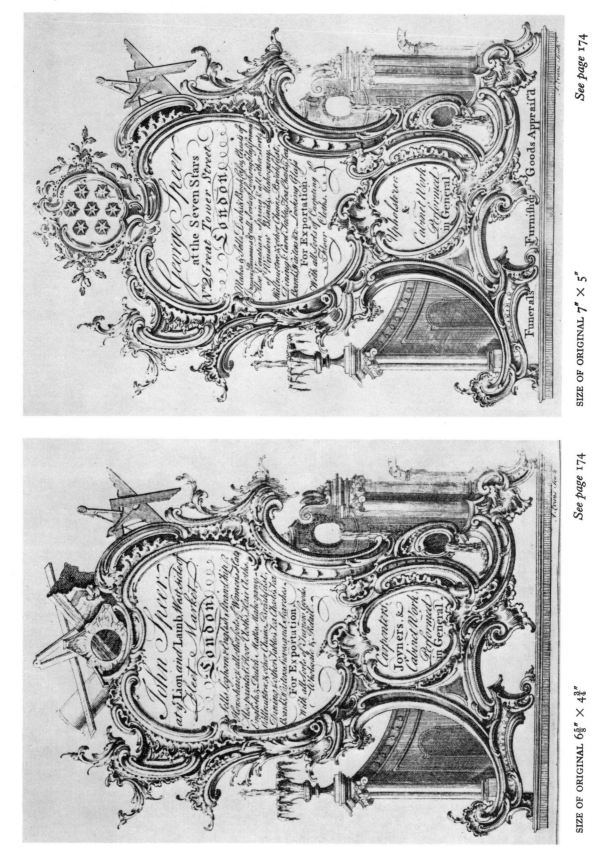

SIZE OF ORIGINAL $6\frac{5}{8}'' \times 4\frac{3}{4}''$ See page 174

SIZE OF ORIGINAL $7'' \times 5''$ See page 174

SENHOUSE AND CO., Upholders and Cabinet-makers, Lambeth. 1768 (2)

SENOLD, JAMES, Upholsterer, No. 23, Fenchurch Street. 1784 (2)
    No. 81, Fore Street. 1790–93

SEVERN, SAMUEL, Upholster, Jermyn Street. 1749 (3)

SEWELL, RICHARD, Carver and Gilder, No. 121, Leadenhall Street, near the
    India House. 1790–93 (1, 2)

SHACKLETON, THOMAS, Upholder, No. 115, Long Acre. 1790–93 (2)
    Partner with his father-in-law George Seddon (q.v.), No. 150,
    Aldersgate Street. 1793–1800 (2)
    Later in partnership of Oakley, Shackleton and Evans (q.v.), No. 8,
    Old Bond Street. 1800–1803 (1)

SHACKLEWORTH, ROGER, Cabinet-maker, Swallow Street. 1749 (3)

SHAPLEY, WILLIAM, Upholder and Cabinet-maker, at *The Crown and Cushion*,
    North side of Cornhill, the third house East of Sun Court. 1765 (33)
    No. 80, Gracechurch Street. 1768–72 (2)
    No. 26, Bishopsgate Street Within. 1774–77 (2)

SHARD (or SHARP), ROBERT, Upholder, in Leadenhall Street. 1724–34 (3)

SHATFORD (or SHAFTFORD), SAMUEL, Cabinet-maker, in Long Acre.
    1749–55 (3, 18)

SHAW AND SON, Upholsterers, No. 34, Hatton Street. 1803 (20)

SHEARER, THOMAS, Designer and Cabinet-maker (address not recorded).
    1788 (49)
    A skilful designer of furniture of whom no more is known other than the engraved
    plates in the *Cabinet-Makers' London Book of Prices*, printed for the London
    Society of Cabinet Makers (1788), which were re-issued under Shearer's name
    as *Designs for Household Furniture*.

SHEFFREY, W., Upholder in general, No. 184, Fleet Street. *c.* 1790 (1)

SHELTON, JOSEPH, Cabinet-maker, in Villiers Street, Strand. 1749 (3)

SHENTON AND SMITH, Chair makers, No. 27, Wardour Street. 1794 (2)
    See also SMITH of the same address.

SHEPHERD, —, Upholsterer, next door to *The Three Tuns* Tavern, in West
    Smithfield. 1746 (5)

SHEPHERD, JOHN, Turner, at *The Straw Hat and Floor Cloth Warehouse*,
    opposite St. Clement's Church, in the Strand. 1751–56 (1)

SHEPHERD, JOHN, Upholder, No. 69, Leadenhall Street. 1777–84 (2)

SHEPHERD, WILLIAM, Upholder, Leadenhall Street. 1724 (5)

SHEPHERD, WILLIAM, Upholder, at *The Rising Sun*, in Mark Lane.
    died suddenly 1733 (5)

SHERATON, THOMAS, Designer of furniture, No. 41, Davies Street, Grosvenor
     Square.   1793 (1, 51)
     No. 106, Wardour Street.   1795
     No. 8, Broad Street, Golden Square.   Died 1806 (49, 56, 62)
                              (Plate, page 167)
Though brought up as a cabinet-maker it is doubtful whether he ever set up a
workshop of his own. He mainly devoted himself to the production of designs
which he published between 1791 and 1805. His principal work appeared in
The Cabinet Makers' and Upholsterers' Drawing Book originally issued in four
parts between 1791 and 1794. To this work he prefixed a lengthy list of subscribers
which included almost all the principal craftsmen of his time. In 1803 he brought
out *The Cabinet Dictionary*, to which he appended a very useful list "of most of
the Master Cabinet-makers, Upholsterers and Chair Makers in and about
London." Of his last work the *Cabinet Maker, Upholsterer and General Artists'
Encyclopaedia* only about one-fourth of the projected issue appeared just before
his death. His rather undistinguished trade-card announces: "T. Sheraton teaches
Perspective, Architecture and Ornaments, makes Designs for Cabinet-makers
and sells all kinds of Drawing Books." A posthumous publication appeared in
1812, *Designs for Household Furniture by the late T. Sheraton, cabinet maker*,
consisting largely of plates from his previous works.

SHERRAN, ROBERT, Cabinet-maker, No. 38, Margaret Street, Oxford Street.
                                                                  1803 (20)

SHERWIN, GEORGE, Cabinet-maker, next the corner in Leadenhall Street.
     Previously he was in Cornhill at the corner of Birchin Lane.   1749 (5)

SHERWOOD, J. H., Cabinet-maker, No. 42, Bartholomew Close.
                                                         1795–1803 (5, 17, 20)

SHERWOOD, SAMUEL OAKLEY, Cabinet-maker, Clapham.   1778 (7)

SHIPLEY, THOMAS, Cane chair maker, Knuckles Alley, Drury Lane.   1709 (4)

SHIPMAN, JAMES, Cabinet-maker and Upholder, No. 15, Rood Lane,
     Fenchurch Street.   1790–96 (2)

SHIPMAN AND SON, Cabinet-makers, No. 9, George Yard, Lombard Street.
                                                              1803–17 (2, 20)

SHORT, ROBERT, Cabinet and Looking-glass Warehouse, in Fore Street,
     near Cripplegate.   (Plate, page 167)   *c.* 1780 (1)

SHOTTER, GAWEN, Upholder, No. 1, Budge Row, Cannon Street. 1790–96 (2)

SHREEVE, —, Upholsterer, at *The Cabinet*, Within Smithfield Bars.   1760 (5)

SHREEVE, WILLIAM, Upholsterer, etc., three doors from Ludgate Hill, in the
     Old Bailey. "The only Inventor and Maker of Venetian Curtains."
                                                             c. 1780 (1)

                              (Plate, page 167)

SHROUDER, JAMES, Papier mâché manufacturer, in Great Marlborough Street,
     Carnaby Market.   1763 (2)

Nath.ᴸ Skinner
At the Black Lyon yᵉ South-
Side of Sᵗ Pauls, LONDON.
Makes & Sells all sorts of Cain-
Rush, & Cover'd-Chairs, and Bed-
Chairs, & Tables, with all Sorts of
Cabinet-work, & Painted-Window-
Blinds, all sorts of Looking-
Glasses, Wholesale, or Retaile,
As Resonable as any whare in
LONDON.

SIZE OF ORIGINAL 5¾″ × 3¾″   *See page 170*

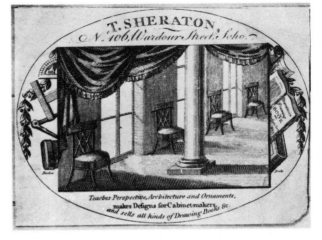

T. SHERATON
N.⁰ 106, Wardour Street, Soho.

Teaches Perspective, Architecture and Ornaments,
makes Designs for Cabinet-makers,
and sells all kinds of Drawing Books, &c.

SIZE OF ORIGINAL 2¼″ × 3⅛″   *See page 166*

William Shreeve
Upholsterer, Appraiser and Undertaker,
Three doors from Ludgate Hill in the Old Bailey
London.
Makes and Sells all Sorts of Cabinets, Glasses,
and Chairs, in yᵉ best manner at Reasonable Rates.
N.B. The only Inventor and Maker of Venetian Curtains,
to Common Windows, to hang in the same Form as yᵉ Right
Venetian Curtains.

SIZE OF ORIGINAL 3⅝″ × 5⅛″   *See page 166*

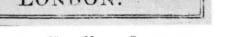

Robert Short
at his Warehouse in Fore Street, near Cripplegate,
LONDON.
Makes & Sells all Sorts of Looking Glass & Cabinet
Work which he Manufactures himself to
supply Merchants for Exportation or Home
Consumption, on the most reasonable Terms.

SIZE OF ORIGINAL 4⅛″ × 5¼″   *See page 166*

SIZE OF ORIGINAL $2\frac{3}{8}'' \times 3\frac{5}{8}''$ *See page* 173   SIZE OF ORIGINAL $3\frac{1}{8}'' \times 4\frac{7}{8}''$ *See page* 177

SIZE OF ORIGINAL $6\frac{1}{8}'' \times 3\frac{1}{4}''$ *See page* 175   SIZE OF ORIGINAL $5\frac{1}{4}'' \times 4''$ *See page* 177

SHUFFREY, W., Upholster, No. 36, Aldgate Street. 1794–96 (2)

SIBTHORPE, CHRISTOPHER, Cabinet-maker, at *The Japan'd Cabinet*, in Aldermanbury. deceased 1730 (5)

SIDDALL, JOHN, Cabinet and Blind maker, No. 35, Upper Bryanston Street, Edgware Road. 1817 (2)

SIDDON [*sic*], GEORGE, is the spelling in the entry of a boy bound to G. Clemapon (*q.v.*) in the list of names of children apprenticed by the sons of the clergy. This evidently refers to the apprenticeship of George Seddon (*q.v.*). 1742–43 (14)

SIDGIER, HENRY, Carpenter, Cabinet-maker and Upholsterer, at *The Carpenters' Arms*, in Great Shere Lane, near Temple Barr. *c.* 1760 (1)

SILK, THOMAS, Cabinet-maker and Upholder, at his Inlaid Cabinet and Upholstery Warehouse, No. 4 on the south side of St. Paul's Church Yard, next door to *The Queen's Arms* Tavern. 1772–96 (1, 2)

(Plate, page 163)

SIMMONS, —, Upholsterer, near Middle Temple Gate, in Fleet Street. 1745 (5)

SIMMS, —, Upholsterer. deceased 1729 (5)

"A very rich quaker reputed to be worth £50,000—he was formerly an upholsterer in Wych Street." (*Daily Post*, 5th Feb., 1729.)

SIMMS, JOSEPH, Wholesale Upholsterer, No. 1, Blackman Street, Southwark. 1767–96 (1, 2)

SIMPSON, BENJAMIN, Cabinet-maker, No. 96, High Holborn. 1790–93 (2)

SIMPSON, BENJAMIN, AND HOUGHTON, MICHAEL, Cabinet-makers, No. 96, High Holborn. 1794 (2)

SIMPSON, GEORGE, *see* G. SIMSON.

SIMS, JOSEPH, *see* J. SIMMS.

SIMS, WILLIAM, Cabinet-maker and Upholder, No. 145, High Holborn. 1774–1808 (1, 2)

SIMSON, GEORGE, Upholder and Cabinet-maker, No. 19, South side of St. Paul's Church Yard. 1790–1827 (1, 2)

(Plates, pages 253, 254)

SIMSON, WILLIAM, Cabinet-maker and Upholder, No. 4, New Bond Street. 1796–1817 (2)

SIVILL, —, Upholder, in Chiswell Street, fronting the Artillery Gate. 1725–31 (2, 5)

SKELTON, HUMPHREY, Upholsterer, in the Haymarket. 1709–23 (4)

A fire occurred on these premises "caused by an experiment which was being carried on to smother bugs." (*London Gazette*, 17th Aug., 1723.)

SKELTON, HUMPHREY—*continued*.

In the Strand. 1727 (3)

Exeter Street, Strand. 1734 (3)

He was admitted Freeman of the Upholders' Company in 1698. Chaloner Smith's *British Mezzotinto Portraits* records a fine mezzotint portrait of Humphrey Skelton engraved by J. Faber, after a painting by H. Hussing, which was first published in 1728 and twice reprinted. A six-line verse below the portrait beginning

When Philosophic Thoughts engage the Mind
A serious Brow and looks intense We find

suggests a studious character which is well borne out by the aspect of the man portrayed. In 1727 *The Daily Courant* reports: "To be sold under a Commission of Bankruptcy awarded against Humphrey Skelton, upholder, three small copyhold farms in the Manor of Woodham Walter and Ingatestone in the County of Essex, late the estate of the said bankrupt." Despite this order he was still in business in 1734.

SKERRET, GEORGE, Upholder, No. 30, Bedford Street, Covent Garden.
1790–96 (2)

SKERRET, THOMAS, Upholster, Bedford Street. 1749–83 (2, 3)

SKINNER, NATHANIEL, Chair maker, etc., at *The Black Lyon*, ye South side of St. Paul's. *c.* 1730 (1)

(Plate, page 167)

SKURRAY, JOHN, Upholsterer, in Princes Street, St. James's. 1749 (5)

SLATER, —, Upholsterer, in Budge Row. 1748 (5)

SMALL, JAMES, Upholsterer, No. 189, Piccadilly. 1790–93 (2)

SMALLWOOD, J., AND CO., Cabinet-makers, No. 40, King Street, Covent Garden. 1790–94 (2)

SMALLWOOD, JOHN, Cabinet-maker, No. 5, Greenfield Street, Field Gate, Whitechapel. 1774–1803 (2, 20)

SMART, GEORGE, Cabinet-maker, No. 16, Bell Alley, Colman Street.
1790–93 (2)

SMARTFOOT, BENJAMIN, Cabinet-maker, at *The Lion and Lamb*, near the Ram Inn, in West Smithfield. 1725 (5)

SMEE, WILLIAM, Cabinet-maker and Upholder, The Pavement, Moorfields.
1817–51 (2)

Later SMEE AND COBAY, Wardour Street.

SMITH, —, Upholder, at the sign of *The Chair*, in Fleet Street. 1744–48 (5)

The "Widow Smith" was succeeded by WILLIAM JELLICOE (*q.v.*).

SMITH, —, Mahogany turner, near the Mews, in Castle Street. 1747 (2)

SMITH, —, Chair maker, No. 27, Wardour Street. 1794–1803 (2, 20)

See also SHENTON AND SMITH.

SMITH AND CO., Upholsterers, No. 7, Great East Cheap.   1803 (20)

SMITH AND SON, Upholders and Carpet manufacturers, No. 82, Holborn.
1790–93 (2)

SMITH, ALEXANDER, Carver and Gilder, No. 11, Orange Street, Red Lion
Square.   1825–27 (1, 2)
> Succeeded at above by W. S. SMITH.

SMITH, CHARLES, Cabinet-maker and Upholsterer, Marshall Street
((?) Carnaby Market).   1749 (3)
> In January, 1759, Ince and Mayhew (q.v.) advertised that they had "taken the
> house of Mr. Charles Smith, cabinet-maker and upholsterer in Carnaby Market,
> who has left off that branch of business." He is probably the same CHARLES SMITH,
> later of Portugal Street (q.v.).

SMITH, CHARLES, Upholsterer and Cabinet-maker, in Portugal Street,
Lincoln's Inn Fields.   1763 (64)
> Charles Smith, upholsterer, of Portugal Street was one of the two executors to
> the will of WILLIAM VILE (q.v.) in 1763. (R. W. Symonds' article in Connoisseur,
> April 1938.)

SMITH, CHARLES AND CO., Upholders to His Majesty, No. 69, Lower
Grosvenor Street.   1791–94 (1)
> *See also* SMITH AND KEY.

SMITH, EDWARD, Turner to Her Royal Highness Princess Amelia, No. 45,
Wimpole Street.   1776 (1)

SMITH, EDWARD, Upholder, No. 53, Gracechurch Street.   1779–93 (2)

SMITH, GEORGE, Upholder, Ratcliffe Highway.   1727

SMITH, GEORGE, Cabinet-maker, in Castle Street.   1749 (3)

SMITH, GEORGE, Cabinet and Upholstery Warehouse, No. 99, New Bond
Street.   1789 (1, 3)

SMITH, GEORGE, Upholder and Cabinet-maker to H.R.H. Prince of Wales,
"Draughtsman in Architecture," No. 15, Prince's Street, Cavendish
Square.   1808 (1)
No. 41, Brewer Street.   1826
> Published *A Collection of Designs for Household Furniture and Interior Decoration*
> in 1808, *A Collection of Ornamental Designs after the Manner of the Antique*
> (1812) and in 1826 *The Cabinet-Makers' and Upholsterers' Guide, Drawing Book
> and Repository of New and Original Designs for Household Furniture*, from No. 41,
> Brewer Street, Golden Square.

SMITH, J., Upholsterer, in the Haymarket, against Pall Mall.   1730 (5)

SMITH, J., Cabinet-maker, No. 13, Charles Street, Grosvenor Square.
1794 (2)
> *See also* SMITH AND BRERETON.

SMITH, JAMES, Cabinet-maker, of St. Paul's, Covent Garden.   1744 (14)

SMITH, JOHN, Upholder, Featherstone Buildings, Holborn.   1734 (3)

SMITH, JOHN, Upholsterer, at *The Three Tents*, by Fleet Ditch, near Holborn
Bridge. 1709 (5)

SMITH, JOHN, Wholesale Upholsterer, No. 7, Great Eastcheap.
1779–1803 (2, 20)

SMITH, JOHN, Upholder, No. 1, Berkeley Square. 1790 (2)

SMITH, JOHN, AND SONS, Carvers and Gilders, No. 137, New Bond Street.
1840 (2)

SMITH, MARY, Bedding and Upholstery Warehouse, No. 282, Holborn,
at the corner of Great Turnstile. 1779–90 (1)

SMITH, MATHEW, Chair maker, St. Martin's Street, Leicester Fields.
1709 (4)

SMITH, R., Carver, Gilder and Printseller, No. 7, Cockspur Street.
1794–96 (2)

SMITH, ROBERT, Carver, Gilder and Printseller, No. 17, Duke's Court,
St. Martin's Lane. 1790–93 (1, 2)

SMITH, SAMUEL, Cabinet-maker and Upholder, at *The Inigo Jones's Head*, in
Compton Court, near Soho. 1749 (5)

SMITH, SAMUEL, in Compton Street. 1760–70

SMITH, SAMUEL, Cabinet-maker, No. 38, Beech Street, Barbican.
1790–93 (2)

SMITH, T., Carver, Gilder and Frame maker, No. 16, Cleveland Street,
Fitzroy Square. *c.* 1800 (1)

SMITH, THOMAS, Upholsterer, in Gracechurch Street. 1723 (5)

SMITH, CAP^T. THOMAS, Upholder, at the corner of Great Queen Street.
1725 (5)

SMITH, THOMAS, Turner, at *The Golden Hand*, Swan Court, Grub Street.
1725 (6)

SMITH, THOMAS, Cabinet-maker, opposite *The Ship* Tavern, at Ratcliff
Cross. 1747 (5)

SMITH, THOMAS, Upholder, in Aldersgate Street. 1779 (7)

SMITH, W. S., *see* ALEXANDER SMITH.

SMITH, WILLIAM, Carpet, Upholstery and Bedding Warehouse, near the
end of Chancery Lane, near Gray's Inn Gate, in Holborn. 1763 (1, 2)

SMITH, WILLIAM, Cabinet-maker, Queen Street, Mint [(?)Southwark].
1794 (2)

SMITH, ZACHARIAH, Upholsterer and Cabinet-maker, within five doors of
Durham Yard, in the Strand. 1742 (5)

SMITH AND BRERETON, Cabinet-makers, No. 13, Charles Street, Grosvenor Square.   1790–93 (2)
   See also J. SMITH.

SMITH AND KEY, Upholsterers, No. 69, Lower Grosvenor Street.   1803 (20)
   See also CHARLES SMITH AND CO.

SMITHER, JOSEPH, Turner, No. 11, Kent Street, near St. George's Church, Southwark.   *c.* 1780 (1)

SMYTHURST, ROBERT, Cabinet-maker, in Litchfield Street, Soho.   1725 (5)

SNAP, JOSEPH, Chair and Cabinet-maker, No. 25, Paul Street, Finsbury Square.   1817 (2)

SNELL, MESSRS., Albemarle Street.   1822
   A secretaire bookcase made by this firm is illustrated in Ackerman's *Repository of Arts, etc.,* for January–June, 1822.

SNELL, WILLIAM, Upholsterer, No. 15, Hanover Street, Long Acre.
                                                              1790–1817 (2, 20)

SNUGGS, J., Upholder and Cabinet-maker, Minories, Tower Hill.   1817 (2)

SOEDERBERG, T., Cabinet-maker and Ebonist [*sic*], No. 19, Tottenham Court Road.   1794–96 (2)

SOLDAN, FRANCIS, Cabinet-maker, West End, Hampstead.   1766 (5)

SOLOMON, ELIJAH, Upholder and Cabinet-maker, in Castle Street, Long Acre.   1790–93 (2)

SOLOMON AND BROWN, as above.   *c.* 1800 (1)

SOMERVILLE, JOHN, Cabinet-maker, No. 22, Chancery Lane.   1803 (20)

SOTHEBY, —, Carver, Gilder and Picture frame maker, No. 13, Strand, opposite Hungerford Market.   *c.* 1780 (1)
                        (Plate, page 168)

SOUNDY, BENJAMIN, Upholster, No. 26, Gracechurch Street.   1772–83 (2)
   No. 5, Clement's Lane.   1784 (2)

SOWERBY, —, Cabinet-maker, near Beaufort Buildings, in the Strand.
                                                           deceased 1746 (5)

SPANE, THOMAS, Carver, of St. Giles' without Cripplegate.
                                                                   1682 (65)

SPANGER, — (?) SPANE, as above.   1700 (49)
   "Paid Spanger ye Dutch carver in full for picture frames." Extract from Lord Bristol's Diary, 5th Nov., 1700.

SPARKES, EDWARD, Upholsterer, in Wych Street, near Lyon's Inn.   1685 (5)

SPARROW, THOMAS, Cabinet-maker, No. 19, Charterhouse Lane.
                                                                   1790–93 (2)

SPARROW AND RAVENHILL, Cabinet-makers, No. 87, Great Bartholomew Close.   1790–93 (2)

SPEER, GEORGE, Cabinet-maker and Upholder, at *The Seven Stars*, No. 2, Great Tower Street.   *c.* 1770, 1779–1803 (1, 2)

See also JOHN SPEERS.

(Plate, page 164)

SPEER, JOHN, Cabinet-maker, etc., at ye *Lion and Lamb*, the West side of Fleet Market.   *c.* 1760 (1)

(Plate, page 164)

"Sells Leghorn and English Straw, Chip, Horsehair and all other sorts of Women's hats, English and Dutch Matts, Mahogany, Wallnut-tree and other Chairs, Breakfast, Dining and other Tables, Tea Chests and Tea Boards, Sieves and Scarches (?) for Exportation with all sorts of Turners' Goods. Wholesale and Retail. Carpenters, Joyners and Cabinet Work Performed in General."

SPEER, JOHN, Cabinet-maker, etc., at *The Seven Stars*, in Great Tower Street.   *c.* 1765 (1)

See also GEORGE SPEER.

SPENCE, JOHN, Cabinet-maker, Husband Street, Carnaby Market.   1774 (3)

SPENCE, JOHN, Upholder, No. 26, Peter Street, Soho.   1790–93 (2)

SPENCE, THOMAS, Upholsterer, at *The Grasshopper*, at Charing Cross.
1660 (33)

SPENCER, JOHN, Chest maker, No. 116, Fenchurch Street.   1792 (2)

SPENCER, SAMUEL, Chair maker, at *The Golden Chair*, Aldermanbury.
1725 (6)

SPENCER, WILLIAM, Carpenter, "at a corner messuage, formerly called *The Crown* and now *The Rowe Buck*, in Cheapside."   1657 (35)

SPICER, ARTHUR, Upholder, in Tower Street.   1734 (3)

SPICER, JOHN, Upholder, at *The Golden Angel*, Wych Street, near Temple Bar.   1724–27 (5)
Removed to *The Golden Angel*, in Fenchurch Street.   1730–32 (5)
In Old North Street ((?) Red Lion Square.)   1734 (3)

SPINNAGE AND HOWARD, Upholders and Paperhanging makers, in Gerard Street, Soho.   1774–77 (2)

See also CROMPTON AND SPINNAGE.

SPRAGG, RICHARD, Cabinet-maker, No. 98, Leadenhall Street.   1783 (2)

SPRATLEY, THOMAS, Cabinet-maker, No. 96, Fore Street.   1790–93 (2)

SPURRIT, WILLIAM, Upholster, in St. James's Street.   1749 (3)

SQUIRE, WILLIAM, Upholsterer and Cabinet-maker, at *The Three Tents and Lamb*, within Bishopsgate, near Cornhill.   *c.* 1730 (1)

From a later trade card we see that he was principally concerning himself with the making of wallpapers "Also all sorts of upholstery and Cabinet Goods." By that time he had moved to *The Three Tents and Lamb* in the Poultry.   *c.* 1760 (1)

STAIN, SAMUEL, Cabinet-maker, in Pall Mall.   1749 (3)

STAINES AND CARPENTER, Upholstery warehouse, No. 5, Ironmonger Lane.
                                                            1796–1803 (2, 20)

STALKER, JOHN, Maker of japanned furniture, at *The Golden Ball*, St. James's
    Market.   1688 (5, 49)
    He published, in conjunction with G. Parker, *A Treatise of Japanning and
    Varnishing*, with twenty-four plates (1688).

STAMFORD, J., Upholder, No. 2, Goodge Street, Tottenham Court Road.
                                                                      1794 (2)

STAMFORD, JEREMIAH, Cabinet-maker, Windmill Street (Tottenham Court
    Road).   1749 (3)

STAMPA AND SON, Carvers and Gilders, No. 74, Leather Lane, Holborn.
                                                               1811–17 (1, 2)

STANDAGE, T., Upholder and Cabinet-maker, No. 8, Little Russell Street,
    Covent Garden.   1796 (2)

STAPLES, JOHN, Cabinet-maker, Upholsterer and Mahogany merchant,
    John Street, Minories.   1790–93 (2)

STEEL, JOHN, Upholsterer and Cabinet-maker, No. 205, Oxford Street.
                                                                 1794–96 (2)

STEINFIELD, H., Cabinet-maker, Warwick Street, Golden Square.   1759 (7)

STENT, ELIZ. BARTON, Turner, at *The Turner's Arms*, in Little Britain.
                                                                   c. 1750 (1)
                            (Plate, page 168)
    Daughter and successor to the late
STENT, ROBERT, at above.

STEPHENS, —, Looking-glass maker, between *The White Bear* and *The Golden
    Sugar Loaf*, in Long Acre.   1705 (5)

STEPHENS, EDWARD, Carver and Gilder, No. 85, Park Street, Grosvenor
    Square.   1790–93 (2)

STEPHENS, GEORGE, Cabinet-maker, Brooke House, the upper end of Brooke
    Street, Holborn.   deceased 1743 (5)

STEPHENS, JOHN, Upholsterer, No. 71, Fleet Market.   1770

STEPHENS, JOHN, No. 127, Houndsditch.   1772

STEPHENS, SAMUEL, Carver and Gilder, No. 18, Lower Brook Street,
    Grosvenor Square.   1790–1803 (5, 20)

STEPHENS, WILLIAM, Upholsterer and Cabinet-maker, No. 217, Piccadilly.
                                                             1803–17 (2, 20)

STEPHENSON, —, Cabinet-maker in Greek Street, Soho.   1803 (20)
    see also William Stevenson at above address.

STERRY (or STIRRIDGE), JAMES, Upholder and Cabinet-maker, in George Yard, Lombard Street.   1783–96 (1, 2)

STEVENSON, WILLIAM, Cabinet-maker, No. 43, Greek Street, Soho.
1803–17 (2, 20)

STEWARD, CHARLES, Cabinet repository, No. 115, St. Martin's Lane.   1817 (2)

STEWARD, JOHN, Cabinet and Chair maker, Clifton Street, Finsbury Square.
1817 (2)

STEWART, ROBERT, Upholster, Bow Street.   1749 (3)

STINTON, —, Looking-glass maker, Moorfields.   1730 (5)

STIRRIDGE, see STERRY.

STOKES, —, Cabinet-maker, No. 26, Tooley Street.   1803 (20)

STOKES, J., Carver and Gilder, No. 21, Newcastle Street, Strand.   1790 (2)
In 1829 was published a "Complete Upholsterers and Cabinet Makers Guide" by a "J. Stokes".

STOKES AND WALLINGTON, Cabinet-makers, Cavendish Court, Houndsditch.
1790–93 (2)

STOLWORTHY, EDMOND, Upholsterer and Cabinet-maker, No. 3, Onslow Street, Hatton Garden.   1809–17 (1, 2)

STOLWORTHY AND MARTIN, Cabinet-makers, No. 21, Vine Street, Hatton Garden.   1824–27 (2)

STONE, RENÉ, Carver and Gilder, at The Golden Head, in Berwick Street, near the French Church (successor to DUFFOUR (q.v.)).   c. 1765 (1)

STONE, RENÉ, Frame maker to His Majesty, at The King's Arms, in Berwick Street.   1772 (1, 8)

STONE, WILLIAM, Cabinet-maker, in Hatton Garden.   1726 (5)

STONESTREET, HENRY, Upholder, in Friday Street.   1734 (3)

STORER, ANTHONY, Upholder, parish of St. Mary Woolnoth.   1683 (65)

STOUT, M., Cabinet and Chair factory, No. 45, Wells Street, Oxford Street.
1817 (2)

STOVELL, G., Upholsterer and Tent maker, to H.R.H. Prince of Wales, No. 3, Lower Grosvenor Street.   1796–1803 (2, 20)

STRAHAN, PATRICK, Cabinet-maker, at The King's Arms and Ball, Fleet Ditch.   1723 (6)

STRICKLAND, —, Upholsterer and Cabinet-maker, No. 75, Long Acre.
1773–93 (26, 56)

Strickland was "nephew to the late Mr. Vile" (q.v.). He appears to have worked with Jenkins, "late foreman to Mr. Cobb," who was Vile's partner. In the Strawberry Hill accounts kept by Horace Walpole, under date 1773, details are given of the costs of an elaborate plumed bed hung with Aubusson tapestry for the Great North Bed-chamber and a set of white or gold elbow chairs which were brought over from Paris through the agency of Mme du Deffand in 1770 and supplied to Strawberry Hill by Strickland.

STRICKLAND AND JENKINS, Cabinet-makers and Upholsterers, No. 75, Long Acre. 1780–93 (1, 2)
> Their trade card announces: "Strickland, nephew to the late Mr. Vile, and Jenkins, late Foreman to Mr. Cobb, cabinet-makers, upholders, appraisers and undertakers at 75 Long Acre."
> *See* VILE AND COBB, *also* JOHN JENKINS.

STRODE, JOHN, Cabinet-maker, at *The Queen's Head and Blue Ball*, Fleet Ditch. 1722–27 (6)

STRONG, FRANCIS, Cabinet-maker, in Swallow Street. 1749 (3)

STUART, CHARLES, Cabinet-maker, in Norris Street. 1749 (3)

STUART, FRANCIS, Cabinet-maker, in Coventry Court (Haymarket). 1749 (3)

STUBBS, JOHN, Chair manufactory, in the City Road and in Brick Lane, Old Street. 1790–1803 (1, 2)
> (Plate, page 168)
> "For all sorts of Yew Tree, Gothic and Windsor Chairs, Alcoves and Rural Seats, Garden Machines (*i.e.* wheeled chairs), Dyed Chairs, etc."

STUBBS, RICHARD, Cabinet-maker and Upholder, in Anchor Street, in Windmill Street, near the Haymarket. *c.* 1780 (1)

STURGIS, JOHN, Chair maker, at *The Rose and Crown*, next door to *The White Rose* Inn, Fleet Market. *c.* 1750 (1)
> (Plate, page 168)

STYFIELD, THOMAS, Carver and Glass grinder, No. 35, Old Compton Street, Soho. 1790–93 (2)

SURMAN, JEREMIAH, Cabinet-maker, in York Street, Covent Garden.
1734 (5)

SUTTON, THOMAS, Upholsterer, in St. Olave Street, Southwark. 1725 (5)

SWAIN, —, Upholder, at *The Wool Pack*, near Bedlam Walk, between Old Broad Street and Old Bedlam, Moorfields. 1764–67 (1, 2)

SWAIN, ELIZABETH, Upholsterer, Nos. 8, 9 and 10, Brokers Row, Moorfields.
1794–96 (2)

SWAIN, SAMUEL, Upholder, No. 9, Brokers Row, Moorfields. 1770–90 (2)
> He was apprenticed to JAMES RODWELL (*q.v.*) 1762, and elected Alderman of the City of London. 1784 (21)
> Master of Upholders' Company. 1787–88

SWAIN, WILLIAM, Upholsterer, at *The Sun*, in Moorfields. 1726 (6)

SWAINSON, JOHN, Cabinet-maker, No. 15, Harp Alley, Fleet Market.
1803–1807 (2, 20)

SWAN, ROBERT, Cabinet-maker, Long Acre. 1774 (3)

SWIFT, GRANT AND HURLEY, Upholsterers, etc., No. 226, Piccadilly.
1803 (20)

SYERS, JOSEPH, Cabinet-maker and Upholder, No. 3, Duffour Place, Broad Street, Carnaby Market.   1817 (2)

SYMPSON, Joiner and Cabinet-maker (address unrecorded).   (22)

> There were many occasions when Mr. Pepys employed the services of "Sympson the joiner" between 1662 and 1668 at his house in Seething Lane, but in none of the entries in the *Diary* is any indication given of where Sympson lived. The fine bookcases which are still to be seen in the Bibliotheca Pepysiana at Magdalene College, Cambridge, were made by Sympson in 1666. On the 16th Aug., 1666, he records: "I find one of my new presses for my books brought home which pleases me mightily." On the 24th Aug., 1666: ". . . then comes Sympson to set up my other new presses for my books." Two years later (14th Aug., 1668): "At home I find Symson [*sic*] putting up my new chimney-piece in our great chamber which is very fine, but will cost a great deal of money, but it is not flung away."   (22)

(Plates, pages 222, 223)

TABOR, JOHN, Upholsterer, near *White Horse Inn*, in Fleet Street.
                                              deceased 1725 (5)

TAIT, GEORGE, Cabinet-maker, in New Round Court, Strand.   1774 (3)

TAITT, JOHN, Upholsterer and Cabinet-maker, in partnership with William Gordon [*q.v.*] in King Street, Golden Square.   1768–70 (2)
In Little Argyle Street, Golden Square.   1772–79 (2)
After 1779 Gordon's name drops out and Taitt moves to No. 75, Swallow Street, Piccadilly.   1779–85 (1, 64)
After 1785 he is found at No. 254, Oxford Street.   1785–99 (8)

> A John Taitt, Upholsterer, of Hanover Street, appears in Westminster Poll Book of 1774 (3).

TAITT, RICHARD, Upholsterer, No. 92, Jermyn Street, St. James's.
                               1788, 1793–1803 (2, 20, 56)

TANTUM, JOSEPH, Cabinet-maker, in Gravel Lane, Houndsditch.   1740 (2)

TAPWELL AND HOLLAND, Cabinet-makers, No. 25, Great Pulteney Street, Golden Square.   1817 (2)

TARLFORD, RICHARD, Upholsterer, at the sign of *The Bell*, in the parish of St. Mildred's-in-the-Poultry.   1565

> A twenty-one years' lease of these premises was granted to him in 1565 by Alderman Sir Thomas Leigh who was elected Lord Mayor of London in 1544 and again in 1552. He died in 1571.
> The above is my earliest record of an upholsterer with a dated address.

TARN AND SON, Cabinet-makers, No. 24, London Wall.   1790–96 (2)

TATE, WILLIAM, Cabinet-maker, No. 5, Fleur-de-luce Street, Norton Falgate.   1783 (2)

TATHAM AND BAILEY, Cabinet-makers, No. 13, Mount Street, Grosvenor Square.   1802–17 (51A, 56)

> *See also* ELWARD, MARSH AND TATHAM.

TATHAM, THOMAS, AND MARSH, WILLIAM, Cabinet-makers, No. 13, Mount Street, Grosvenor Square. *c.* 1795–1809 (56)

Principal Cabinet-makers to Prince of Wales (later George IV) from 1795 onwards. They also supplied furniture for Carlton House and Southall, Bedfordshire. (Clifford Smith's *Buckingham Palace*, p. 111.)

Marsh retired in 1809 and later the firm became

TATHAM, BAILEY AND SAUNDERS, Cabinet-makers, No. 13, Mount Street. 1811–17 (2, 56)

Succeeded by BAILEY AND SAUNDERS (*q.v.*), Thomas Tatham having died in 1818. (12)

TATNALL, JOHN, Upholder, in Ironmonger Lane, Cheapside. 1722–40 (5, 6)

TAYLER, MATTHEW, Cabinet and Chair maker, No. 8, Sun Street, Bishopsgate Street. 1817 (2)

TAYLER AND WRIGHT, Upholders and Cabinet-makers, No. 157, Fenchurch Street. Successors to Mr. Chesson. 1774–77 (1, 2)

See CHESSON AND BATHURST.

TAYLOR, B., Cabinet-maker and Upholder, No. 81, Kent Street, Borough. 1817 (2)

TAYLOR, DANIEL, Cabinet-maker, in Shakespear Walk (Upper Shadwell). 1790–93 (2)

TAYLOR, DAVID, Cabinet and Chair maker, No. 14, Wardour Street. 1817 (2)

No. 26, Berners Street. 1824 (2)

See JOHN TAYLOR.

TAYLOR, GEORGE, Cabinet-maker and Upholder, No. 156, St. John's Street, Smithfield. 1774–77 (2)

TAYLOR, HYNMERS, Upholsterer and Cabinet-maker, at *The Crown and Cushion*, over against Lord Monson's, in Piccadilly. 1758–72 (1, 2, 5)

Another billhead of Hynmers Taylor gives *The Crown and Cushion* as "by St. James's Church." The house of the second Lord Monson stood on the east side of Burlington House in Piccadilly, the site now occupied by·Albany. He bought it in 1746 and sold it to Henry Fox (the first Lord Holland) in 1763. In 1792 Wilkes' Directory gives Hynmer [*sic*] Taylor, Upholder, in Portland Street. (2)

TAYLOR, JOHN RICHARD, Upholsterer, No. 16, Bedford Court, Covent Garden. 1824 (2)

He published an oblong octavo volume of engraved designs of sofas and chairs from the above address, *c.* 1822.

A drawing room sofa and two chairs by this maker are illustrated in colour in Ackermann's *Repository of Arts* for July–Dec., 1824.

TAYLOR, JOHN, Cabinet-maker, No. 14, Wardour Street.   1774–93 (2, 3)
    Succeeded by DAVID TAYLOR (*q.v.*).

TAYLOR (or TAYLER), JOSEPH, Upholsterer and Cabinet-maker, No. 157,
    Fenchurch Street.   1777–84 (2)

TEARNLEY, —, Chair maker, No. 1, Garden Row, near the Obelisk, Lambeth.
                                                                    1803 (20)

TEASDALE, WEBB AND CO., Wholesale Upholsterers, No. 29, Gracechurch
    Street.   1777–84 (2)
    See WEBB AND LAWFORD.

TELLING, —, Carver, Gilder and Frame maker, No. 13, Piccadilly.
                                                                    1790–93 (2)

TEMPEST, MICHAEL, Upholder.
    St. Mary Woolchurch Hawe Burial Register.   1599

TENNANT, THOMAS, Chair maker, in Long Lane.   1732 (2)

TERRY (or TARRY), GEORGE, Upholder, Whitecross Street.   1724–34 (3)

TERRY, HENRY, Cabinet-maker and Upholder, No. 16, Ave Maria Lane.
                                                                    1779–93 (2)

THACKER, BENONI, Cabinet-maker (address unrecorded).
                                                       1726 and 1755 (18, 49)
    Employed by Sir William Chambers for work at Carrington House in Whitehall
    and elsewhere.

THACKTHWAITE, DANIEL, Cabinet-maker, Marshall Street.   1749 (2)

THACKTHWAITE, MICHAEL, Upholder, No. 7, Marylebone Street.
                                                                 1774–94 (2, 3)

THACKTHWAITE, WILLIAM, Cabinet-maker, Carnaby Street.   1749 (2)

THARP, —, Upholsterer, at the end of Dover Street, in Piccadilly.   1720 (5)

THARRAT, THOMAS, Cabinet-maker, No. 17, Shepherd Street, Oxford Street.
                                                                    1817 (2)

THOMAS, JOHN, Cabinet-maker, Poland Street.   1790–93 (2)

THOMAS, JOSEPH, Cabinet-maker and Upholsterer, No. 15, Charles Street,
    Grosvenor Square.   1803–17 (2, 20)

THOMAS, WILLIAM, Cabinet-maker, No. 17, Greek Street, Soho.
                                                                    1790–93 (2)

THOMAS AND FLINT, Cabinet-makers, No. 17, Greek Street, Soho.
                                                                    1794–96 (2)

THOMAS AND WALLACE, Cabinet-makers, No. 17, Greek Street, Soho.
                                                                    1784 (2)

THOMPSON, ALEXANDER, Cabinet-maker, Great Hermitage Street, Wapping.
                                                                    1790–93 (2)

At THORN's,
Cricket Bat, Turnery, and Patten Warehouse,

At the ·BEEHIVE and PATTEN, in John-ſtreet, Oxford Market;

ARE MADE AND SOLD,

Floor Cloths of all Patterns
Dutch and Engliſh Matting
Lift Carpets and Hair Cloths
Garden Mats
Night Gown Baskets
Fine Cradles
Childbed and Work Baskets
Bread and Fruit ditto
China Baskets and Sallad ditto
Tin Coal ditto
Tin Knife ditto
Powder Puffs and Bags
Mahogany Voiders
Butlers Trays
Tea Boards and Tea Cheſts
Coffee and Chocolate Mills
Spice Cupboards
Silver-top Cruet Frames
Black Lead Pencils
Bottle Stands
Ivory Fiſh and Counters
Backgammon Tables
Umbrelloes
Cribbage Boards
Comb Trays
Box, Ivory, and Horn Combs
Cloſe-ſtools
Chairs of all Sorts
Tin'd Fire Screens
Tin Duſt Pans
Iron Shovels
Japan'd Coal Scoops
Iron ditto
Bellows and Coal Tubs
Salt Boxes and Flour Tubs
Bowls and Platters
Plate Racks and Pye Peels
Chopping Blocks
Pails and Piggens
Churns and Milk Pails
Waſhing Tubs and Stools
Flaskets for Clothes, Clothes Horſes, and Hair Lines
Malt Shovels and Scoops
Buffalo Drinking Horns
Shoe and Powder Horns
Wool and Cotton Curry-Combs and Bruſhes
Jewellers Bruſhes
Lawn, Hair, and Wire Sieves
Wig Stands and Boot Jacks
Clothes Bruſhes
Rat and Mouſe Traps
Squirrel Houſes, Chains and Collars
Blacking Balls and Sponges
Shop-ſtools and Garden Sticks
Venice Wiſp Cloth Bruſhes

** Rocking Horſes, Chairs for Children, with all Sorts of Mops, Brooms, and Bruſhes: Cricket-Bats, Pattens and Clogs, Wholeſale or Retale, at the moſt reaſonable Rates.

See page 183

SIZE OF ORIGINAL 6⅜" × 5"

FRANCIS THOMPSON,
Turner and Chair-Maker,

(From Mr. AYLIFFE, Turner to His Majeſty)

At the THREE CHAIRS, in St. JOHN's LANE, near HICKS's HALL;

MAKETH and SELLETH all Sorts of dy'd Beach Chairs, Bruſhes, Brooms, Mops, and Matting, Wholeſale and Retail. Likewiſe Pails, Waſhing-Tubs, Iron hoop'd Coal-Tubs, Fire-Screens, Plate-Racks, Shop-Stools, Cloſe-Stools, Coal-Boxes, Knife-Boxes, Knife-Whetters, Salt-Boxes, Wainſcot and Nottingham Voiders, Comb-Trays, Tin-Plate-Baskets, Tin Scuttles, plain and painted; Iron Duſt-Pans, Cradles, Flaskers, Child-bed-Baskets, China Plate Baskets, Work Baskets, Kitchen and Chamber Bellows, Hair Cloth, and many other Things too tedious to mention. Painted Floor-Cloths of all Sorts and Sizes, of the neweſt Pattern, warranted to be done well in Oil, and wear well; and to be ſold as cheap as any Adveꞇiſer in LONDON. Likewiſe Ready Money for Bees Wax.

See page 183

SIZE OF ORIGINAL 7⅞" × 4¼"

SIZE OF ORIGINAL 4⅞" × 5"
See page 189

SIZE OF ORIGINAL 6⅞" × 5⅝"
See page 184

THOMPSON, B. R., Dyed Chair maker, No. 62, Red Lion Street, Clerkenwell.
                 1794–1803 (2, 20)

THOMPSON, FRANCIS, Turner and Chair maker from Mr. Ayliffe, Turner
 to His Majesty, at *The Three Chairs*, in St. John's Lane, near Hicks's
 Hall.   *c.* 1750 (1)

(Plate, page 181)

THOMPSON, JAMES, Upholder, in Cullum Street (Fenchurch Street). 1753 (7)

THOMPSON, JAMES, Upholsterer, No. 146, Fenchurch Street. 1768–70 (2)
 No. 133, Fenchurch Street.   1772–74 (2)

THOMPSON, WILLIAM, Upholsterer, No. 57, Fleet Street.   1790 (2)

THOMSON, GUY, Cabinet and Case maker, No. 2, Duke Street, Smithfield.
                  1790–96 (1, 2)

THOMSON AND FISKE, Cabinet and Case makers, No. 2, Duke Street,
 Smithfield.   1803 (20)

THORLEY, JAMES, Upholder, at *The Golden Head*, against the Church, in
 St. Martin's Lane.   1748 (5)

THORN, —, Turner and Small Furniture maker, at *The Beehive and Patten*,
 in John Street, Oxford Market.   1764 (1)

 Thorn was a maker of cricket bats and no earlier maker of them in London has
 been recorded.

(Plate, page 181)

THORNHILL, RICHARD, Upholder, Limehouse.   1734 (3)

THORNTON, CHRISTOPHER, Looking-glass maker, at *The Looking Glass*,
 Peter Street in the Mint, near the Square, Southwark. 1707 (1)

THORNTON, CHRISTOPHER, Glass grinder, Piccadilly. 1723 (6, 10)

THORNTON, T., Cabinet-maker, No. 8, South Street, Manchester Square.
                    1817 (2)

THOROLD, JOHN, Upholder, in Old Street.   1724–34 (3)

THORP, —, Upholster, on Fish Street Hill, by the Monument.
                 1740–47 (5)

THORP, FRANCIS, Upholder, in Aldersgate Street. 1724–34 (3)

THORP, ROBERT, Upholder, in Gloucester Street, Red Lion Square.
                 1724–34 (3)

THORPE, JOSEPH, Upholder, in Pall Mall. 1725 and 1726 (5)

THROTMAN, ANDREW, Cabinet-maker, No. 71, Tottenham Court Road.
                   1796 (2)

THURSFIELD, EDWARD, Upholsterer, at *The Plow*, in Russell Street, Covent
 Garden.   1685 (5)

TIBBS, SAMUEL, Carver and Gilder, No. 88, Bartholomew Close.

1790–93 (2)

TIDD, THOMAS, Cabinet-maker, in Old Street Square. 1769 (15)

TIJOU, MICH, Carver and Gilder, No. 22, Greek Street, Soho. 1796 (2)

TILBE, SAMUEL, Upholsterer, in Leadenhall Street. 1727 (5)

TILLIER, JOHN, Upholster, in Bedford Street. 1749 (3)

TOD, THOMAS, Cabinet-maker, in Great Trinity Lane. 1747 (5)

TOLPUT, JOSHUA, Upholsterer, No. 115, Long Acre. 1803 (20)

TOMBS, BARTHOLOMEW, Upholder.
Registers of the Parish of St. Mary Woolnoth. 1679 (65)

TOMKINS, WILLIAM, Upholsterer, at *The Royal Bed*, the corner of New
Broad Street, near Little Moorgate, in Moorfields. *c.* 1760 (1)

(Plate, page 182)

His card bears a close resemblance to that of JAMES RODWELL (*q.v.*) at *The Royal
Bed and Star*, in New Broad Street (*q.v.*).

TOMKINS, WILLIAM, Upholder and Cabinet-maker, No. 14, Brokers Row,
Moorfields. 1772–deceased 1778 (2)

TOMKINS, WILLIAM, Upholder and Cabinet-maker, No. 14, Brokers Row,
Moorfields. 1779–96 (2)

TOMLIN, ROGER, Upholster, at *The Crown and Cushion*, over against Stock's
Market, Great Lombard Street. 1723–26 (5, 6)

TOMLIN, ROGER, Upholsterer, at *The Crown and Cushion*, in Fenchurch
Street, near the Ipswich Arms, Cullum Street. 1726–32 (5)

TOMSON, WILLIAM, Upholder, No. 57, Fleet Market. 1784–96 (2)

TONKINS, RICHARD, Turner, nephew and successor to Thomas Newton
[*q.v.*] at the corner of Clifford Street, Saville Row. 1783 (1)

TONKINS, ESTHER, Turner, successor to Richard Tonkins (*see* above).

1805 (1)

TOPLIS AND WOOLFIT, Upholders, No. 22, St. Paul's Church Yard. 1817 (2)
Being next door to No. 23 this firm may have been connected with the old
established business of the Bell family (*q.v.*).

TORBUT, —, Cabinet-maker, No. 12, Red Lion Street. 1803 (20)

TORRENT, GEORGE, Upholsterer, at *The Golden Ball*, Houndsditch. 1723 (6)

TOULMIN AND KERR, Upholstery warehouse, No. 28, Brokers Row, Moorfields. 1803 (20)

TOWLER, JAMES, Upholder and Cabinet-maker, No. 25, Greek Street, Soho.
1796 (2)

TOWN AND EMANUEL, Manufacturerers of Buhl Marquetrie, Reisner and
Carved Furniture, No. 103, New Bond Street. 1839 (1, 2)

See page 193

SIZE OF ORIGINAL 4⅝" × 3"

See page 190

SIZE OF ORIGINAL 4⅝" × 3"

SIZE OF ORIGINAL $3\frac{7}{8}'' \times 5\frac{7}{8}''$

See page 193

SIZE OF ORIGINAL $4\frac{1}{4}'' \times 6''$

See page 193

TOWNE, LAURENCE, Upholster, Cornhill Ward. 1640 (16)

TOWNSEND, JOHN, Cabinet-maker, at *The Cabinet*, in the Minories.
1725 (6)

TOWNSEND, WILLIAM, Upholder, in Charles Street, near Grosvenor Square.
1749–74 (3)

TOWNSEND, WILLIAM, Upholsterer, in Wimpole Street. 1792 (2)

TRAHERNE, EDWARD, Cabinet-maker, employed by Charles II (address unrecorded). *c.* 1660 (64)

TREGOE, JOHN, Cabinet-maker, at *The Hand and Chair*, the East end of St. Paul's. 1749 (5)

TREHERN, GEORGE, Cabinet-maker and Upholsterer, No. 12, Charlotte Street, Rathbone Place. 1817–25 (1, 2)
In Drake Street, Red Lion Square. (1)

TRIGGEY, JOHN, Cabinet-maker and Upholder, No. 19, Butcher Hall Lane, Newgate Street. 1817 (2)

TROLTEN, JOHN, Upholsterer (address unrecorded). 1750–56 (8)

TROTTER, JOHN, Upholder and Cabinet-maker, appointed Upholder to George II, No. 43, Frith Street, Soho. 1755–92 (2, 8)

TROUGHTON, NATHANIEL, Upholsterer, at *The Lamb*, under the Royal Exchange, in Cornhill. 1705 (33)

TUBB, JOHN, Upholsterer and Cabinet-maker, No. 11, Catherine Street.
1783 (2)

TUCKER, JOHN, Upholder, at *The Angel*, in Houndsditch. 1753 (5)

TUCKER, THOMAS, Upholsterer, Somerset Street East. 1792 (2, 20)
No. 24, Hatton Street. 1803

TUCKER AND BRAITHWAITE, Upholders, High Holborn. 1768–72 (2)

TUCKER AND LITTLE, Upholders, No. 315, High Holborn. 1790–96 (2)

TUELLY, CHARLES, Cabinet-maker and Upholder, No. 49, Kenton Street, Brunswick Square. 1817 (2)

TULL, SAMUEL, Upholder, Parish of St. Ann's, Westminster. 1710 (5)

TURING, WILLIAM, Looking-glass and Cabinet-maker, at *The Eagle and Child*, in Bedford Street, Covent Garden. before 1721 (5)
Removed to the Strand, "over against the New Exchange, two doors from *The Half Moon* Tavern." 1723–26 (5, 49)
From the year 1721 he was in partnership with JOHN GUMLEY (*q.v.*) and in 1729 he was working with Gumley's widow when they were dismissed from the employment of the Great Wardrobe. (56)

TURLEY, —, Cabinet-maker, in Lamb's Conduit Street, Red Lion Square.
1803 (20)

TURNER, —, Upholsterer, at *The Royal Tent*, in Compton Street, Soho.
1721 (5)

TURNER, —, Cabinet-maker, in Dean Street, Soho.   died 1752 (61)

TURNER, —, Upholder and Tent maker, No. 19, Providence Row, Moorfields.
1790–93 (2)

TURNER, —, *see* WILKINSON AND TURNER.   1790–93 (2)

TURNER, HENRY, Upholder and Cabinet-maker, No. 132, New Bond Street.
1790–96 (2)

    Later TURNER, SMITH AND CO., at above.   1803 (20)

TURNER, J. AND H., Upholders and Cabinet-makers, No. 139, New Bond
Street.   1813–40 (2)

TURNER, JOHN, Cabinet-maker, in High Holborn.   1763 (2)

TURNER, JOHN, Upholder, in Searle Street, Lincoln's Inn Fields.
1790–93 (2)

TURNER, JOHN, Cabinet-maker, No. 16, Titchfield Street, Marylebone.
1803 (20)

TURNER, RICHARD, Upholster, in Henrietta Street.   1783–84 (2)

TURNER (TURNOR or TURNOUR), THOMAS, Cabinet-maker, at *The Two
Golden Balls*, near James Street, in Long Acre.   1746–48 (1, 5)

TURNER, WILLIAM, Carver and Gilder, No. 40, Snow Hill.   1790–93 (2)

TURNER AND HULLOH, Cabinet-makers, No. 27, Brokers Row, Moorfields.
1803 (20)

TURNER, SMITH AND CO., *see* HENRY TURNER.   1803 (20)

TURNLY, —, Chair maker, in Garden Row, near the Obelisk (in Blackfriars
Road).   1803 (20)

TURNOUR, THOMAS, *see* THOMAS TURNER.

TUTOFT, CHARLES, Cabinet-maker, in Broad Way, Westminster.   1749 (3)

TUTOP, CHARLES (*cf*. TUTOFT), Upholder, Tothill Street, Westminster.
1755–93 (2, 18)

TYLER, JOSEPH, Cabinet-maker, Carver and Upholder, in Wardour Street,
Soho.   1763 (2)

TYSSE, JAMES, Cabinet-maker, No. 29, Chancery Lane.   1790–93 (2)
Or

TYTE, JAMES, as above.   1796 (2)

ULLMAN, —, Cabinet-maker, at the corner of Little Wild Street, Lincoln's
Inn Fields.   1747 (5)

UNDERDOWN, PHILIP, Cabinet-maker, No. 254, Strand.   1790–93 (2)

UNDERWOOD, RICHARD, Cabinet-maker, Villiers Street, York Buildings, in
the Strand.   1763–64 (2)

UNDERWOOD, THOMAS, Cabinet-maker, at above. 1774 (3)

VAN DEN HELM, A "Dutch table maker," over against Compton Street, by St. Ann's Wall, Soho. 1711 (5)

VANDERGUCHT, G., Carver, Gilder and Picture dealer (address not recorded) 1761 (1), 1779 (23)

VAN HAESEN, Cabinet-maker, in Jermyn Street. 1737 (5)

VAN RUYVEN, SAMUEL, Cabinet-maker, at the sign of *The George*, on the South side of St. Paul's Church Yard. 1722–28 (5, 6)

VAUGHAN, —, Upholder, in Prince's Street, Leicester Fields. 1760 (5)

VAUGHAN, GEORGE, Chair maker ((?) sedan chairs), to the Prince of Wales, in Coventry Street, near Haymarket. 1730–47 (5)

VAUGHAN, SAMUEL, Sedan Chair maker, Coventry Street, Piccadilly. 1762–72 (2, 7)

VAUT, THOMAS, Upholster, Coventry Street. 1749 (3)

VENTRIS, WILLIAM, Upholder, in Salisbury Court, Fleet Street. 1724–31 (5)
In Essex Street. 1734 (5)

VERNON, EDWARD, Cabinet-maker, Long Acre. 1709 (4)

VERNON, MATTHEW, Upholder, in Ludgate Street. 1724–34 (3)

VERNON, THOMAS, Upholder and Cabinet-maker, No. 22, Piccadilly. 1779 (1, 2)

VICKERS AND RUTLEDGE, Upholders and Cabinet-makers, successors to Thomas Bailey [*q.v.*] at their manufactory in Conduit Street, Hanover Square. *c.* 1775–80 (1)
(Plate, page 182)
See also WILLIAM RUTLEDGE.

VILE, WILLIAM, AND COBB, JOHN, Cabinet-makers and Upholsterers to His Majesty, (No. 72) the corner of St. Martin's Lane and Long Acre. 1750–67 (1, 2, 8, 56)
At the beginning of the reign of George III the firm of Vile and Cobb held a pre-eminent position among the cabinet-makers to the Royal Household, due mainly to the superb quality of Vile's cabinet work and the individual character of his designs. The prices they charged for their work were notoriously high, but nevertheless the firm maintained a flourishing business among the aristocracy for many years. The Strawberry Hill Accounts show that the firm was supplying furniture to Horace Walpole between 1760 and 1771. The superb four poster (*see* under COBB) and other items in the Strawberry Hill Accounts are all referred to as "Pd. *Vile's* bill for etc." Vile died in 1767 and Cobb carried on the business until his death in 1778. The trade card of WILLIAM BEAUMONT (*q.v.*) describes him as "nephew and successor to the late Mr. Vialls" [*sic*] but the card of STRICKLAND AND JENKINS (*q.v.*) also states that Strickland was Mr. Vile's nephew and that Jenkins was late foreman to Mr. Cobb. (1)
(Plates, pages 246, 247)

VILLENEAU, CHARLES, Upholder, the corner of Duke Street, in Piccadilly.
1748 (5)

VILLENEAU, JOSIAS, Upholsterer, at *The Golden Leg*, near St. Thomas'
Hospital, Southwark.   1733 (5)
Also against *Ye Bull's Head* Tavern, in the Borough of Southwark.
c. 1740 (1)

VIPOND, NICHOLAS, Upholsterer, No. 87, Bartholomew Close.   1760–74 (5)

WADE, WILLIAM, Carver and Gilder, No. 86, Leadenhall Street.
1802–26 (1, 2)

(Plate, page 185)

WADE, WILLIAM JOHN, Carver and Gilder, No. 86, Leadenhall Street.
1827–39 (2)

WAKE, —, Upholsterer, in Long Acre.   1730 (5)

WAKELIN, DANIEL, Cabinet-maker, at *The Cabinet*, in Knave's Acre, near
Golden Square.   1763 (1)

WAKELING, GILES, Upholsterer to the Admiralty, No. 36, Gerrard Street,
Soho.   1832–39 (2)

WAKELING, THOMAS, Upholsterer to the Admiralty, No. 36, Gerrard Street,
Soho.   1825–32 (1, 2)

WALBANCKE, EDWARD, Upholder, No. 1, Rathbone Place, Oxford Street.
1774 (2)
No. 24, Oxford Street.   1783

WALBANCKE AND SMITH, Upholders, No. 4, John Street, Oxford Street.
1790–94 (2)

WALDRON, THOMAS, Upholder, No. 11, Catherine Street, Strand.
1784–96 (2, 5)
"Patent bedsteads upon a new and elastic construction," Broad Street, Carnaby
Market.   1803 (20)

WALKER, —, Upholsterer, in Leadenhall Street.   1748 (5)

WALKER, G., Cabinet-maker and Upholsterer, No. 134, St. John's Road,
Clerkenwell.   *c.* 1830 (1)

WALKER, JA., Cabinet-maker, No. 122, Jermyn Street.   1794 (2)

WALKER, JOHN, Upholsterer, No. 246, Shoreditch.   1790 (2)

WALKER, JOSEPH, Upholsterer and Bedding manufacturer, No. 96, High
Holborn.   1826 (2)
No. 109, High Holborn, opposite New Turnstile.   1832–39 (1, 2)

WALKER, MARTIN, Cabinet-maker, No. 18, Pitfield Street, Hoxton. 1817 (2)

WALKER, MELLICANT, Upholder, No. 71, Fleet Market.   1790–1803 (2, 20)

WALKER, SAMUEL, Upholder, No. 17, Aldgate Within.   1770–74 (2)

SIZE OF ORIGINAL $2\frac{1}{2}'' \times 3\frac{1}{4}''$ *See page* 197

SIZE OF ORIGINAL $3'' \times 7\frac{5}{8}''$ *See page* 197

CHARLES WHARTON

Picture Frame Maker.

at the Crown & Two Sceptres in Queen-street in the Park, Southwark. Makes & sells all Sorts of Picture Frames, either in Gold, Lacquerd or Black, which Country Chapmen may be furnishd by Wholesale or Retail, at the lowest Prices.

We also has great Choice of Maps & Prints Ready Fram'd, and a variety of Paintings or Glass.

See page 198

SIZE OF ORIGINAL 5⅜″ × 3⅝″

Alex.ʳ Wetherstone

CARPENTER, JOYNER and TURNER,

at y.ᵉ Painted Floor Cloth & Brush in Portugal street, Near Lincolns Inn Back Gate.

Sells all sorts of Floor Cloths, Hair Cloths, List Carpets, Royal & other Matting, Mahogany Caterns with Brass hoops, Desks & other Stands, Writers hand boards, Tea Boards, Tea Trays, Tea Chests, Back Gammon Tables & Draught Boards, Childs Bed China Plate & other Baskets, Cradles & Chairs, Oval Frames, & all sorts of Lignum Vitæ & Tunbridge Wares, Mops, Brooms, Brushes, Sieves, Hampers, Bellows, Wood Platters, Bowls, Pails, Washing Tubs, Coal & Corn Measures, Spunge, Iron and Tin Coal Scoops Sand Scuttles & Horses for Cloths, Fire Skreens, Plate Racks, Umbrellas, Cotton & Wool for Quilting, Hair Lines, Cords, Pack, Thread, Black Balls & Turnery Wares of all Sorts, Likewise English & Dutch Toys wholesale and Retail, at the most Reasonable Rates.

See page 198

SIZE OF ORIGINAL 7¾″ × 5⅛″

WALKER, WILLIAM, Cabinet-maker and Upholsterer, No. 7, James Street, Covent Garden.   1774–1814 (1, 2, 3)

WALKINGTON, *see* JENNINGS AND WALKINGTON.

WALLACE, J., Upholder and Cabinet-maker, No. 5, Great Portland Street.
                                    1803 (20)

WALLE, HENRY, Upholder, Carver and Gilder, at *The Royal Pavilion*, No. 109, St. Martin's Lane.   1786 (1)

WALLIN, RICHARD, Upholder, at the shop of Mrs. Bird, Turner, Without Newgate.   (1)
    See WILLIAM BIRD.   1724
                    (Plate, page 186)

WALLIS, —, Cabinet-maker, at *The Elephant*, opposite the South Door, No. 66, St. Paul's Church Yard.   1757 (33)

WALLIS, CHARLES, Upholsterer, at *The Crown and Cushion*, in New Bond Street.   1722 (6)
    "One of the earliest shops to be occupied in New Bond Street, the latter an extension, north, of Old Bond Street, was built *circa* 1721, in which year it is rated for the first time in St. Martin-in-the-Fields."
                    (Wheatley and Cunningham's *London Past and Present*.)

WALLIS, CHRISTOPHER, Cabinet-maker, at *The Blue Flower-de-Luce*, next Drury Lane, Long Acre.   c. 1760 (1)
    Formerly in Dirty Lane (or Charles Street), Long Acre.   1749 (3)
                    (Plate, page 186)

WALSH AND MOODY, Upholders, No. 277, High Holborn.   1783 (2)

WALTER, JOHN, Upholsterer, at *The White Lyon*, Little Old Bailey.   1724 (6)

WALTER, —, Upholsterer, in Kensington.   1749 (5)

WALTER, THOMAS, Upholder, Kensington.   1776 (7)

WALTERS, DAVID, Cabinet-maker, in Grosvenor's Mews.   1749–55 (5, 18)

WARD, CHARLES AND CO., Carvers and Gilders, Nos. 3 and 4, Dean Street, Soho.   c. 1800 (1)

WARD, JAMES K., Carver and Gilder, No. 66, King Street, St. Ann's, Soho.
                                    c. 1780 (1)

WARD, JOHN, Upholder, in Red Lion Square.   1727 (3)

WARD, THOMAS, Upholsterer, at *The Boar's Head*, in Cornhill.
                                    1690–96 (5)

WARING, —, Carver and Gilder, No. 139, Long Acre.   c. 1780 (1)
    The same card with the address altered reads: No. 69, Margaret Street, Cavendish Square.   c. 1790–1803 (1, 20)
                    (Plate, page 185)

WARING, BASIL, Chair and Cabinet-maker, next door but one to *The White Hart* Brew House, in King Street, Bloomsbury.   1740 (5, 61)

WARNER, HENRY, Upholder (address not recorded).   1705 (9)

WARNSLEY, JOHN, Cabinet-maker, No. 22, Shug Lane.   1790–93 (2)

WARREN, EDWARD, Upholsterer, at *The Crown*, in Wych Street.

1724–26 (2, 3)

WARREN AND CO., Proprietors of a Warehouse, for all sorts of elegant Furniture, Pictures, China, etc., in Vine Street, Piccadilly.   1763 (2)

WARREN AND RANDALL, Upholsters, No. 18, Coventry Street, Haymarket.

1796 (2)

WARREN AND VENSON, Turners and Carvers of oval frames, No. 9, New Round Court, in the Strand.   1796 (2)

WARWICK, JOSEPH, Turner, at *The Chair*, Upper Shadwell.   1721 (6)

WATERFALL, ROBERT, Pinker, Cutter and Raiser of satin, at *The Rising Sun*, in Bedford Street.   (?) 1711 (1)

WATKINS, HENRY, Upholsterer, No. 63, Holborn Hill.   1790–93 (2)

WATKINS, T., Upholder and Cabinet-maker, No. 39, Berwick Street, Soho.

1817 (2)

WATSON, —, Carver and Gilder, By His Majesty's Royal Letters Patent, at *The King's Arms*, No. 21, Long Acre.   *c.* 1780 (1)

WATSON, —, Cabinet-maker, No. 21, Wardour Street, Soho.   1803 (20)

WATSON, DAVID, Upholsterer, No. 51, Parliament Street.   1803 (20)

WATSON, DAVID AND SON, Upholsterers, No. 14, Bridge Street, Westminster.

1774–96 (2, 3)

WATSON, ELIZABETH, Embroideress, The Corner House of Cherry Tree Alley on Bunhill, by the New Artillery (Ground).   1696 (5)

WATSON, ELIZABETH, Embroideress, at the sign of *The Wrought Bed*, in Sword Bearers' Alley, in Chiswell Street.   1706 (5)
"Wrought beds from £7 to £40 per bed, with all sorts of fine chain-stitch work...."

WATSON, ELIZABETH, Embroideress, in Crown Court, in Old Change, near St. Paul's.   1710 (5)
"Wrought beds, curtains and quilts."

WATSON, GEORGE, Cabinet-maker, No. 36, Fetter Lane.   1817 (2)

WATSON, J., Cabinet-maker and Upholder, No. 14, Green Street, Theobalds Road.   1817 (2)

WATSON, JOHN, Upholsterer, at *The Red Lyon*, over against the Royal Exchange, Cornhill.   1689–97, died 1722 (2, 33, 49)

WATSON, JOHN, Upholsterer, in Wood Street.   1727–30 (3, 5)
In King Street.   1734

Willerton & Roberts

TURNERS

to their Royal Highness's y.ͤ Duke of Gloster. Pr: Henry & Pr: Fred.ᵏ &

Toy Makers;

to his Royal Highness the Prince of Wales &c at y.ͤ Original Manufactory
Y.ͤ Corner of Conduit Street in Old Bond Street Sell Wholesale & Retail with great Variety of Dutch Toys
Usefull & Ornamental Trinkets, & every Article in the Toy Way

NB as this Manufactory is opend on a new Construction by y.ͤ Original Makers
'tis hoped 'twill call the Attention of the Curious as no Pains or Expence
will be spared to give Satisfaction

TOYS and TRINKETS mended at the SHORTEST NOTICE.

SIZE OF ORIGINAL 7″ × 6″

See page 203

Will.ᵐ Witton Upholsterer
Appraiser & Undertaker
at the Royal Bed, on S.ᵗ Margarets Hill
In the Borough of
SOUTHWARK

Makes & sells all sorts of Upholstery
Goods Wholesale & Retail viz Fashionable
Standing Beds, Feather Beds, Quilts
Rugged Blankets Coverlets Flanders
& English Ticking Also Leather Cane &
Matted Chairs at very Reasonable Prices.

See page 206

SIZE OF ORIGINAL 6¾″ × 4¾″

John Whitcomb
Cabinet-Maker and Upholsterer,
at the Crown & Cushion in Princes Street,
near the end of Compton Street, S.ᵗ Anns Soho.
LONDON.

Makes & Sells all sorts of Cabinet Chair and Uphol-
stery work, in the best manner & on the lowest Terms.
Likewise all Sorts of Blankets, Quilts, Cotton Coun-
terpanes, Coverlids & Bed-ticks, & Also ready made
Feather beds, Mattrasses, Bedsteads, & Furnitures made as
well as if bespoke; and as cheap as at any Warehouse.
All sorts of Window Blinds & Spring Curtains made
and Paper Hangings in general.
N.B. Goods carefully Appraised, Bought and Sold.
& Funerals performed at reasonable rates.

See page 199

SIZE OF ORIGINAL 6⅝″ × 4⅝″

WATSON, PETER, AND MARTEN, —, Cabinet-makers, No. 12, Bartholomew Close, West Smithfield. 1790–93 (1, 2)

(Plate, page 191)

WATSON, THOMAS, Cabinet-maker, in Queen Street (Westminster). 1749 (3)

WATTS, JAMES, Upholsterer, No. 3, Brokers Row, Moorfields. 1790–93 (2)

WEALE, DANIEL, Upholder, No. 50, Snow Hill. 1779 (2)
No. 23, Lower Holborn. 1783–84

WEATHERALL, JOHN, Upholder, No. 26, Haymarket. 1774–94 (1, 2, 3)
No. 52, Dean Street, Soho. 1796–1803 (20)

WEBB, CHARLES, Cabinet-maker, No. 6, Beech Street, Barbican. 1790–93 (2)

WEBB, I. AND M., Bedstead and Cabinet-makers, Old Bethlem. 1790 (2)

WEBB, JOHN, Upholsterer and Cabinet-maker, No. 8, Old Bond Street. 1840 (2)

WEBB, ROBERT, Upholsterer, at *The Queen's Head and Three Tents*, in Bedford Street, Covent Garden. 1712–24 (1, 3, 15)

(Plate, page 191)

WEBB, TEASDALE, Wholesale Upholder, No. 29, Gracechurch Street. 1774–84 (2)

Followed by WEBB AND LAWFORD (*q.v.*).

WEBB, WILLIAM, Upholsterer and Cabinet-maker, No. 227, Strand. 1790–96 (2)

WEBB, WILLIAM, near the Turnpike, Newington, Surrey.
"Maker of Yew Tree, Gothic and Windsor chairs, China and Rural Seats, single and double angle and Garden Machines, Children's Chaises . . . N.B. For Exportation." (*Cf.* WILLIAM WOOD.) 1792–1808 (1, 2)
He was succeeded by R. Webb (later Webb and Bruce). 1811

WEBB AND BRUCE, Windsor and Garden and Rustic Chair Manufactory, Kings Road, Chelsea. 1817–23 (2)
And at Hammersmith.

WEBB AND LAWFORD, Wholesale Upholsterers, No. 29, Gracechurch Street. 1783–96 (2)

WEBB AND SAMPSON, Wholesale Upholsterers, Threadneedle Street. 1763–65 (2)
No. 1, George Street, Mansion House. 1768–70 (2)

WEBSTER, JO., Upholsterer and Cabinet-maker, No. 21, Poland Street, Oxford Road. 1794 (2)
Great Portland Street. 1796 (2)

WEBSTER, JOHN, Cabinet-maker, Mercer Street. 1774 (3)

WEIGHT, JOHN, Cabinet and Chair maker, Savoy Steps, Strand.   1796 (2)

WEIR, DAVID, Cabinet-maker, in Silver Court, Silver Street.   1803 (20)

WELCH, JAMES, Glass grinder and Looking-glass maker, behind *The Rose and Crown*, in the Broad Way, Black-Fryers.   1724 (5)

WELCH, JOSEPH, Upholder, Shoreditch.   1724–34 (3)

WELLS, GEORGE, Upholsterer, in Castle Street, Long Acre.   1790–94 (2)

WELLS, JAMES, Upholder, in Paternoster Row.   1724–27 (3)

WELLS, JOHN, Upholsterer, at *The King's Head*, end of Fetter Lane, Fleet Street.   1685–89 (1, 33)

WEST, CHARLES, AND SON, Upholsterers, No. 35, Bucklersbury.   1790–93 (2)

WEST, JOHN, Cabinet-maker, King Street, Covent Garden.

    1745 (36), 1749 (3), died 1758

This is probably the house that was occupied by Thomas Arne, upholsterer (*q.v.*), father of Dr. Arne, the composer, where the four "Indian Chiefs" were accommodated (*c.* 1710). Nicholas Rowe, the Poet Laureate, lived and died here (1718), and "at his lodgings at Mr. West's, the cabinet maker in King Street, Covent Garden," David Garrick was living here in 1743–45. West died in 1758 and was succeeded by SAMUEL NORMAN (*q.v.*) of Whittle, Norman and Mayhew. William Ince (*see* INCE AND MAYHEW) was one of John West's apprentices.   (31)

WEST, STEPHEN, Upholsterer, at the corner of Blackmoor Street, in Drury Lane.   1720 (5)

WESTWOOD, M., Upholsterer, No. 32, Crooked Lane.   1803 (20)

WETHERELL AND WILSON, Carvers and Gilders, No. 64, Leadenhall Street.   1790 (2)

WETHERSTONE, ALEXANDER, Carpenter, Joyner and Turner, at *The Painted Floor Cloth and Brush*, in Portugal Street, near Lincoln's Inn Back Gate.   1760–65 (1, 2)

(Plate, page 192)

WHALLEY, THOMAS, Cabinet-maker, Rose Street, Long Acre.   1774 (3)

WHARTON, CHARLES, Carver and Gilder, at *The Crown and Two Sceptres*, in Queen Street, in the Park, Southwark.   *c.* 1750 (1)

(Plate, page 192)

WHEATLEY AND RIDSDALES, Upholsterers, at *The Lamb*, in Clement's Lane.   *c.* 1760

WHEATLEY AND RIDSDALES, Wholesale Upholsterers, No. 25, Clement's Lane, Lombard Street.   1760–77 (2)

WHEATLEY, RISDALES AND BELL, Wholesale Upholsterers, No. 25, Clement's Lane.   1768 (1, 2)

WHEELER, FELSTEAD, Upholsterer, No. 73, Old Broad Street, opposite New Court.   1763–70 (2)

WHEELER, RICHARD, Upholder, No. 26, Ivy Lane. 1783 (2)
    No. 151, Fleet Street. 1784–96

WHITAKER, ANN, Upholsteress, No. 19, Castle Street, Leicester Fields.
    1794 (2)

WHITBY, JOHN, Joiner (address unrecorded). 1661 (8, 64)
    Supplied couch and chair frames to the Royal Household.

WHITBY, JOHN, Upholster, in Mount Street. 1749 (3)

WHITBY, JOHN, "Cabinet-maker and Upholsterer of London." 1756 (52)
    He is thus referred to in Oliver Brackett's *English Furniture Illustrated* as making a set of chairs for Lord Langdale, but probably as of Mount Street (*see* above).

WHITCOMB, JOHN, Cabinet-maker and Upholsterer, at *The Crown and Cushion*, in Prince's Street, near the end of Compton Street, St. Ann's, Soho. *c.* 1760 1774–76, (1, 3)
    A billhead of 1776 with address in Prince's Street, opposite Gerrard Street, Soho, was made out to Revd. Mr. Drake, of Shardeloes, Amersham, for a goose feather bed and bolster, £7 10s. od.

(Plate, page 196)

WHITE, —, Cabinet-maker, next door to *The Cross Keys* Tavern, in Holborn.
    1748 (5)

WHITE, JEREMIAH, Upholder, No. 12, Wardour Street, St. Ann's, Soho.
    1790–93 (1, 2)

WHITE, JOHN, Cabinet-maker, in Long Acre. 1748 (5)
    The name of a John White, cabinet-maker, appears in the list of subscribers to Chippendale's *Director*. 1755

WHITE, JOHN, Cabinet-maker and Upholsterer, near Slaughter's Coffee House, in St. Martin's Lane. *c.* 1760 (1)

WHITE, JOHN, Upholder, in Queen Street, Westminster. 1784–93 (2)

WHITE, JOHN, Upholder, No. 3, Storey's Gate, Westminster. 1803 (20)

WHITE, NATHANIEL, Cabinet-maker, at *The Desk and Bookshelf*, ye corner of Thavies Inn Gate, Holborn. *c.* 1750 (1)

WHITE, RICHARD, Cabinet-maker and Upholsterer, No. 76, Oxford Street.
    1790–94 (2)

WHITE AND HICKMAN, Cabinet-makers, in Houndsditch. 1740 (5)
    A serious fire occurred on these premises and the damage was assessed at £3,000. "Mr. Bylis White, an eminent cabinet-maker in Houndsditch, died having acquired a genteel fortune." 1751 (5)

WHITEFOOT, PHINEAS, Upholster, in Warwick Street, by Golden Square.
    1733 (5)

WHITEHEAD, T., Cabinet-maker, No. 43, Aldermanbury. 1817 (2)

WHITEHORNE, RICHARD, Upholsterer, late partner of T. NASH and E. HALL [*q.v.*], at *The Royal Bed*, on Holborn Bridge. died 1740 (5)

WHITEHORNE, WILLIAM, Cabinet-maker (address unrecorded).   (5)

In an advertisement of sale of stock (1740) he is referred to as "well known for his curious Workmanship in Mahogany and Walnut-Tree."

WHITING, SAMUEL, Upholsterer, in Watling Street.   deceased 1748 (5)

WHITING, SAMUEL, Cabinet manufactory, No. 140, Houndsditch.   1817 (2)

WHITLEY, THOMAS, Cabinet-maker and Upholder, No. 29, John Street, Tottenham Court Road.   1817 (2)

WHITROE, ABRAHAM, Cabinet-maker, in Peter Street [Westminster].

1749 (3)

WHITTLE, JAMES, Carver and Gilder, King Street, Covent Garden.

1743–61 (2, 5, 56)

See WHITTLE, NORMAN AND MAYHEW.

WHITTLE, JAMES, NORMAN, SAMUEL, AND MAYHEW, JOHN.   1758 (2, 5, 56)

"Having purchased the lease of the late Mr. West's [*q.v.*] house and warehouses in King Street [Covent Garden], beg leave to acquaint the Nobility, Gentry and Others that they continue to carry on the Upholstery and Cabinet as well as the Carving and Gilding Businesses in all their branches. . . ." James Whittle is first heard of as a carver and gilder in 1742–43 when he supplied some tables and mirrors to the Earl of Cardigan. Later he was joined by Norman and they were then working for the Duke of Bedford at Woburn and at Bedford House, Bloomsbury, in 1757. Mayhew's connection with the firm must have been a short one as we find him in partnership with Ince (*q.v.*) in 1759 at Broad Street, Carnaby Market. Whittle is further traceable by his work for the Earl of Leicester at Holkham in 1761. Norman set up for himself in Soho Square after the King Street premises had been burnt down in 1758.   1758

WICK, CULLUM, Upholder, in Bishopsgate Street.   1727 (3)

WICKS, CHARLES, Upholsterer, at the sign of *The Ship*, on Snow Hill.

1713 (5)

WICKSTEED, G., Cabinet and Bedstead maker, No. 10, Broad Street, Carnaby Market.   1817 (2)

WIGGAN, RICHARD, Cabinet-maker, in Silver Street, Golden Square. 1749 (3)

Canaletto, when in London, lodged at Mr. Wiggan's and it was there that he exhibited *A View in St. James's Park* in 1749 and views of the Thames in 1751.

(23)

WILD, DANIEL, Cabinet-maker, in St. Paul's Church Yard.   *c.* 1725

(Plate, page 235)

WILDGOOSE, JOHN, Cabinet-maker, in North Audley Street, Grosvenor Square.   1745 (5)

WILKIE, JOHN, Cabinet and Chair maker, No. 1, Norfolk Street, Fitzroy Square.   1817 (2)

WILKINSON, CHARLES, Cabinet-maker, No. 21, St. Paul's Church Yard.

1760–72 (2)

Later WILKINSON AND TURNER (*q.v.*).

Stephen Wood
At the CABINET near the
Bridge foot Southwark:
Makes and sells, all sorts of
Cabinet work, Looking Glasses,
Peer Glasses and Sconces;
Where Gentlemen, Merchants, &
Country Chapmen, may have the
best of Goods, Wholesale or Retail
at the lowest Prices.
N.B. Old Glasses mended or Alter'd.

SIZE OF ORIGINAL 5⅝" × 3⅝"

See page 206

James Woodroff
Upholder Undertaker & Sworn Appraiser,
at the Royal Bed & Blanket Warehouse, near
the Spread-Eagle Inn, in Grace-church Street,
London.

Sells all sorts of Upholstery & Cabinet Goods, four Post & other Bedstead,
with Damasks, Harrateens, Cheneys, Linceys & Washing Furniture: Feather
Beds, Blankets, Quilts, Cotton & Linnen Counterpains, Rugs, Coverlids, Turkey
English & other Carpets; Paper-Hangings; Mahogany & Wallnut-Tree Chest of Drawrs,
Dining, Drawing & Card Tables, Mahogany Wallnut-Tree & other Chairs,
Looking Glasses &c. Wholesale & Retail, at the Lowest Prices.
—— Likewise Funerals Compleatly Furnished. ——

See page 206

SIZE OF ORIGINAL 7" × 5⅛"

201

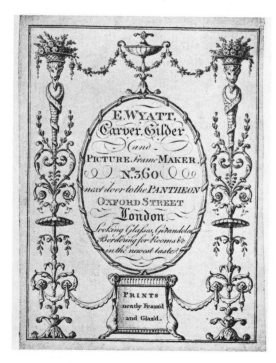

SIZE OF ORIGINAL 4⅝″ × 2¾″ *See page* 209

SIZE OF ORIGINAL 3¾″ × 2¾″   *See page* 210

SIZE OF ORIGINAL 4⅝″ × 6¾″

See page 204

WILKINSON, JOHN HENRY, Wholesale Upholsterer, No. 25, Budge Row.
1796 (2)

WILKINSON, JOSHUA, Upholsterer, at the sign of *The Easy Chair*, No. 7, Brokers Row, Moorfields, at the corner of Bell Square, between Old Bethlem and New Broad Street. 1784 (1, 2)
And at No. 107, Cheapside. 1784

WILKINSON, JOSHUA, junior, Upholder, No. 107, Cheapside. 1784 (2)
No. 7, Brokers Row. 1785

WILKINSON, THOMAS, Looking-glass maker, in Stonecutter Street, near Fleet Ditch. 1725 (5)

WILKINSON, THOMAS, AND CO., Cabinet-makers, No. 9, Brokers Row, Moorfields. 1814–17 (2)
Nos. 7, 8, 9 and 10, Brokers Row, also at No. 1, Finsbury Square.
1823–27 (2)

WILKINSON, WILL[M] AND THO[S], Cabinet-makers, Nos. 9 and 10, Brokers Row, Moorfields. 1790–1811 (1, 2)

WILKINSON, W., Upholsterer, No. 14, Ludgate Hill. 1814–38 (2)

WILKINSON AND TURNER, Upholders and Cabinet-makers, No. 21, St. Paul's Church Yard. 1790–93 (2)
See also CHARLES WILKINSON.

WILKINSON AND WORNUM, No. 315, Oxford Street. 1812
An upright piano by this firm is illustrated in Ackerman's *Repository of Arts* for January–June 1812.

WILKS, —, Turner and Maker of Kentish cricket bats and balls, No. 220, Strand (burnt out from No. 234). 1778 (1)

WILLERS AND WARNER, Wholesale Upholders, in Leicester Square.
1790–93 (2)

WILLERTON AND ROBERTS, Turners to their R.H.H. the Duke of Gloster, Prince Henry and Prince Frederick. Toymakers to H.R.H. Prince of Wales. At ye corner of Conduit Street, in Old Bond Street. 1768 (1)
(Plate, page 195)

WILLEY, SAMUEL, Upholder, in Chancery Lane. 1749 (5)

WILLIAMS, —, Cabinet-maker, in Glass-House Yard, Aldersgate Bars.
1747 (5)

WILLIAMS, CHARLES, Upholsterer, Leicester Fields. 1709 (4)

WILLIAMS, CHARLES, Upholder, in Red Lion Street. 1727 (3)

WILLIAMS, G., Cabinet-maker and Upholder, No. 69, King Street, Golden Square. 1817 (2)

WILLIAMS, HENRY, Joiner and Chair maker (address not recorded).   (1)
>   He supplied chairs to Sir Paul Methuen in 1728 and various chairs and stools
>   to the Royal Palaces from 1729 to 1758.   1728–58 (8, 56)

WILLIAMS, JOS., Cabinet-maker, opposite Beaufort Buildings, in the Strand.
>   deceased 1760 (61)

WILLIAMS, MORGAN, Joiner, in King Street, Covent Garden.   1803 (20)

WILLIAMS, RICHARD, Cabinet and Chair maker (Sedan), Cucumber Court,
>   Shipyard [by *The Ship* tavern] in the Strand.   1749 (3)

WILLIAMS, ROBERT, Upholder and Cabinet-maker, in Bow Street. 1774–77 (2)
>   No. 28, King Street, Covent Garden.   1779–84 (2)
>   No. 40, King Street, Covent Garden.   1790–93 (2)
>   *See also* THOMAS WILLIAMS.

WILLIAMS, THOMAS, at his Cabinet, Upholstery and Carpet warehouse, in
>   Bow Street, Covent Garden.   1763 (1, 2)
>   (Plate, page 202)

WILLIAMS, THOMAS, Cabinet-maker and Upholsterer, Hermitage Bridge.
>   1768 (2)
>   No. 8, Great Tower Street.   1770–74 (1)

WILLIAMS, WILLIAM, Upholster, in St. Martin's Lane.   1749–55 (3, 18)

WILLIAMS, WILLIAM, Upholder, No. 13, Berwick Street, Soho. 1790–93 (2)

WILLIAMS, WILLIAM, Cabinet-maker, No. 4, Chapel Street, Spitalfields.
>   1790 (2)

WILLIAMSON, JOHN, Upholsterer, in Bedford Court, Covent Garden.
>   1790 (2)

WILLIS, JOHN, Cabinet-maker and Upholsterer, Hermitage Bridge. 1768 (2)

WILLIS, JOHN, Cabinet-maker, No. 19, St. Paul's Church Yard.
>   1770–92 (2)

WILLMOTT, W., Cabinet-maker, No. 53, Blackman Street, Southwark.
>   1794–96 (2)

WILLS, F., Cabinet-maker and Upholsterer, South Street, Southampton
>   Street, Pentonville.   (1)

WILLSON, —, Upholder and Cabinet-maker, No. 20, Aldersgate Street,
>   nearly opposite the Church. Remov'd from Jewin Street.   *c.* 1790 (1)
>   His trade-card announces that he sold Organs, Harpsichords and Piano Fortes
>   and likewise was a "Dealer in Coals."

WILMOTT, THOMAS, Cabinet-maker and Upholsterer, No. 16, John Street,
>   Oxford Street.   1802 (1)

WILSON, —, Cabinet-maker and Upholsterer, No. 90, Charlotte Street,
>   Fitzroy Square.   1811–14 (1, 2)
>   No. 6, Welbeck Street, corner of Wigmore Street.   1817–39 (1, 2)

WILSON, BENJAMIN, Upholder, No. 1, Brokers Row, Moorfields (later WILSON AND DAWES). 1790 (2)

WILSON, J., Cabinet-maker, No. 3, Walker's Court, Poultney Street. 1794 (2)

WILSON, J. WEATHERALL, Carver and Gilder, No. 64, Leadenhall Street. 1790–93 (2)

WILSON, JACOB, Cabinet-maker and Upholsterer, No. 90, Charlotte Street, Fitzroy Square. 1811–14 (1, 2)
Later with James Wilson of Welbeck Street.

WILSON, JAMES, Cabinet-maker, Castle Court (?) Leicester Square. 1749 (3)

WILSON, JAMES, Cabinet-maker and Upholsterer, No. 6, Welbeck Street, at corner of Wigmore Street. 1817–39 (1, 2)

WILSON, RICHARD AND ROBERT, Cabinet-makers, No. 93, Gray's Inn Lane. 1790–93 (2)

WILSON, SAMUEL AND W., Upholsterers, No. 144, High Street, Borough, near the Church. 1825–27 (1, 2)

WILSON, T., Cabinet-maker, No. 20, King Street, Borough. 1803 (20)
See also WILSON AND REED.

WILSON, WILLIAM, Carver, St. Mary's, Newington. 1767 (7)

WILSON AND BROWN, Cabinet-makers and Upholsterers, No. 405, Strand. 1770–77 (2)
No. 376, Strand. 1779–83 (2)
See also BROWN AND WILSON; WALTER WILSON AND CO.

WILSON, WALTER, AND CO., Cabinet-makers and Upholsterers, No. 376, Strand. 1774–96 (2, 3, 20)
Nos. 128 and 376, Strand. 1803
See also WILSON AND BROWN.

WILSON, WALTER, AND CO., Cabinet-makers and Upholsterers, No. 376, Strand. 1790–96 (1, 2)
No. 128, Strand. 1810

WILSON AND DAWES, Upholders, No. 1, Brokers Row, Moorfields. 1793 (2)
See also BENJAMIN WILSON.

WILSON AND READ, Cabinet-makers, Princes Street, Leicester Fields. 1790–93 (2)

WILSON AND REED, Cabinet-makers and Upholsterers, No. 20, King Street, Borough. 1790–93 (2)
No. 102, Borough High Street. 1794–96 (2)

WINSTANLEY, RICHARD, Upholsterer, No. 10, Paternoster Row, Cheapside. 1792–96 (2), 1803 (20)

WINTERTON, JOHN, Upholsterer, No. 78, Fleet Street. 1768–72 (2)

WINTON, HENRY, Upholder, Essex House, in the Strand.

deceased 1740 (5)

The last portion left standing of Essex House was finally demolished in 1777.

WISE, CHRISTOPHER, Upholster, in Queen Street, Golden Square. 1749 (3)

WITHERS, WILLIAM, AND DEEBLE, Upholders, No. 85, Cannon Street.
1790–96 (2)

WITHEY, SAMUEL, Cabinet-maker, No. 53, Leather Lane, Holborn. 1794 (2)

WITTON, WILLIAM, Upholsterer, at *The Royal Bed*, on St. Margaret's Hill, in the Borough of Southwark. *c.* 1750 (1)
(Plate, page 196)

WOLLASTON, —, Cabinet-maker, in Long Acre. *c.* 1710–20 (12, 62)
Wollaston is reputed to have made the earliest use of mahogany in this country. Dr. William Gibbons (*see D.N.B.*, 1649–1728), having received a consignment of this timber, commissioned Wollaston to make him a candle box of it and subsequently a bureau. A second mahogany bureau was made for the Duchess of Buckingham. The references to these personages suggest a date towards the end of the reign of Queen Anne or early in that of George I.

WOOD, EDWARD, Upholsterer, in Shug Lane. 1732 (5)

WOOD, EDWARD, Cabinet and Chair maker, No. 23, Old Silver Road, Old Street. 1817 (5)

WOOD, JOHN, Upholder, in Crown Court (Wardour Street). 1749 (3)

WOOD, RICHARD, Upholder, Fleet Ditch. 1724 (3), 1727 (5)

WOOD, STEPHEN, Cabinet and Looking-glass maker, at *The Cabinet*, near the Bridge Foot, Southwark. 1725 (1, 6)
(Plate, page 201)

WOOD, THOMAS, Bedstead maker, No. 122, Old Street, St. Luke's, near the Turnpike. *c.* 1790 (1)

WOOD, WILLIAM (address not given). (1)
A label found on a yew tree Windsor chair reads: "Maker of all sorts of yew tree Gothick and Windsor chairs, China and Rural seats, single and double angle, and Garden Machines, Children's Chaises . . . N.B. for exportation." *c.* 1800
See also WILLIAM WEBB.

WOODCROFT, — [(?) WOODROFFE, below], Upholder, at *The Cross Keys*, in Fleet Street. 1722 (5)

WOODROFF, JAMES, Upholder, at *The Royal Bed*, near the Spread Eagle Inn, in Gracechurch Street. 1764 (1, 2)
(Plate, page 201)
Name engraved on trade-card reads "James Woodroff," but the receipt on back of bill, *twice* written, is spelt James Woodroffe. The 1763 Directory gives James Woodroffe.

See page 211

SIZE OF ORIGINAL 6⅜" × 4⅝"

See page 211

SIZE OF ORIGINAL 6⅝" × 5"

208

The Coach and
LOOKING GLASS MANUFACTORY
By Lake Young
in James Street, Covent-Garden:
or at his Warehouse near the Pump in
WATLING STREET, LONDON.

Where Merchants, Captains of Ships, Country Chap-
men &c, may be supply'd on reasonable Terms with
all Sorts of Looking Glasses, Viz.t Sconces, Pier &
Chimney Glasses, Dressing Boxes & Swingers,
in Mahogany, Walnut-tree, & Painted, or in rich Carv'd
& Gilt Frames, in the neatest Taste & newest fashion.
All Sorts of Window Glass,
Wholesale and Retail, or for
Exportation.

SIZE OF ORIGINAL 8⅜″ × 6½″

See page 211

WOODROFFE, DANIEL, Upholsterer, at *The Cross Keys*, over against Serjeant's Inn, in Fleet Street. deceased 1724 (5)

WOODROFFE, DANIEL, Upholsterer, late of Panton Street. deceased 1749 (5)

WOODROSE, —, Upholsterer, at *The Sun*, in Fleet Street. 1702 (5)

WOODWARD, J., Cabinet-maker and Upholder, No. 121, Borough, Southwark. 1817 (2)

WOODWARD, WILLIAM, Upholsterer, at *Ye Crown and Cushion*, near Old Bedlam in Moorfields. *c.* 1750 (1)

WOOF, E., Chair and Cabinet-maker, in Old Street Road. 1817 (2)

WOOLASTON, —, *see* WOLLASTON.

WOOLF, BENJAMIN, Cabinet-maker, in Princes Street, near Covent Garden. 1688 (5)

WOOLFORD, J. JOHN, Upholster, in St. Paul's Church Yard. dated label 1772 (1)

WOOLLETT, HENRY, Upholder and Cabinet-maker, No. 33, Fore Street, Cripplegate. 1817 (2)

WOOLLEY, GEORGE, Cabinet and Upholstery manufactory, No. 196, Piccadilly. 1803–17 (2, 20)

WOOTOM, JOHN, Carver and Gilder, No. 5, Long Acre. 1790–93 (2)

WORNUM, *see* WILKINSON AND WORNUM.

WORSLEY, THOMAS, Cabinet-maker, in Glasshouse Street, Golden Square. 1790–93 (2)

WORTHY, JOHN, Cabinet-maker, Hemings Row. 1749 (3)

WORTLEY, WILLIAM, Cabinet-maker, in Whitechapel. 1774 (7)

WOSTER, THOMAS, Cabinet-maker, at *The White Swan*, in St. Paul's Church Yard. *c.* 1715, died 1736 (1)

He was in partnership with G. COXED (*q.v.*) at above, where they were followed by HENRY BELL (*q.v.*) and his successors.

WRAUGTON, ANN, MRS., Sale of Indian and Japanned cabinets, at *The Blue and White Balls*, in King Street, Covent Garden. 1694 (5)

WRIDE, WILLIAM, Cabinet manufacturer, No. 68, Curtain Road, Shoreditch. 1817 (2)

WRIGHT, —, Upholder, in Buckingham Street, York Buildings (Strand). 1747 (5)

WRIGHT, —, Carver and Gilder, No. 26, Leadenhall Street. 1794 (2)

WRIGHT, ABRAHAM, Upholsterer and Cabinet-maker, No. 410, Oxford Street, opposite Rathbone Place. 1796–1802 (1, 2)

(Plate, page 202)

WRIGHT, ADAM, Cabinet-maker and Upholsterer, No. 55, Long Acre. No. 51, Long Acre. 1774–93 (1, 2, 3)

WRIGHT, F. AND W., Upholsterers and Cabinet-makers, to H.M. Stamp Office, No. 410, Oxford Street, opposite Rathbone Place. 1803–1808 (1, 2)

WRIGHT, W., Upholsterer and Cabinet-maker, No. 410, Oxford Street, opposite Rathbone Place. 1809–25 (2)

WRIGHT, HENRY BOXLY, Joiner, at *The Three Kings and Star*, Crispin Street, Spitalfields. 1723 (6)

WRIGHT, JOHN, Upholder, No. 40, Great Russell Street, Bloomsbury. 1790–1803 (2, 20)

WRIGHT, JOHN, Cabinet manufacturer, No. 1, Bowling Green Lane, Clerkenwell. 1817 (2)

WRIGHT, JOSEPH AND RICHARD, Upholders, Brokers Row, Moorfields. 1792 (2)

WRIGHT, RICHARD, Upholder and Cabinet-maker, at *The White Lion*, in Lower Moorfields. *c.* 1760 (1)

WRIGHT, RICHARD, Cabinet warehouse, No. 63, Charlotte Street, Fitzroy Square. 1817 (2)

WRIGHT, S., Carver and Gilder and Looking-glass manufacturer, No. 388, Strand, corner of Southampton Street. *c.* 1830 (1)

WRIGHT, THOMAS, Upholder and Cabinet-maker, No. 32, Swithins Lane, Cannon Street. 1772 (2)

WRIGHT, THOMAS, Upholsterer, No. 47, South Moulton Street. 1839 (2)

WRIGHT, TIMOTHY, Upholster, Duke Street. 1749 (3)

WRIGHT, W., *see* F. AND W. WRIGHT, No. 410, Oxford Street. 1809–95

WRIGHT, W., Cabinet and Chair maker, No. 82, Titchfield Street, Fitzroy Square. 1817–39 (2)

WRIGHT, WILLIAM, Cabinet-maker, in Porter Street, Newport Market. 1774–93 (2, 3)

WRIGHT AND SNELL, Upholders, No. 40, Great Russell Street, Bloomsbury. 1794–96 (2)

WYAT, MRS., Upholsterer [*sic*], in Wine Office Court, Fleet Street. 1748 (5)

WYATT, EDWARD, Carver and Gilder, No. 360, Oxford Street, next door to the Pantheon. 1790–1811 (1, 2, 17, 57)

(Plate, page 202)

Executed chimney frame, etc., at Litchfield House in 1794 and carving and gilding at Carlton House to the extent of £756 in 1811.

WYATT, JAMES, Upholsterer and Cabinet-maker, No. 37, Eagle Street, Red Lion Square, Holborn. label *c.* 1800 (1, 56)

WYBURD AND TERRY, Japan chair manufactory, City Road.   1803 (20)

WYMAN, JAMES, Carver and Gilder, in Blackmoor Street, near Clare Market.
c. 1760 (1)

(Plate, page 207)

WYNDE, JAMES, Upholder, in Golden Lane.   1734 (3)

YARDLEY, ANDREW, Upholster, Cornhill Ward.   1640 (16)

YARDLEY, GEORGE, Carver and Gilder, in Noble Street, near Aldersgate.
c. 1770 (1)

(Plate, page 207)

YATE, ELISHA, Upholder, No. 57, Little Britain.   1790 (2)

YATEMAN (or YEATEMAN), W., Cabinet manufacturer, No. 18, Green Street,
Leicester Square.   1794–1817 (2)

YATEMAN, WILLIAM, Upholsterer and Cabinet-maker, No. 24, Leadenhall
Street.   1790–94 (2)

YATEMAN, WILLIAM, Upholsterer, No. 12, St. Paul's Church Yard.
1797–1803 (1, 20)

YEATES, ROBERT, Turner, at *The Woolpack*, corner of Old Gravel Lane.
1723 (6)

YEATS, JOHN, Cabinet-maker, in St. Martin's Lane.   1749 (3)

YEWD, WILLIAM, Cabinet-maker and Mahogany turner, at *The Golden Lyon*,
three doors from Somerset House, in the Strand.   1763 (1, 2)

YOULE, JOHN, Cabinet-maker, at *The Cabinet*, in Drury Lane.
"leaving off trade" 1694 (5)

YOUNG, —, Upholsterer, in Ironmonger Lane, Cheapside.   1747 (5)

YOUNG AND FALL, Upholsterers, No. 4, Ironmonger Lane, Cheapside.
1760 (2)

YOUNG, HICKMAN, Upholsterer, No. 4, Ironmonger Lane, Cheapside.
1763–68 (2)

YOUNG AND BROOKS, Upholsterers, No. 4, Ironmonger Lane, Cheapside.
1770 (2)

YOUNG AND BROOKS, Upholsterers, No. 51, Hatton Garden.   1772 (2)

YOUNG AND HICKMAN, Upholsterers, No. 51, Hatton Garden.   1777 (84)

YOUNG, JAMES, Cabinet-maker, in Piccadilly.   1749 (3)

YOUNG, LAKE, The Coach and Looking-glass manufactory, James' Street,
Covent Garden, or at his Warehouse near the Pump in Watling Street.
1769 (1)

(Plate, page 208)

No. 54, Watling Street.   1774–1802 (2)

Succeeded by BROWN, YOUNG AND SON, Glass cutters.   1808–25 (2)

YOUNG, WILLIAM, Cabinet-maker, King Street, Little Sanctuary.   1774 (3)

YOUNG, WILLIAM, Cabinet-maker and Upholsterer, No. 160, Ratcliffe Highway.   1790–93 (2)

YOUNG AND HOWARD, Upholders and Cabinet-makers, No. 14, Oxford Street

                                                   1790–93 (2)

YOUNGE, JOHN, Upholster (address not recorded).   1660–61 (8)

      Quoted by R. W. Symonds in *Connoisseur*, January 1934.

The following two entries have been noted from

      The *London Gazette*, 18th March, 1688, and the *Daily Courant*, 24th March, 1709, without further identification:—

      [NO NAME], an Upholsterer, at *The Royal Bed*, between the two Turnstiles, in High Holborn.   1688 (5)

      [NO NAME], an Upholsterer, in Wych Street.   1709 (5)

OLD ENGLISH FURNITURE
AND ITS MAKERS

THE PROBLEM OF IDENTIFICATION

By R. W. SYMONDS, F.S.A.

OLD ENGLISH FURNITURE AND ITS MAKERS: THE PROBLEM OF IDENTIFICATION

By R. W. SYMONDS, F.S.A.

VERY FEW FURNITURE MAKERS IDENTIFIED their work either by labelling or stamping; for in England, as opposed to France, chair- and cabinet-makers were not obliged by law to put their mark on their wares.*

The result is that we have a mass of old English furniture on the one hand, and a mass of joiners' and cabinet-makers' names (see the lists in this book) on the other hand, and the two, for the most part, are unrelated. The finest walnut or mahogany arm-chair or bureau-bookcase, the star piece in a collection, is ascribed a date and a place of origin, but who actually made it no one knows. "Made by a London cabinet-maker of the first rank" is the nearest description that we can safely apply; or, in the case of furniture with provincial characteristics, "The work of a Yorkshire or Midlands cabinet-maker or joiner."

There are two certain methods of identifying the maker of a piece of old English furniture: the maker's label pasted on the piece; and the preservation, with the piece, of the original bill. The name of a craftsman on a piece of furniture is also another method of identification, but furniture signed in this way is seldom found. Of the few examples I have seen, it has been done by inlaying (fig. 15, p. 233), or by being cut in the gesso ground and gilded. There is also the signature proper, written by the craftsman with brush or pen. But it must be remembered that labelled pieces of furniture are rare, and signed pieces of furniture are exceedingly rare.

The labelled piece of furniture presents a number of problems to the student. First of all there are two types found on furniture: one is a trade-card, or handbill, and the other a label proper. The trade-card was not printed, like the modern business card, on a small piece of pasteboard, but on a sheet of good quality paper which ranged in size from a small octavo to a large quarto. It was handed to prospective customers. Many of these cards or handbills have been preserved with memoranda on the back of prices or of an amount owed by a customer. From those illustrated in this

---

* Foreign smiths, joiners and coopers were an exception to this according to a Statute of the fourteenth and fifteenth year of Henry VIII, 1522–23. "And that no Stranger born out of the King's Obeisance, using any of the Mysteries or Occupations of Smiths, Joiners, or Coopers, shall make any Manner of Wares or Vessels concerning the same Mysteries or Occupations, except that they and every of them put such Marks to every of the same Wares and Vessels, before they shall be put to Sale or Use." To what extent this law was observed, we do not know; and the restriction no longer applied as soon as the stranger was enfranchised by the mistery or company of the craft in question.

book, it can be seen that they were often highly decorative in their design, and frequently contain the sign of the craftsman's shop. They often listed the articles the craftsman made or sold and the different varieties of work —joinery, cabinet-making, undertaking, upholstery—that he carried out. Although these cards were primarily handbills and were not made for the purpose of pasting on to pieces of furniture, some craftsmen occasionally used them in this way.

The second type of label was much smaller, was usually circular, and sometimes only gave the name and address of the craftsman, omitting all reference to his wares (figs. 16, 19, pp. 234, 237). Such labels appear to have been cut by scissors from a sheet on which they were printed like the early, unperforated postage stamps. They must have been purposely designed for pasting on to furniture, which makes it odd that so few pieces of furniture with this type of label have been preserved; in fact, a piece with the handbill type of label is more often found. Being small they were perhaps more easily peeled or scraped off than the larger handbill labels. Often a label will show, from its mutilated edges, that someone has tried to remove it.

It is a very curious fact that about two-thirds of the extant pieces of labelled furniture were made, or sold, by craftsmen who worked in St. Paul's Church Yard. Why did this particular colony of chair-makers, cabinet-makers and upholsterers, between the years 1720 and 1790, paste their handbills or circular labels on to furniture? Also, why was it that the fashionable cabinet-makers and upholsterers of St. Martin's Lane and Long Acre never used handbills or labels at all? For no piece of furniture bearing the label of Gerreit Jensen, John Bradburn, Thomas Chippendale, William Vile, John Cobb, William Hallet or Benjamin Goodison has, so far, been recorded. The inference is, that being patronised by the best of English society they had no reason to advertise themselves in this way.

Thomas Chippendale, however, chose the grand manner of publicising himself by illustrating his furniture designs in his famous *A Gentleman and Cabinetmaker's Director*. A handbill or trade label was beneath his notice; he even had a distaste for a rococo billhead which was liked by the cabinet-makers in the City, and the headings of his bills were written instead in a flourishing hand on a plain folio.

Judging by the number of his extant labelled pieces, Giles Grendey, who was not a member of the St. Paul's Church Yard colony, was particularly fond of labels. This joiner and cabinet-maker was born in 1693 and died in 1780. His workshop and home were in part of an old mansion called Aylesbury House, in St. John's Square, Clerkenwell. In 1731 Aylesbury House caught fire. We learn from the newspaper accounts of the accident that Grendey lost a thousand pounds' worth of furniture which he "had pack'd for Exportation against the Morning." This, then, was Grendey's reason, or one of his reasons, for labelling his furniture: in order that his foreign customers should know his name and address.

The scarcity of labelled furniture is partly due to the labels having been worn away by the rubbing of articles placed in the drawers (for it was in a drawer, i.e. in a noticeable but not too conspicuous place, that the label was generally affixed), or to their having been deliberately removed by the owners who thought them unsightly.

The comparison of several pieces of furniture which can definitely be attributed to one cabinet-maker will reveal certain ornamental *motifs* and certain stylistic treatments in common. Once a cabinet-maker's predelictions for design and ornament have been established, we can then search for other pieces of his handiwork among the unidentified mass of old furniture which has been preserved. This line of research has met with success in America; for labels were popular with colonial and federal craftsmen.

The labelled furniture of Giles Grendey provides an opportunity for following this method of identification. Let us start with the mahogany cabinet (fig. 24, p. 242); it was made by Grendey, for his label is pasted on one of the trays in the lower cupboard. The carved apron piece surmounted by a frieze decorated with a Grecian scroll is a very unusual ornament for decorating the plinth of a cabinet. I noticed that a similar apron piece, with Grecian scroll frieze, decorated the front rails of two large marble-topped side tables (fig. 26, p. 243). I also noticed that the same design of carved apron was on two dwarf wardrobes (figs. 25, 27, pp. 243–4). Another connecting link between this mahogany cabinet and the two wardrobes is that the panels of the doors of all three pieces are serpentine shaped. Furthermore, I found a third wardrobe of identical design to the other two, except that it is slightly later in date for the apron piece has rococo ornament (fig. 28, p. 245). All three wardrobes have the outer edges of the doors carved with rose and ribbon ornament, just like the doors of the cabinet. Also the panel mouldings of all three pieces are carved with the egg and tongue *motif*. Grendey's partiality for the serpentine-shaped panel is proved by a mahogany wardrobe (see fig. 23, p. 241), and a japanned bureau bookcase, both bearing his labels and having doors with the same shaped panels.

An account of labelled furniture would be incomplete without considering whether the label is original to the piece on which it is pasted. In other words, has somebody removed the label from a poor quality piece of furniture, or one in a bad condition which would be very expensive to repair, and pasted it on to a rare and saleable piece in order to give it additional value from the collector's point of view?

A little more than twenty years ago a walnut bureau, with a decorative label of an early maker pasted on the outside of one of the drawer bottoms, appeared in a dealer's shop. It was bought by a collector and was illustrated and commented upon in articles written by me and others. We had no reason to think that the label was not put there by the actual maker. Recently, however, I was told on very good authority that this label had been transferred from another piece of furniture of little value.

This deception has probably been practised a number of times. The collector who is considering a piece of labelled furniture should therefore make careful inspection of the label. The one and only test is to lift up the edge of the label in order to see whether the wood underneath has, compared with the wood surrounding the label, a clean and fresh tone, which is the condition it should be in if the label was pasted on when the wood was new. It seems that this kind of cheat has, so far, confined his activities to removing labels from one piece of furniture to another. He has not, as far as we know, applied a loose handbill, of which a number are occasionally advertised for sale in a bookseller's catalogue, to a nameless piece. In this case he would have the added task of treating the label itself, for a label preserved in a bundle of labels has a clean and fresh appearance.

The earliest labelled examples of furniture so far recorded are three chests of drawers of Hugh Granger of The Carved Angel, Aldermanbury. One of them, decorated with olive-wood parquetry, is illustrated (fig. 10, p. 228). Granger was churchwarden of St. Mary's, Aldermanbury.

Cabinet-makers who followed the new craft of veneering, seem to have introduced trade cards and labels during the Restoration. Joiners, on the other hand, never used printed labels; some of them continued to brand their wares with their initials as a means of identification, a method which we know was used in the sixteenth century and probably before. In the seventeenth century branded initials were particularly common on joined chairs and stools, but not so common on tables and carcass furniture. Walnut and beech cane chairs were very often branded with the makers' initials*. The point has been raised that these branded initials were the owners' and not the makers', but this is not so, for the branding of chairs and stools was too widespread to be anything else but a trade custom. Chair-makers, particularly provincial chair-makers, continued to brand their chairs into the eighteenth century, for several mahogany chairs bearing the makers' initials on the seat rails are known. Giles Grendey is the only chair-maker, as far as we know, who used labels for his chairs, but this was due to the fact that he was also a cabinet-maker.

There were two reasons for a craftsman marking his furniture with his initials: as a means of identification and in order "to prevent abuses." For instance, Thomas Granford, tool maker, who lived at the sign of the "3 Plane-makers" in Queen Street, near Cheapside, London, advertised in *The Post-man* during 1703, that he "maketh and selleth all sorts of Joyners and Carpenters Tooles, where any Artificers or Merchants may be fur-

---

* Sometimes cane and joined chairs are found with two sets of initials, the second set being, one presumes, either that of the carver or the turner who added the decoration.

nished with greater or lesser quantities of the best sort, and to prevent abuses, I mark with my Name at length instead of T.G."

It has been suggested that the initials R.P., branded on several cane chairs, stand for Richard Price, who was the chair-maker and joiner to the Crown in the reign of Charles II. Price died about 1684. But no one has yet made a study of makers' initials and tried to establish correspondences.

At the very end of the eighteenth century stamping (not branding) the maker's name in full was used as an alternative to a label. Gillow of Lancaster was one of the first to make a practice of this method. The position chosen for the stamp "Gillows Lancaster" was usually on the top edge of a drawer front (fig. 46, p. 259). In the nineteenth century this stamping of the full name was adopted by a number of London firms.

In the late eighteenth and early nineteenth centuries a brass plaque was sometimes used in place of a stamp or label. The famous firm of Seddon appears occasionally to have made use of this more permanent form of identification (fig. 47, p. 260). This did not, however, prevent them from using a paper label as well (see fig. 48, page 260).

When the maker can be identified by his bill, the student of old furniture then knows the date of the piece (which is of the greatest value for establishing when this or that design was current), and what it cost originally. Other fascinating details may also be revealed.

For example, we know through the Bill Books in the Public Record Office that the beautiful jewelled cabinet, the gift of George III to Queen Charlotte (fig. 29, p. 246), was made by the cabinet-maker William Vile in 1762, and that it cost £138 10s. 0d.

But more of Chippendale's furniture than that of any other maker can be identified through the preservation of his bills. The most complete range of his bills (from 1766 to 1771) is for the furnishing of Nostell Priory, for Sir Rowland Winn, the fifth baronet. From these invaluable accounts we are able to prove that pieces of superb mahogany furniture, which are still at Nostell, were actually made in Chippendale's workshop. In addition, we learn from these accounts that he made ordinary furniture as well, such as "a deal stool, 1/3"; "A Wainscot pillar and Claw Table, 15/–"; and "A Large strong Elm Chopping block for the kitchen, 10/–." Of course Chippendale made much plain household furniture for the use of the servants of his rich patrons, but who today, in the light of his *Director*, would associate such stuff with his name?

A study of the furniture at Nostell reveals a number of little conceits which are peculiar to Chippendale alone. For instance, the oval panels on each of the two outer corners of the blocks at the top of the legs not only appear on the set of japanned chairs and stools (fig. 33, p. 249), but on the mahogany drawing table (fig. 35, p. 250). The sunk shaped panel decorating the tapered legs of this table is also reproduced on the square legs of the

Pembroke table (fig. 36, p. 251). Another device was to shape in the Chinese style the two upper corners of the two panels of the clothes press (fig. 32, p. 248), and leave the lower corners square. This shaped corner at the top of the panel was also used by Chippendale on the doors of a bookcase at Nostell, and is a design shown in the *Director*.

The mouldings of Chippendale's furniture, when compared with the furniture of lesser makers, have a character of their own. They have a delicacy of profile caused through the fine quality of the mahogany, and are of a more intricate section. A study of the mouldings can be made from the *Director* plates where the sections are drawn full size.

A bill of Chippendale's is a rarity, and most Chippendale furniture, unlike that at Nostell Priory, has been removed from its first home. What evidence, therefore, have we for believing that any pedigree-less piece of furniture came from Chippendale's workshop? Apart from the similarity of its design to a plate in the *Director*, which anyone might have copied, the evidence must reside in Chippendale's handwriting; that is to say, in the refinements of the mouldings, the fine quality of the craftsmanship in general, and the use of "very fine wood"—an expression that occurs often in Chippendale's accounts.

There are many extant pieces, particularly chairs, which have been copied from the *Director*, but the majority of them are the work of provincial cabinet- and chair-makers. Although such furniture will have Chippendale's design, it will lack his handwriting. A London cabinet-maker with an organisation which could produce beautiful furniture of fine wood would certainly not have sought inspiration from a competitor's catalogue. He would have had his own designs and, like Chippendale, his own draughtsmen-designers. Therefore a piece of *Director* design with Chippendale's handwriting can safely be said to have come from the Master's workshop.

The furniture of William Vile, like that of Chippendale, also has a definite character both in the treatment of the design and ornament, and in the beautiful quality of the craftsmanship and timber.

Whenever possible the name of a particular cabinet-maker is attached by auctioneers, dealers and collectors to a piece of old furniture. A decade ago everything was Chippendale; nowadays it is Vile, Chippendale's great contemporary. The pretext on which Vile's name is hung is frequently very slender. As Sir Ambrose Heal's scholarly work amply shows Chippendale and Vile did not make all the best furniture during the middle years of the eighteenth century. There is a host of other makers to consider, as is now evident by the vast number of names which Sir Ambrose's many years' patient research has brought to light and recorded in this volume.

A careful study of the characteristic conceits and devices adopted by various makers provides clues which cannot be neglected.

PLATES

FIG. 1.—SAMUEL PEPYS'S BOOKCASE "1" MADE BY "SYMPSON THE JOYNER."
Circa 1666–7

FIGS. 2, 3, 4.—CORNICE OF PEPYS'S BOOKCASES 1 AND 12, AND DETAIL OF INTERIOR, NOTE THE IRON STAY AND HINGE

FIG. 5.—QUEEN MARY'S WRITING-TABLE OF "FINE MARKATREE," MADE BY GERREIT JENSEN IN 1690

FIG. 6.—GLASS CASE FOR QUEEN MARY'S USE AT KENSINGTON, MADE BY GERREIT JENSEN IN 1693

FIG. 7.—WRITING-DESK TABLE INLAID WITH SILVER AND BRASS MADE BY GERREIT JENSEN IN 1695

FIG. 8.—FOLDING TOP OF MARQUETRY WRITING-TABLE (FIG. 5)

FIG. 9.—INLAID SILVER AND BRASS TOP OF WRITING-DESK TABLE (FIG. 7)

228

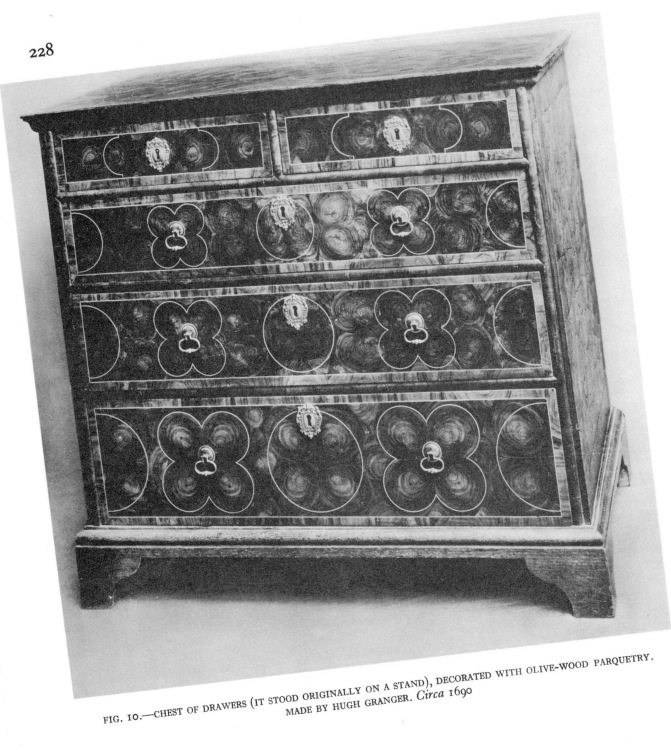

FIG. 10.—CHEST OF DRAWERS (IT STOOD ORIGINALLY ON A STAND), DECORATED WITH OLIVE-WOOD PARQUETRY. MADE BY HUGH GRANGER. *Circa* 1690

FIG. 11.—WRITING CABINET OF VENEERED MULBERRY DECORATED WITH CROSS BANDINGS OF KINGWOOD AND INLAID PEWTER LINES. MADE BY JOHN COXED. *Temp.* QUEEN ANNE

FIG. 12.—BURR MULBERRY CABINET WITH CROSS BANDINGS OF KINGWOOD AND INLAID PEWTER LINES. MADE
BY G. COXED AND T. WOSTER. *Temp.* GEORGE I

FIG. 13.—BURR MULBERRY WRITING CABINET WITH KINGWOOD BANDINGS AND PEWTER LINES. MADE BY
G. COXED AND T. WOSTER. *Temp.* GEORGE I

FIG. 14.—CABINET OF FIGURED WALNUT WITH WRITING DRAWER BY WILLIAM OLD AND JOHN ODY. *Temp*. GEORGE I

233

FIG. 15.—WALNUT WRITING CABINET OF ARCHITECTURAL DESIGN, SIGNED "SAMUEL BENNETT
LONDON FECIT." *Temp.* GEORGE I

234

FIG. 16.—WRITING CABINET VENEERED WITH FIGURED WALNUT (THE DOOR ORIGINALLY HAD A LOOKING-GLASS
PANEL), BY JOHN PHILLIPS. *Temp.* GEORGE I

FIG. 17.—TABLE VENEERED WITH WALNUT, SOLID WALNUT LEGS BY DANIEL WILD. *Circa* 1730

236

FIG. 18.—WRITING CABINET OF GREEN GROUND JAPAN BY JOHN BELCHIER. *Circa* 1730

FIG. 19.—DETAIL OF FIG. 18 SHOWING FITTED INTERIOR

FIG. 20.—WAINSCOT DESK BY BENJAMIN CROOK. *Circa* 1735

FIG. 21.—WALNUT CARD TABLE WITH VENEERED TOP AND FRIEZE AND SOLID WALNUT LEGS.
MADE BY BENJAMIN CROOK. *Circa* 1730

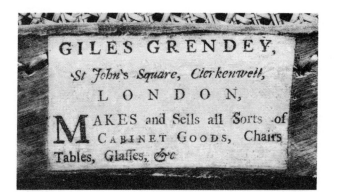

FIG. 22.—SIDE-CHAIR OF SCARLET JAPAN, ONE OF A SET MADE BY
GILES GRENDEY. *Temp.* GEORGE I

FIG. 23.—MAHOGANY CLOTHES PRESS BY GILES GRENDEY. *Circa* 1740

FIG. 24.—MAHOGANY PRESS ON CUPBOARD BASE, BY GILES GRENDEY. *Circa* 1735

FIG. 25.—DWARF CLOTHES PRESS ATTRIBUTED TO GILES GRENDEY.
Circa 1735

FIG. 26.—MARBLE TABLE ON MAHOGANY FRAME ATTRIBUTED TO GILES GRENDEY.
Circa 1735

244

FIG. 27.—DWARF CLOTHES PRESS ATTRIBUTED TO GILES GRENDEY. *Circa* 1735

FIG. 28.—DWARF CLOTHES PRESS WITH ROCOCO ORNAMENT ON APRON PIECE
ATTRIBUTED TO GILES GRENDEY, *Circa* 1745

FIG. 29.—QUEEN CHARLOTTE'S JEWEL CABINET MADE BY WILLIAM VILE. *Circa* 1762

FIG. 30.—TOP OF JEWEL CABINET SHOWING THE QUEEN'S ARMS INLAID IN IVORY

FIG. 31.—INTERIOR OF JEWEL CABINET

FIG. 32.—LARGE MAHOGANY CLOTHES PRESS MADE BY THOMAS CHIPPENDALE FOR SIR ROWLAND WINN IN 1767

FIGS. 33 AND 34.—CHAIR AND STOOL JAPANNED GREEN AND GOLD, PART OF A SUITE MADE BY THOMAS
CHIPPENDALE FOR SIR ROWLAND WINN IN 1771

FIG. 35.—MAHOGANY DRAWING-TABLE WITH RISING TOP MADE BY THOMAS CHIPPENDALE
FOR SIR ROWLAND WINN IN 1767

FIG. 36.—"A VERY NEAT PEMBROKE TABLE" WITH DRAWER FITTED WITH BACKGAMMON BOARD, MADE BY
THOMAS CHIPPENDALE FOR SIR ROWLAND WINN IN 1769

FIG. 37.—MAHOGANY CLOTHES PRESS WITH BASE OF DRAWERS MADE BY PHILIP BELL.
Circa 1770

FIG. 38.—PEMBROKE TABLE BY GEORGE SIMSON.
Circa 1790

FIG. 39.—MAHOGANY CHEST OF DRAWERS BY
PHILIP BELL. *Circa* 1770

FIG. 40.—TABLE WITH PAINTED DECORATION IN CLASSIC STYLE BY GEORGE SIMSON LATE EIGHTEENTH CENTURY

FIG. 41.—MAHOGANY TABLE WITH VENEERED TOP BY HENRY KETTLE LATE EIGHTEENTH CENTURY

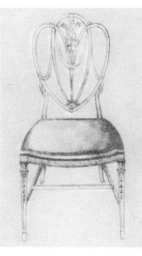

FIG. 42.—DINING-ROOM AT WORKINGTON HALL, CUMBERLAND. THE MAHOGANY FURNITURE WAS SUPPLIED
BY RICHARD AND ROBERT GILLOW OF LANCASTER

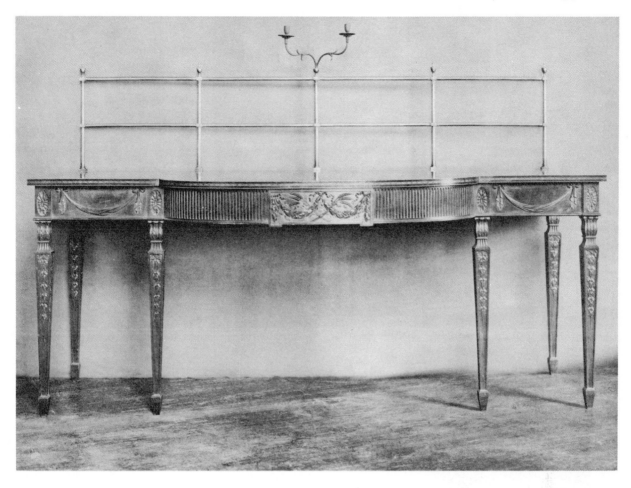

FIG. 43.—MAHOGANY SIDE-BOARD TABLE WITH ITS ORIGINAL DRAWING FROM GILLOW'S COSTS BOOKS
"FOR J. CHRISTIAN ESQ. SEPT. 26TH, 1788"

FIG. 44.—MAHOGANY URN AND PEDES-
TAL IN THE DINING-ROOM AT
WORKINGTON HALL. MADE BY RICHARD
AND ROBERT GILLOW

FIG. 45.—DETAILS OF SIDE-BOARD TABLE
(FIG. 43)

FIG. 46.—LADY'S WRITING-TABLE OF SATINWOOD MADE BY GILLOW. LATE EIGHTEENTH CENTURY

FIG. 47.—WRITING-CUM-PEMBROKE TABLE WITH MAKER'S
BRASS TABLET EARLY NINETEENTH CENTURY

FIG. 48.—SMALL WRITING-TABLE BY THOMAS
AND GEORGE SEDDON. *Circa* 1825

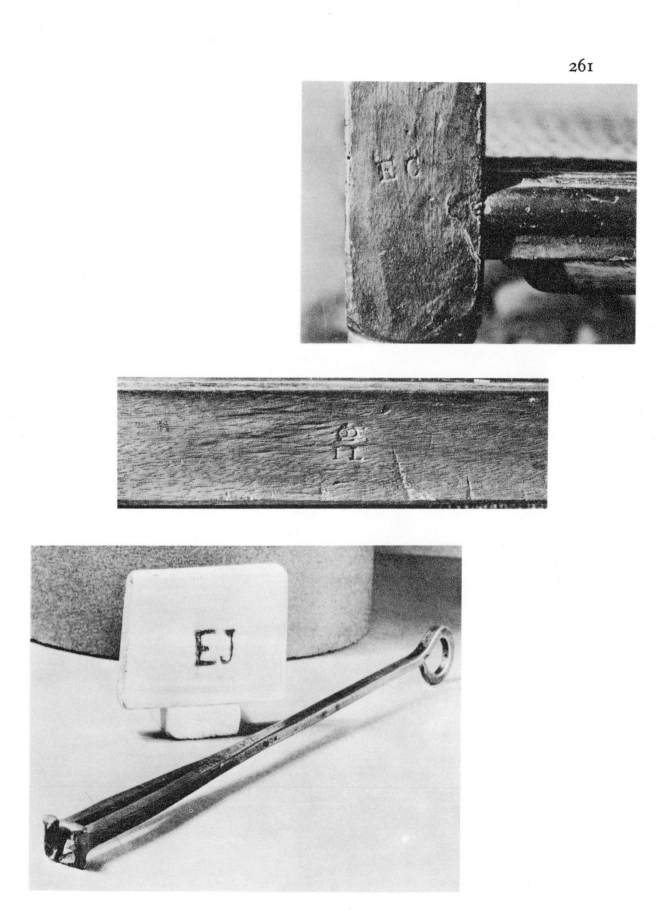

FIGS. 49, 50, 51.—CHAIR-MAKERS' MARKS AND BRANDING IRON

FIG. 52.—BABY CHAIR BRANDED WITH MAKER'S INITIALS. *Temp*. CHARLES II

NOTES ON THE
ILLUSTRATIONS

(Pages 222–262)

NOTES ON THE ILLUSTRATIONS
which appear on pages 222–262

Figures 1, 2, 3 and 4 (pages 222, 223)

One of the many new furniture designs of the time of Charles II was a bookcase with doors which resembled a glazed window. It was divided into rectangular panes formed by moulded glazing bars.

It is likely that this type of bookcase was conceived by a bibliophile who wanted to enclose his books in order to keep them from dust, but still be able to see them. A window with wooden glazing bars, in place of the leaded casement window, was first made on the Continent, but as the earliest glazed bookcases which have been preserved are English, it was probably an Englishman who first thought of housing his books behind glazed doors.

On 23rd July, 1666, Pepys recorded: ". . . Sympson, the Joyner; and he and I with great pains contriving presses to put my books up in; they now grow numerous and lying, one upon another, on my chairs. . . ."

The sliding panel enclosing the base (probably adapted from the new Dutch sash windows) was certainly a novel idea and one which was quite likely to have sprung from the ingenious mind of Mr. Pepys. But whether he also invented the glazed door, or whether it was an innovation of the time which he merely adopted, we shall never know.

The Pepys presses show very little variation one from another, the main difference being in the carved ornament (see the difference between the two cornices illustrated). They were designed so that a number of them could stand round a large room, and they were originally placed like sentinels in Pepys's "closett" in Seething Lane, and later at York Buildings. The advantage of this design of bookcase was that more cases could be added as the library increased. Pepys started with three or four; added to them later and finally he had twelve.

Figures 5, 6, 7, 8 and 9 (pages 224–227)

Although these three pieces of furniture bear no label, they are undoubtedly the work of Gerreit Jensen, and can be identified from his bills in the Royal Accounts. The bill for the writing-table is dated 30th October, 1690, and headed "For her Ma^{ts} Service att Kensington."

> For a Folding writeing table of fine Markatree with a Crowne & Cypher, £22 10 0.

The top folds (fig. 8, p. 227), and the marquetry panel decorating it contains the crown and the cypher WM. The quality of the inlay is in accordance with the description "fine Markatree." The close-grained hard wood which has been used for the drawer linings is difficult to identify. It may have been imported from the East Indies.

The design of this table, which is supported on eight legs (the legs, unfortunately, are modern restorations), with its folding top and an independent unit of small drawers, is more in keeping with a French table.

> For a glass case of fine markatree upon a Cabonett with doors for Kensington, £30.

This china, or curiosity, cabinet appears in Jensen's account for 24th July, 1693. As it is the only "glass case" inlaid with marquetry which appears in his bills, it must be the cabinet which is now at Windsor Castle. In the seventeenth century a cabinet had solid doors, and a piece of furniture with glazed doors was called a "glass case." Hence this china cabinet is described as if it is two pieces of furniture: a cabinet (i.e. the base) and a glass case.

The writing-desk table appears in an account dated *Michaelmas to Lady Day, 1694–5*. "For a fine writing desk Table inlaid wth mettall, £70." The metal is silver and brass and the inlaid woods are of numerous kinds, now difficult to recognise under the polish. An almost identical desk table (it lacks only the frieze with the circular medallion in the middle, containing the cypher WM) is at Boughton House, Northamptonshire. It was made for Ralph, the first Duke of Montagu, 1638–1709.

An unusual feature of the top (see detail, fig. 9, p. 227), which is constructed of a single plank of wainscot oak framed at the ends, is that it is held to the carcass by means of four dowels. This was done in order to prevent the wood splitting through shrinkage. A number of pieces of this "inlaid with metall" furniture appear in Jensen's bills. This was an expensive treatment as the £70 for the writing-desk table shows. Metal inlay furniture was inspired by the work of the French *ébéniste* André Charles Boulle. The strong French influence in the design of Jensen's furniture reveals his Continental background. The fine quality of marquetry and metal inlay work, combined with the French design, suggests that his training (and that of some of his journeymen) had been in France. He was probably a Huguenot refugee.

All three pieces of furniture are at Windsor Castle and are reproduced by gracious permission of Her Majesty the Queen.

Figure 10 (page 228)

This chest of drawers veneered with olive-wood parquetry and enlivened with geometrical panels formed of inlaid lines of boxwood, must have been mounted originally on a low stand with turned legs and stretchers. The section of the moulding of the top clearly indicates this.

Two other chests of drawers bearing the label of Hugh Granger have also been preserved. One is like the example illustrated here, and the other is decorated with inlaid panels of floral marquetry. The parquetry and marquetry and the section of the mouldings of these chests suggest that Granger made them during the decade 1680–90. In the late seventeenth century this chest of drawers and the chest on stand were very popular pieces of furniture. They were made by the joiners in wainscot, by the japanners in paint and varnish with black and coloured grounds, and by the cabinet-makers in veneered walnut, olive-wood and marquetry.

Figures 11, 12 and 13 (pages 229–231)

Bureau writing cabinets, veneered with the burr wood of the mulberry tree and decorated with bands of kingwood contained within inlaid pewter lines, appear to have been the speciality of John Coxed, also G. Coxed (probably the son of John) who was in partnership with T. Woster (see page 40). A number of these mulberry bureau bookcases with kingwood bandings and pewter lines have been preserved, but not all of them are labelled. That the unlabelled examples were also made by Coxed and Woster there is no doubt.

The emphasis given to the mottled figure of the burr wood by staining it with boiled oil darkened by colouring matter is the chief characteristic of this mulberry veneered furniture. The oil affects the variations in the texture of the wood by darkening the porous ground (i.e. the end grain) and leaving light the non-porous. Other woods which give the same effect when treated with oil, are burr ash and bog oak.

Coxed and Woster also made veneered walnut furniture and "Wainscot-Work of all sorts" which suggests that they employed joiners who made wainscot furniture and house joinery.

Another branch of Coxed and Woster's business, according to their trade card, was the making of looking-glasses and "Large sconces." These were candle sconces, probably with looking-glass backs to reflect the light of the candle. "Old glass New polished, and made up fashionable" is a footnote to one of Coxed and Woster's two recorded labels. This meant replacing an old-fashioned frame with one in the latest style. This new fashioning of looking-glass was often practised in an age when looking-glass plates were expensive.

Figure 14 (page 232)

A walnut veneered cabinet with writing drawer. The upper part is fitted with small drawers enclosed by doors with looking-glass panels. This cabinet bears the label of William Old and John Ody who, like their contemporaries Coxed and Woster, produced veneered furniture of fine workmanship.

By courtesy of Messrs. Pratt & Sons.

Figure 15 (page 233)

A writing cabinet veneered with walnut. "Samuel Bennett London Fecit" is inlaid on the back of the bookcase door at the base of the two pilasters. This form of a maker's signature is exceedingly rare, and indicates a vanity unusual with a craftsman. A similar writing cabinet also by Samuel Bennett and signed in the same manner is recorded. Unlike the example illustrated it has the lower part of *bombé* shape, which was a favourite design with the Dutch cabinet-maker, but only very seldom used here.

By permission of the Victoria and Albert Museum.

Figure 16 (page 234)

A narrow writing bureau bookcase of veneered walnut by John Phillips. The walnut bureau and the bureau with a bookcase were made in two standard widths: 2 feet or a little over and about 3 feet.

What was the reason, one might ask, for this narrow size? Writing upon a bureau of this width is neither very comfortable nor convenient, and in the reigns of George I and II, when most of them were made, the house with small rooms was the exception and not the rule. It seems, therefore, that they were designed for a position which did not afford much width. This could only have been against the pier wall between the windows of the standard type of brick house which was built in large numbers during the first half of the eighteenth century, a position which would have the advantage of catching the light from both windows.

That many of these bureaux were used for dressing as well as writing is suggested by the fact that the top drawer is fitted with toilet boxes and often a small toilet glass.

The large bureau which had no dressing drawer was placed against one of the side walls of the parlour. It was the most important piece of furniture in the room and required, therefore, a more prominent position than that between the windows.

Figure 17 (page 235)

This table with three drawers supported on cabriole legs must have been used for a specific purpose. Examples veneered with walnut, japanned, of wainscot oak and solid mahogany have been preserved; but most, by far, are of walnut, ranging from the coarsest to the best cabinet work. The problem is, for what purpose did our ancestors use this table? Its popularity during the first half of the eighteenth century meant that it played a very definite part in the furnishing of ordinary homes as well as those of the wealthy classes.

As the centre drawer is usually shallower than the two side drawers, this suggests that it was a table designed to sit at, but not with great comfort.

The two uses to which it might have been put were as a dressing-table or as a wash-stand for shaving, which was a laborious business in those times and probably done sitting. One cannot press the view that it was a dressing-table for we certainly know that a small pedestal knee-hole table, on the top of which was placed the toilet glass, was used by men for this purpose, the equivalent for women, called a "Toylet," having a fabric skirt surround. Were there, then, two types of men's dressing tables? Or was it a wash-stand? Our ancestors must have used some kind of wash-stand and none, with the exception of a tripod stand with a circular rim into which the basin fitted (erroneously thought to be a wig-powdering stand), has so far been recognised. Unfortunately we do not know.

In the collection of Mrs. Ronald Gilbey.

Figures 18 and 19 (pages 236, 237)

It is difficult to say whether the japanned bureau bookcase was as popular in the first half of the eighteenth century as the walnut bureau bookcase, owing to the former's high rate of destruction. When the japanned surface became scratched and rubbed and worn away by use (it was only paint and varnish) and, at the same time, the piece became old-fashioned, it was banished to the servants' quarters where the process of decay and ill usage continued rapidly.

The example illustrated is in an almost perfect state, which means that for two hundred years it must have been little used. The two platforms seen each side of the curved pediment were originally designed for china vases or figures. The open pediment had also a platform, now missing, for a piece of china. The decoration of the tops of cabinets and scrutoires with china was much in favour during the first half of the eighteenth century. Defoe says that it was Queen Mary who introduced the "Custom or Humour, as I may call it, of furnishing Houses with China-Ware, which increased to a strange degree afterwards, piling their China upon the Tops of Cabinets, Scrutores, and every Chymney-Piece, to the Tops of the Ceilings and even setting up Shelves for their China-Ware, where they wanted such Places, till it became a grievance in the Expense of it, and even injurious to their Families and Estates."

In the collection of Mr. G. N. Charrington.

Figures 20 and 21 (pages 238, 239)

A class of furniture cheaper than the veneered furniture of the cabinet-maker was made by the joiner. It was called "wainscot" because it was made of imported oak from the Baltic. It was a milder and straighter grain than the English-grown oak, and for this reason was used extensively by joiners for house fitments and furniture.

Benjamin Crook, the maker of the bureau and the walnut card table illustrated, was, it appears from the wording of his label, a craftsman who did cabinet-work, made mahogany tables, looking-glasses and chairs and, like many makers of St. Paul's Churchyard, added to his income by the production of wainscot furniture and joinery. It is unusual for a piece of wainscot furniture to bear a maker's label. This bureau and card-table, both of which bear Crook's labels, show the range of his production—from a plain inexpensive utilitarian bureau for a citizen's home, to an expensive card-table with veneered walnut top and frieze supported on elegant cabriole legs.

A feature of the card-table which is by no means common to all walnut card-tables, is that the two legs which support the hinged top both fold out in what is known as a "concertina action." This permitted the back legs to be at the corners of the top. It was a refinement which added a little to the cost.

Bureau illustrated by courtesy of Messrs. S. W. Wolsey and card-table by Messrs. Phillips of Hitchin.

Figure 22 (page 240)

A chair of scarlet japan with cane seat, belonging to a large set of six arm-chairs, twenty side-chairs and a day-bed.* On the underside of the seat rail of several of the chairs is pasted the label of Giles Grendey who made this suite of furniture for export to Spain—until 1935 it was in the Duke of Infantado's Castle of Lazcano. Of the many cabinet-makers who made furniture for export, Giles Grendey alone supplies us with the proof.

An advertisement of the sale of household goods in London in 1751† concludes with the statement that "amongst which [furniture] are several capital Pieces design'd for the Spanish and Portugal Trade." This indicates that the Peninsula was recognised as an exploitable market, and that furniture for it was especially designed.

The furniture of this trade that has been preserved is usually japanned— walnut pieces are very scarce and pieces of gilt and gesso are scarcer still.

The japan for the home market was of gold imposed upon sombre grounds of black, dark blue and olive green, colours which, under England's dull skies, took on a richness and brilliancy. But the japan for the bright sunlight of Spain and Portugal was of a vivid scarlet and of the brightest gold which changed to a mellow red and a rich bronze. White and yellow grounds were also used by the English japanner for this oversea trade.

Apart from the brighter colouring of the japan grounds, cane was used for the seats of chairs, stools and settees "design'd for the Spanish and Portugal Trade," owing, no doubt, to their comparative coolness. This is a conspicuous feature at a time when cane was outmoded in England.

By courtesy of the Metropolitan Museum, New York.

* The chairs are now in the Metropolitan Museum, New York, the day-bed in the Victoria and Albert Museum.
† *General Advertiser*, 28th February.

Figure 23 (page 241)

A mahogany clothes press by Giles Grendey, the interior fitted with sliding trays for clothes. In the eighteenth century people did not hang their clothes up, but laid them down. Was it a bust or a piece of china which originally decorated the wide space in the open pediment?

Figure 24 (page 242)

A mahogany press on a cupboard base. By Giles Grendey. An unusual piece of furniture, perhaps made to the special instructions of a customer. Note the similarity of the apron piece with the apron pieces of the two dwarf clothes presses (figs. 25, 27, pp. 243–4), and the side-table (fig. 26, p. 243).

Figure 25 (page 243)

A dwarf clothes press with interior fitted with sliding trays. *Circa* 1735. Attributed to Giles Grendey, see pages 69, 71. This design of clothes press was far less favoured than the press in two carcasses, similar to the example fig. 23, p. 241. One is able, however, to place things in the top tray without standing on a chair, as was necessary with the taller press.

Figure 26 (page 243)

A marble table on massive mahogany frame with cabriole legs, attributed to Giles Grendey, see page 217.

Figure 27 (page 244)

A dwarf clothes press very similar in design to the press fig. 25, p. 243. Attributed to Giles Grendey. *Circa* 1735.

Figure 28 (page 245)

A dwarf clothes press attributed to Giles Grendey. The stand is decorated with rococo ornament, indicating that it was made about 1745.

By permission of the Victoria and Albert Museum.

Figures 29, 30 and 31 (pages 246, 247)*

Vile and Cobb, Cabinet makers

For the Queens Apartment at St James's

For a very handsome Jewel Cabinet made of many different kinds of Wood on a Mohogy Frame very richly Carved all the Front, Ends & Top Inlaid with Ivory in Compartments & neatly Ingraved the Top to lift up & two drawers under the doors all lined with fine Black Velvet with fine Locks & the Brass Work Gilt, £138 10s.

Although Vile and Cobb were in partnership, it was "William Vile,

---

* *Photographs lent by Mr. H. Clifford-Smith, F.S.A.*

Cabinet Maker" who supplied cabinet work, and "William Vile and John Cobb, Upholsters," who charged for upholstering chairs, supplying carpets and curtains, linen and so forth. In other words, Cobb was the upholsterer and Vile the cabinet-maker. The reason why Queen Charlotte's jewel cabinet was supplied by both of them must have been on account of Cobb's lining of the interior with "fine Black Velvet."

This jewel cabinet was given to Queen Charlotte by George III for the safe keeping of the diamonds which she wore at their Coronation in 1761—the bill for the cabinet is under the date of 1761–66 and was probably made in 1762. Did Vile, one wonders, employ an ornamentalist to design this remarkable cabinet, as Chippendale employed Matthias Lock for his rococo ornament?

By gracious permission of H.M. The Queen.

1767
Novr 12

Figure 32 (page 248)

To a very large mahogany cloaths press with a Pediment top folding doors & sliding shelves cover'd with marble paper & Bays aprons drawers in the under part made of fine wood & Good locks &c. £18 18s.

This is the description in Chippendale's bill of the wardrobe which he made for Sir Rowland Winn's Yorkshire home, Nostell Priory. It appears to have been customary for Chippendale to line the sliding trays or shelves of his clothes presses with marbled paper. The "Bays aprons" were pieces of green cloth which hung down the front of the open tray to prevent dust from entering. From contemporary accounts this appears to have been a feature with other cabinet-makers as well, although no press is known with its aprons intact.

By permission of the Trustees of the late Lord St. Oswald.

Figures 33 and 34 (page 249)

SIR ROWLAND WINN Bart   Dr
1771   To Chippendale Haig & Co.
April 8

to 8 Chairs with India feet and Arms neatly Japan'd Green and Gold, the backs & Seats in linen for Anti Room, £21.

May 6

To 2 dressing Stools Japan'd Green & Gold to match the Chairs and Stuff'd in Linnen, £3 12s.

This suite of chairs and stools, and the sofa at £8 6s., had originally chintz covers which were "lin'd, bound & fring'd." Chippendale was a little wide of the mark when he described the feet as Indian, by which he meant Chinese. He was probably thinking of the Chinese fret panels in the arms.

By permission of the Trustees of the late Lord St. Oswald.

1767
June 30

Figure 35 (page 250)

To a very neat mahogany drawing Table of very fine wood the top made to rise, & doors with drawers within at each end & a large drawer at the end with a slider the top cover'd with green velvet, £8 8s.

This beautiful little table has all the elegance in design, and skill in craftsmanship, of furniture which indubitably came from Chippendale's workshop, see page 219. It is in the library at Nostell Priory, for which it was probably designed.

By permission of the Trustees of the late Lord St. Oswald.

1769
July 3rd

Figure 36 (page 251)

To a very neat Pembroke Table of fine yellow & other woods with a very good Backgammon Table fitted as a drawer & good locks & Castors &c., £7 10s.
A Set of Ivory Men & Ivory Boxes & Dices, £1 10s.

This must have been one of the earliest uses of the name "Pembroke," for the majority of tables of the same design date from the last quarter of the eighteenth century. According to Sheraton the term was "given to a kind of breakfast table, from the name of the lady who first gave orders for one of them." The gilt brass drop handles on the drawer were liked by Chippendale at this period, and they appear on a number of other pieces of furniture with small drawers at Nostell Priory.

By permission of the Trustees of the late Lord St. Oswald.

Figure 37 (page 252)

A clothes press with sliding trays and a base with drawers. It bears the label of Philip Bell, see page 6. This was the most common design of clothes press in the eighteenth century. Judging by the large number that have been preserved, it must have been familiar in most bedrooms.

By courtesy of Messrs. Mallett & Son.

Figure 38 (page 253)

This Pembroke table, made by George Simson about 1795, compared with the Pembroke table made by Thomas Chippendale in 1769, shows the evolution in their design during a quarter of a century. The earliest tables have rectangular tops and straight legs. Later the tops changed to oval and the legs became tapered. The next change was that the flaps became D-shaped, and with this design the legs were sometimes turned instead of tapered. The simple and elegant design of the eighteenth-century Pembroke table was lost when the cabinet-makers of the Regency racked their brains to design something novel and striking.

Figure 39 (page 253)

Mahogany chest of drawers by Philip Bell. Like the clothes press made by the same maker (fig. 37, p. 252), this chest of drawers also shows a simple design combined with good cabinet work. The serpentine front was called by Chippendale and other cabinet-makers of his time "a commode shape," probably because the contemporary French commodes also had their fronts of serpentine shape.

By courtesy of Mr. Leonard Knight.

Figure 40 (page 254)

Table by George Simson with painted decoration in the classic manner. This very active craftsman was an undertaker as well as a maker of mahogany and painted furniture. The oval medallion is after a painting by Reynolds of Hope (Miss Morris) nursing Love which was shown at the Royal Academy in 1769. The surround to the medallion is chocolate colour, and the flowers in the border and the festoons in the frieze are green on a pale yellow background.

By courtesy of Messrs. Mallett & Son.

Figure 41 (page 255)

A plain rectangular table of simple design, the top veneered with mahogany and decorated with an oval panel. This table bears the label of Henry Kettle, who was the successor to Philip Bell at 23, St. Paul's Church Yard, see pages 14, 100. The efforts of a past owner to remove Kettle's label by scoring its surface explains why so few labelled pieces of furniture have been preserved.

By courtesy of Messrs. Phillips of Hitchin.

Figures 42, 43, 44 and 45 (pages 256–258)

When John Christian of Ewanrigg Hall, Cumberland, married in 1782 Isabella, the daughter and sole heiress of Henry Curwen, he came to live at Workington Hall, his wife's ancestral home. He also assumed the name of Curwen. During the next ten years they modernised much of the decoration and largely refurnished the house. From Richard and Robert Gillow of Lancaster they bought the dining-room furniture.

Between 1780 and 1790, architecture, decoration and furniture were in the Neo-Classic style. Rooms were enriched with Greek and Roman ornament which appeared on cornices, friezes, panel mouldings, chair-rails, skirtings, door and window surrounds, and chimney-pieces. Chimney-pieces were of marble, and doors of mahogany, and rooms were designed with apsidal or recessed ends formed by a screen of columns.

In this style the dining-room and library at Workington Hall were transformed. Whether John Christian employed a local architect to design the new decoration, or left the work to firms who specialised in plastering, joinery and carving, we do not know. But the detail of the design does not exhibit the scholarly handling of Robert Adam.

Although two bills, dated 1782 and 1783, of Richard and Robert Gillow for furniture supplied to John Christian have been preserved, the dining-room furniture is not included in them. There is no doubt that this furniture was made by the Gillows, for a sketch of the actual sideboard table, described as "for Mr. John Christian," and an exact design of the dining-room chair, are in the Gillow cost books. There is also a sketch, dated 1788, of the urn and pedestal.

This dining-room furniture seems to have been supplied between the years 1788 and 1790, but it does not include the dining-table, fig. 42, which, by the design of its turned reeded legs, was made at a later date. The construction answers to the "telescopic dining-table" invented by Richard Gillow in 1800. It must, therefore, have been bought in place of the original table.

This suite of furniture, as it is today, consists of fourteen chairs, a dining-table 18 feet long with seven leaves in a case, a pair of window seats, a sideboard-table, a pair of pedestals with vases, a cellarette, and a pair of half-circular side-tables. It is all made from a hard mahogany, and the carving is of high quality. The fact that the chairs are fourteen in number suggests that the usual pair of arm-chairs was not supplied, and that the set is complete. The chairs have stretchers, which distinguishes their north country origin, for the London-made "parlour chair" of the same type was without stretchers. Chairs illustrated in Hepplewhite's *Guide*, and Sheraton's *Drawing-book*, are proof of this.

A sideboard-table with flanking pedestals and vases, like the set which stood against the wall in the recess behind the columns in John Christian's dining-room, was in fashion in the last quarter of the eighteenth century. Sheraton, in his *Drawing-book*, writes that "in spacious dining-rooms these sideboards are often made without drawers of any sort having simply a rail, a little ornamented, and pedestals with vases, which produce a grand effect, one pedestal is used as a plate warmer and is lined with tin; the other as a pot-cupboard, and sometimes it contains a cellarette for wine. The vases are used for water for the use of the butler. . . ."

This description applies very closely to John Christian's sideboard-table and pedestals. The 7 feet 6 inches long table has its original brass rail at the back which was not to hang a curtain on, but to stand silver dishes and plates against. Sheraton writes that, when the candles are lighted in the branch fixed to the rail, it gives "a very brilliant effect to the silver-ware."

A further feature of interest is that the legs and the tablet in the frieze are carved with a design of vine leaves and bunches of grapes, bacchic symbols appropriate to a table on which stood the wine bottles and decanters.

By courtesy of Messrs. M. Harris & Sons.

Figure 46 (page 259)

Several ladies' writing-tables made of satinwood and stamped "Gillows Lancaster," similar to this example, have been preserved. At the back is a sliding screen (missing in the table illustrated) to protect the writer from the heat when the table is moved in front of the fireplace.

Figure 47 (page 260)

This writing-cum-Pembroke table with rising pigeon holes and drawers at the back was not Seddon's invention, but the brass plaque inscribed "Patent" claims it for him.

Sheraton, in his *Drawing-book*, shows a similar contrivance. In his description he says, "This piece serves not only as a breakfast, but also as a writing table, very suitable for a lady. It is termed a Harlequin Table, for no other reason but because, in exhibitions of that sort, there is generally a great deal of machinery introduced in the scenery." The plate in Sheraton's *Drawing-book* is dated 1792, but he does not claim the invention as his own. When the cord of the Seddon table is pulled the box with the pigeon holes rises.

By courtesy of Messrs. Drury and Drury.

Figure 48 (page 260)

A small mahogany writing-table with compartment at the back of top for ink and pen by Thomas and George Seddon. The turning of the legs suggests it was made about 1825. The turned wooden handles are original.

In the collection of Mr. J. S. Sykes.

Figures 49, 50 and 51 (page 261)

Although thousands of joiners' branding irons must have been made in the seventeenth century, they are exceedingly rare now. The mark "EG" (or "EC") is on the upright of a cane chair; the mark "IL" surmounted by a crown is on the seat rail of a walnut chair made about 1725. No chair-maker or joiner with initials I. or J. L. held the royal warrant at this time. Perhaps the maker's shop was at the Sign of the Crown, which was not uncommon in the eighteenth century.

The branding iron is from the collection of Mr. S. W. Wolsey.

Figure 52 (page 262)

This baby's chair with "Boyes and Crownes" cresting is branded in several places with the chair-maker's mark "RP." It is tempting to think that this may stand for Richard Price, chair-maker to Charles II. He died about 1683.

By courtesy of Messrs. S. W. Wolsey.